T0243921

MURDER BALLADS
old & new
A DARK & BLOODY RECORD
by STEVEN L JONES

fh

Murder Ballads Old & New: A Dark & Bloody Record
by **Steven L Jones**

ISBN: 9781627311335

Designed by Ron Kretsch
Cover art by Steven L. Jones
Printed in USA

FERAL HOUSE
1240 W. Sims Way, #124
Port Townsend, WA 98368

www.feralhouse.com
info@feralhouse.com

DEDICATION

For Susan, who believed in me

For Catherine, who saw it through

For Mojo, who stayed by my side

TABLE OF CONTENTS

Chapter Three:
Game Changers, Outlaws, and Folk Heroes

Chapter Four:
Hard Work and Hard Times: Songs of Labor and Strife

"Dry Spell Blues" by Son House
"Hard Time Killing Floor Blues" by Skip James
"On the Killing Floor" by Doctor Clayton
"Mean Old World" by Little Walter
"This Bitter Earth" interpreted by Dinah Washington

Featuring the songs:
"Dora" by the Mekons
"Ellen West" by Throwing Muses
"Annalisa" by Public Image Ltd

Chapter Five:
Fancies of Love, Fantasies of Death

Featuring the songs:
"Der Erlkönig" (Schubert) interpreted by Dietrich Fischer-Dieskau
    & Gerald Moore
"The Erl-King" by Steve Gillette
"Earl King" by Dom Flemons

Featuring the songs:
"Psycho" interpreted by Elvis Costello, James Kittell, and Eddie Noack
"The Cold, Hard Facts of Life" by Porter Wagoner
"I've Got Someone to Kill" by Johnny Paycheck
"Folsom Prison Blues" by Johnny Cash
"These Hands" by Eddie Noack and interpreted by Hank Snow
"Dolores" by Eddie Noack
"The End of the Line" by Eddie Noack

Featuring the songs:
"Murder in the Red Barn" by Tom Waits
"The Murder of Maria Marten" interpreted by Shirley Collins &
    The Albion Country Band

Featuring the songs:
"Lie Down" by the Handsome Family
"Grandmother Waits for You" by the Handsome Family
"My Beautiful Bride" by the Handsome Family
"Drowned" by the Who
"The Ocean Doesn't Want Me" by Tom Waits
"Down in the Ground" by the Handsome Family
"The Forgotten Lake" by the Handsome Family

Chapter Six:
Lost and Found

FOREWORD

Several of my life's great loves converge at the murder ballad: stories and story-telling, music and songs, my enduring passion for the macabre, flawed protagonists, and tales from the dark side. A good murder ballad can have all or most of those things going simultaneously. Ever since Johnny Cash sang of shooting a man in Reno just to watch him die, many of my favorite songwriters have written songs that, by various degrees, can be construed as murder ballads. Bruce Springsteen used the Charlie Starkweather murder spree from the 1950s to set up an album about Reagan-era disenfranchisement in the early 1980s. In the 1990s, Nick Cave made an entire album of murder ballads.

Most of my favorite songwriters have at least tried their hand at writing a murder ballad, but the tradition dates back through the ages. For as long as there have been songs, there have probably been songs about someone killing someone else. Some are composed in the first person, and many from an outside point of view. A few are even written from the victim's side of the equation.

My first attempts at writing murder ballads came early in my songwriting. In the twelfth grade, I wrote an album of songs in which I killed my true love, then attempted to become her (I called it *Dangerous Obsessions*; it wasn't very good, although probably passable for my tender age). Murder and death were such ubiquitous themes in my writing that, in the '80s, I wrote a song called "Smiling at Girls" with a death reference in every single line, but set to a major key to pass it off as a lighthearted pop song. It worked and became a tiny regional hit and earned my early band, Adam's House Cat, a first-place prize in a national "best unsigned band" contest.

But I digress.

My band Drive-By Truckers have numerous songs that skirt, to varying degrees, the murder ballad sub-genre. These include a trio of songs that feature a recurring obsession with killings and preachers. "Go-Go Boots" and "The Fireplace Poker" tell of a preacher having his wife murdered from two different points of view, and "The Wig He Made Her Wear" tells the true story of a preacher's wife shooting her husband. Ironically, the song featured in this book is somewhat of an outlier. I never really considered it a murder ballad, although I guess technically it is.

I wrote "Two Daughters and a Beautiful Wife" shortly after the terrible slayings that inspired it—a tragedy described elsewhere in this book. To me, there was a personal side to the song as I slightly knew the family who lost their lives, and we had very close mutual friends in Richmond, Virginia. It was possibly the most horrific act that ever happened to someone I knew personally, and I wrote the song in an attempt to find some peace and closure. At the time, I was a new father, and that circumstance figured into the song and how I told its story. My song never speaks of the actual events, instead painting a picture of a family reunited in heaven after an unmentioned incident tore their world apart. It cuts so close that I have friends who still leave the room on the rare occasions we play the song live.

It was through "Two Daughters and a Beautiful Wife" that I met Steven Jones when he profiled the song for *Sing Out!* magazine and, later, *Salon*.

With *Murder Ballads Old & New: A Dark & Bloody Record*, Steven has written an excellent book detailing and paying loving tribute to the art form—the various types of murder ballads, their history and fallout, and their themes, good and bad, beautiful and ugly. His survey dates back hundreds of years but carries forward into the present, encompassing multiple styles and approaches. It looks at its subject matter artistically and sociologically, with a keen eye for historical perspectives and the mores of the day.

The book is also beautifully humanistic, seeking a deeper understanding of its dark subject matter than is often offered up and is all the better for it. It avoids glorification of the grotesque in favor of examining the many levels and layers of grief, pain, and suffering that surround such things, not only for the victims and their families but often the perpetrators too. The book is written with clear-eyed understanding, or at least an attempt at such, giving it a depth of feeling and soul far beyond the surface of its sinister theme.

Murder Ballads Old & New also delves deeper into the musical aspects of these songs than one might expect. The book acknowledges that lyrics are only half of what makes a great song—that sometimes, an unexpected chord change can shape the mood beyond what mere words can convey. Steven writes more deeply about the musical side of songs—melody, harmony, rhythm, and arrangement— than many music journalists.

The result is a book that personalizes a potentially impersonal subject, bringing us closer to the sadness and savagery of its theme than the title might suggest—hopefully as close as any of us ever find ourselves.

—Patterson Hood
(songwriter, essayist and performer, founding
member of the band Drive-By Truckers)

STEVEN L JONES, *OPEN HYMNAL #1*, 2019.

INTRODUCTION

I don't really like happy music. I don't think it says anything. — Charlie Rich

Two brothers, drunk on backwoods whiskey, fall into a violent quarrel on Christmas Day. One of them, stabbed, bleeds to death and the other flees the scene. Apprehended and beaten by the dead man's son, the killer dies in jail leaving a family shattered and a widow scarred.

This really happened—both in reality and in a song. You'll find the story of the song—of the events that inspired it, its composition, its singer, its legacy—within the pages of this book. Unusually, the scarred widow played a critical role in both aspects. First, she lived the event: lost her husband to familial violence, then coped for a lifetime with the tragedy's aftermath. But she also sang the song. Indeed, it seems to have provided her solace for decades, a balm for grief and shock and mourning that she held close to her heart, just under her breath, but also once sang defiantly to her husband's killer. As an old woman, she sang it for an archivist's microphone and, years later, the recording found its way to me. It gripped me so that I was stirred to write about it, hence its inclusion here.[1]

A model for tragic ballads, old and new, lies within this tale of despair, documented, then disseminated. All that's missing is a plethora of cover versions and variations (unlike many such songs, this one has rarely been reinterpreted). A brush with death, real or imagined, inspires a song. The song's creation affords its composer (or performer, or both) a chance to express something penetrating about mortality, which is then shared with listeners. These listeners project their own insights and experiences onto the song. Sometimes they take it up themselves, expanding and adapting until a hybrid emerges. This revision is also shared, and the cycle repeats. The dynamic is both commemorative and cathartic. It serves as an act of remembering, even if the subject is fictional (because fantasies of death are still confrontations with it), but also as a soul-reckoning with the ineffable.

This book is about unhappy music—songs of death and loss caused by sudden, often violent reversals of fortune, celebrated and scrutinized for what each reveals about the human condition, and the role creativity plays in processing trauma and grief. Its epigraph comes from country music's melancholic "Silver Fox," whose gospel blues, "Feel Like Going Home," seeks a deathlike peace from a perceived life of defeat ("I tried and I failed / And I'm tired and weary").[2] Because few of the characters in these songs had the good fortune to prepare for their deaths, I feel my role is to send them off with some kind of posthumous

---

1   See "The Triplett Tragedy" in chapter 1.
2   Recorded twice by Charlie Rich in full-blown arrangements with organ and choir. The definitive, pull-over-your-car version is his breathtakingly spare piano and vocal demo from 1973.

closure and, in the process, elucidate something worthwhile about the drive to document death's impact, in the most tragic of circumstances, in song.

A homicidal couple commits a series of child murders, burying their victims on a desolate moor. Both die in prison, the man unrepentant, the woman contrite but demonized by a community unable to fathom her cruelty. A generation later, their crimes still haunt, their motives mystify.

The Moors Murders also happened, and two unrelated musicians who grew up in the shadow of these ghastly crimes culled youthful memories of headlines, news photos, and hushed dinner-table conversations to create songs about them in adulthood. Unlike the first song, these weren't obscure archival recordings primarily heard by specialists or collectors; they appeared on popular albums of the day and were heard by both ardent and casual fans at rock concerts.[3]

Why do people chronicle such bleak and disturbing events in music— specifically songs, those amiable bursts of lyric and tune linked with holidays, radio hits, and campfire singalongs? On one level, it's a banal question; people write music about all sorts of things, and dramatic accounts drawn from life can grip listeners and translate to cash and cachet for ambitious professionals. But the widow of the first song sought neither remuneration nor a mass audience; the story of her husband's death was a private affair made public, the song previously shared only with family and friends. And the child-murder songs were atypical album tracks by both artists: non-catchy, non-commercial, focused less on commerce than on art.

This is not consistently so; other songs in this book were unapologetic stabs at the big time or at significant statements. But the best of them, whether lurid or restrained, popular or esoteric, spring less from the desire to score hits than from the desire to connect with something tangible, felt, and lived. And the song as a musical unit—concise and reductive, easily shared and learned—provides an ideal currency for this commemorative, cathartic exchange.

Life, we all know, is dictated by death. It lurks behind us, our constant companion, impelling action and reverie both languid and tense. If many trade belief in a literal soul for some notion of psychic essence, few wish to give up the secular ghost too soon, or unexpectedly, or (even) at all. So it makes sense that some souls dictate songs about it—try to capture something key or novel or timeless about the inevitable in as immediate and emotive a form as music. "Man cannot endure his own littleness," wrote Ernest Becker in *The Denial of Death* (1973), "unless he can translate it into something meaningful on the largest possible level."[4] I don't entirely agree; I'd end the sentence after "meaningful"

---

3   See "Suffer Little Children" in chapter 2.
4   Ernest Becker, *The Denial of Death* (New York: Free Press, 1997), p. 196.

because, for every grandiose vision of lasting legacy, there are far humbler hopes of simply not being forgotten.

Anyone who's wandered an old graveyard—sifted through weeds and brambles to read half-sunken tombstones among gnarled tree roots and fallen branches—will know the forlorn sense of lost souls and the efforts families made to memorialize them. "I mattered" or "They mattered," such stones seem to say. Sudden or violent death (or reduced lifespan—old cemeteries teem with graves of children felled by now curable diseases) exacerbates tragedy and the desire to remember. As does poverty. Such graves resonate with the homely folk songs in this book, and I'm drawn to the unpretentious earnestness of both. A hand-inscribed sandstone marker in rural America will always move me more than an elaborate tomb on some funerary Park Avenue.

> *In murder ballads, the magic is in the mystery, the parts left unsaid. Like the wordless, unspeakable parts of our own psyche, murder ballads hold secrets that loom larger the farther down they're pushed. The more holes we cut in these songs, the more powerful they become. —Rennie Sparks[5]*

This book collects (revised) essays I originally wrote for *Murder Ballad Monday,* a blog about old songs of death and disaster and their more modern counterparts.[6] In 2015, the blog was incorporated into *Sing Out!,* the pioneering music journal that documented the postwar folk revival, lauded in its heyday by Woody Guthrie as his favorite magazine. Augmenting those original essays are new ones, written specifically for this book. *Sing Out!* folded as a print journal in 2014, and *Murder Ballad Monday* was a strictly online venture. Its mission was captured in a subtitle: "Reflections on the tougher side of life in old, weird America and the British Isles." More on "old, weird America" in a moment, but note the expanded subject matter: not just murder ballads, the subtitle promises, but songs about the "tougher side of life." If this implies a slight discomfort with the topic plus a desire to broaden its scope, I share both.

Murder ballads are traditional songs about homicide, based in varying degrees on factual accounts, passed between performers and audiences, sometimes over centuries. Many originated in Britain ("Lord Randall," "Matty Groves," "The Twa Sisters") and found their way to America, especially Appalachia, in the 18th and 19th centuries. Others originated in America ("Omie Wise," "Knoxville Girl," "Silver Dagger") but have British forebears. Related are more recent topical broadsides inspired by current events ("Stagger Lee," "Frankie and Johnny," "Delia").

---

5   Rennie Sparks, "Pretty Polly," in Sean Willentz and Greil Marcus, eds., *The Rose and the Briar: Death, Love and Liberty in the American Ballad* (New York: W. W. Norton & Co.), p. 39.

6   Founded by friends and University of Chicago alums Ken Bigger, Patrick Blackman, and Shaleane Gee.

A curious facet of the older songs is how geographic and generational variables alter their narratives over time—performers add and subtract lines, switch places and names, omit critical details. The "holes cut in these songs" mentioned by Rennie Sparks[7] refer to this gradual erosion and consequent confusion about what happens and why. Because songs of murder sat awkwardly with practitioners of old-time religion, morbid and sensational facts were often excised. Their deletion made plots and motivations confusing—at times incomprehensible—but also increased the songs' inherent sense of mystery. Sung and re-sung, these eerie and abridged versions became new standards, uprooted from their progenitors—dark riddles about death, violence, and the human capacity for evil.

These are worthy of study, and a large body of exegetical text exists. But because many concern women killed by men, and because those narrative "holes" obscure "whats" and "whys", too often an air of misogyny imbues them; without clarifying facts, fatalism and sanctimony render them cautionary tales about what happens to sinful (i.e., sexually active) women. For these two reasons—the ubiquity of analysis and the monotony of "dead bad girl" themes—I worked to expand *Murder Ballad Monday*'s purview to include songs about crime sprees, war, illness, car wrecks, and funerary customs and to add modern analogues from Chicago blues, punk, post-punk, and alt-country.

Murder Ballad Monday rode an unlikely wave of interest in these desperate songs that began in earnest with the 1997 re-release (on CD) of the *Anthology of American Folk Music*—a cryptic compendium of musical Americana that helped launch the mid-twentieth-century folk boom, compiled from hillbilly, blues, and other roots music recordings of the '20s and '30s by the eccentric artist, filmmaker, and occultist Harry Smith. The critic Greil Marcus was a crucial figure in the re-release, and excerpts from his same-year chronicle of Bob Dylan and the Band's *Anthology*-influenced *Basement Tapes* (recorded in 1967) were included with Smith's original liner notes.[8] Marcus memorably described Smith's *Anthology* as an "occult document disguised as an academic treatise"—a hermetic work of art organized around schemas both arcane (color-coding, volumes categorized by Water, Fire, and Air) and sociological (Black and white artists desegregated and unidentified by race).[9] He coined the classic phrase "old, weird America" to characterize its oddball characters and oneiric atmosphere and his vision of the collection as a surreal counter-narrative to orthodox history. In 2005 he co-edited a book of essays on American ballads, which further put these songs on the map (and added contemporary counterparts).[10]

Death suffuses Smith's *Anthology*: among its titles are songs about homicide, suicide, assassinations, shipwrecks, and crop blight. It includes traditional murder ballads, rural folk tunes, and topical broadsides. And its reappearance set off a mania in some quarters for tragic old ballads, prompting reissues of

7   One-half of the gothic country duo the Handsome Family (with her husband Brett Sparks) and the band's acclaimed lyricist. Her essay on "Pretty Polly" in Willentz and Marcus's *The Rose and the Briar* is a far-reaching analysis of that ballad.

8   Greil Marcus, *Invisible Republic* (New York: Henry Holt & Company, 1997).

9   Greil Marcus, "The Old, Weird America," liner notes for *Anthology of American Folk Music* (Smithsonian Folkways, 1997), p. 7.

10   Willentz and Marcus, *The Rose and the Briar*.

HARRY SMITH, C. 1965

forgotten recordings, *Anthology*-inspired tribute concerts and recordings, and murder-ballad-themed concept albums by major artists—collective efforts to excavate those secrets that loom largest when pushed down.

An unassuming country boy becomes an unlikely hold-up man and killer. He morphs into a hero for the rural poor despite official pariah status, sharing his plunder and evading authorities until shot dead in a farmer's field. His legend outlives him.

Songs of the topical variety have a newspaper-like tone (and were often based on journalistic accounts). They add details and build tension, line by line, their drama heightened by non-mists-of-time contemporaneity and just-the-facts verisimilitude. But if reportage is their manner, legend looms nearby. The pariah-*cum*-folk hero Pretty Boy Floyd, described above, inspired Woody Guthrie to mythologize his life in ballad form during the Great Depression.[11] The resulting tune—a genial but subversive account of a modern-day Robin Hood—resonated with ancient Child ballads[12] but also inspired '60s rock musicians. The motif of the righteous bandit who champions an oppressed citizenry, timeless and archetypal, found new life in antiauthoritarian times.

I came to these songs mainly via the "old, weird America." Tangentially aware of them for years—through reading, rock covers, and roots music reissues—they were contextualized and revealed to me as part of a greater whole by the post-Smith *Anthology* revival. A lifelong music lover, son of a choir-director father and violinist mother, I was immersed in music from birth: classical, spirituals, show

---

11   See "A Walkin' Chunk a Mean-Mad" in chapter 3.

12   Traditional songs and their variants, collected and studied by the musicologist Francis James Child in *The English and Scottish Popular Ballads* (Houghton, Mifflin and Company, 1882-98), a five-volume bible for folk-song enthusiasts that includes many murder ballads.

tunes, pop, rock, and country—the latter mainly through my mother. If Dad grounded me in *a cappella* choral music, Mom did so with Mozart and Bach but also Tom T. Hall and Dolly Parton. An early memory, around age four, is of my mother, busy in the kitchen, singing along to Tennessee Ernie Ford on the radio, and me trying gamely to join in.

Dad came from a (lower) middle-class background, but Mom was poor. She grew up partly in rural Kentucky, on land her family—mostly dirt farmers—cultivated as best they could for a century and a half. My mother was the first in her family to attend college (on scholarship), and they doted on her musical talent. But she never saw a dentist until adulthood, and an ugly scar on her knee confirmed her deprived upbringing (she split it open as a child, but her parents couldn't afford medical care). This dichotomy between poverty and comfort, rural roots and urban respectability, sat uneasily with me. Decades before *Hillbilly Elegy* and Hillary's basket of deplorables, I knew how society viewed my families. Dad's was bourgeois-aspirant and educated ("good"), and Mom's salt-of-the-earth and struggling ("bad"). In ruder terms, she was white trash, rescued from redneck ignorance and squalor by my upwardly mobile father.

Yet I always preferred her family to his. They were earthier, more openhearted, and less passive-aggressive. They laughed more and, while both families sang, when Mom harmonized with her sisters (she had four full plus three half-sisters), their joy was contagious. Her father was a carpenter who made his own guitars, and at family gatherings he'd play story-songs he'd written or country hits like Dolly Parton and Porter Wagoner's "Jeannie's Afraid of the Dark." Both families were roughly conservative Christian—Mom's evangelical, Dad's middle-of-the-road Methodist. But as I shifted from believer to atheist to spiritual-not-religious over the years, her family was less judgmental. And as I delved deeper into art, bohemia, and radical politics, they seemed less scandalized by pierced ears, ripped clothes, Marxist paperbacks, and AIDS activist buttons. We may have had little to talk about beyond family, but I always felt welcome.

My parents divorced when I was a teenager, and the schism prompted a lifelong passion for genealogy and historical research. Today I recognize this activity as a coping strategy—a quest to find out where I came from as my family fell apart. Always absorbed by lists and charts and unsolved mysteries, my new hobby combined all three. In pre-digital days this required long hours in libraries, interviewing aged kin, and walking graveyards. Years of study uncovered multiple skeletons in multiple closets, including murder. It also spurred a fascination with the genealogy of songs—a desire to map out themes and motifs and find musical ancestors and descendants that culminated in *Murder Ballad Monday* and this book.

More than once in my twenties, I stumbled on this graffito: *Film is art ... TV is furniture ... Rock and roll is life.*[13] It summed up my ethos in the early '80s,

13   No idea where it originated. A Google search uncovers only a variant: "Film is art, *theater* [my italics] is life, TV is furniture." I saw it on a wall at Tewligan's Tavern (Louisville's premier punk club) circa 1983 and a year or so later over a toilet at the School of the Art Institute of Chicago.

Frank Loose

LOUISVILLE'S PREMIER PUNK CLUB, TEWLIGAN'S TAVERN, 1984

when auteurs still made vital films and rock music remained the linchpin of youth culture. I collected rock records, read rock mags and (mimeographed) zines, played in rock bands in high school and beyond, and, before leaving my hometown of Louisville for art school, I celebrated my outsider status with fellow misfits in the local punk scene. Among musicians I met there were Cathy Irwin and Janet Bean—Carter Family enthusiasts who later formed the alt-country band Freakwater. Blending punk and country was rare in those days; the latter genre was too closely linked with reactionary politics and the Moral Majority. But when artists tried, I was thrilled: caught in a tug-of-war between down-home heritage and anarchic demimonde, successful mergers made me feel whole.

Cartoony cow-punk bands had made wiseass efforts, but a sea change occurred in the '80s as cutting-edge artists embraced country roots. Thus L.A.'s X, whose singers John and Exene resembled a punk Johnny Cash and June Carter, launched the Knitters—a side project that played countrified versions of X songs plus covers by Lead Belly and Merle Haggard. R.E.M., actual Southerners inspired by punk, had a lead singer who sang with an undisguised drawl and crooned Charlie Rich and Roger Miller tunes sans irony. The Violent Femmes, snotty folk-punks fronted by an actual evangelical, opened their sophomore LP with a self-penned murder ballad.[14] And in 1985, an obscure album called *Fear and Whiskey* by the British punks the Mekons—less a band than a socialist collective who wrote group compositions and recorded in various configurations—achieved the seemingly impossible, melding punk, left-wing politics, and late-capitalist despair to Hank Williams–style

---

14   "Country Death Song," *Hallowed Ground*, 1984. Basically a rehash of Dylan's "Ballad of Hollis Brown" (1964) and inspired by the singer Gordon Gano's youthful run-ins with murder ballads.

honky-tonk.[15] One such configuration was the Jon Langford–led cover band Pine Valley Cosmonauts—a shifting ensemble of roots rockers (e.g., Dave Alvin, Steve Earle, Alejandro Escovedo) who cut three albums of songs of death and homicide between 2002 and 2013, further raising the profile of murder ballads. Langford and various Mekons (e.g., Tom Greenhalgh, Kevin Lycett, Sally Timms) played critical roles in recasting tragic ballads and the gestation of the alt-country genre, hence their recurrence within this book. By the time I left art school, I was collecting country records and had traded my leather jacket for work shirts and a CAT Diesel Power hat.

This reaffirmation of lineage peaked for me, at least symbolically, in 1989, when my longtime girlfriend and soon-to-be wife—also a Kentuckian and misfit, torn between bourgeois and blue-collar facets of family—hosted with me a "mournful evening" of performance art called the Tragedy Club.[16] Multiple artists staged works on lonely, forsaken themes, and we provided linking bits— songs and vignettes rather than emcee-style introductions—between acts. It was the fullest airing yet of my integrated country-punk self, shared with the life partner who'd accompanied my journey.

We sang "Long Black Veil," lit by gothic candelabra, and "Lost Highway," seated on the bar. But the image burned in my memory is our opening gambit—a kind of visual poem that captured all my conflicted feelings about country and punk, high and low art, left and right politics, and my split-culture background. Dressed in redneck finery (denim, flannel, bandanas, and boots), we laid an American flag on the floor, clinked Coors tallboys together and swigged, then fell into each other's arms and slow-danced on Old Glory to Patsy Cline's "Sweet Dreams."

Mostly it is loss which teaches us about the worth of things.
—Schopenhauer, Parerga and Paralipomena, *1851*

I include this digression about my life and background for two reasons. First, it delineates themes vital to this book and grounds them in my experience. Second, because, for me, art—whether writing, painting, or playing music—is inseparable from life, and, despite inevitable immersion over the years in postmodern thought (I used to teach Intro to Critical Theory), I remain, in many ways, an unrepentant modernist. Without bogging down in tedious debate over this ism vs. that ism, what I mean is I care more about human beings and their inner experience than about fussing about language. I value sincerity over irony, poetry over concept, seek meaning, and reject nihilism. This makes me highly uncool in circles where emotion is routinely derided as "sentiment" and transcendent yearning as "woo

15   In *Revenge of the Mekons*, Joe Angio's 2013 documentary about the band, the critic Mark Kemp nails their accomplishment: "I'm a Southern guy who grew up on country music … I sometimes think that [band co-founder] Jon Langford gets my culture better than I do … I mean, blue-collar country fans shouldn't be conservative … They should be leftists. And only a socialist Brit could get that across."
16   Curated by the artist and composer Robert Metrick and held in a smoky basement dive in Chicago called Club Lower Links–long defunct but then famous for cabaret-style live art.

woo." I'm hardly anti-intellectual, but this all-brain/no-heart trend has dominated cultural discourse for half a century; it doesn't dominate me.

This alignment affects my approach to the book's often homespun, ultra-earnest songs, their stories, writers, and singers. If part of my role is to send off the dead with posthumous closure, I wish to give them dignity and listen respectfully to both the tale of their demise and the teller. In doing so, I can't (and don't want to) be an impartial witness. I've no desire to plant myself squarely in each story. But I, too, project insights and experiences onto the songs in this cycle of commemorative, cathartic exchange.

> *Death is both profound and banal. Like life, it's simultaneously the only thing that matters and of no great importance. Few things affect us more deeply, yet its ubiquity, inevitability, and the cheapness with which it's treated in the sociopolitical sphere conspire to negate its significance. It inspires great art and stupefying clichés. And its omnipresence creates conundrums for the compassionate ...*

I wrote those words in an essay about the twentieth anniversary of my first wife's death.[17] She died of cancer at 34, less than a year after terminal diagnosis, nine years after we slow-danced on the American flag. We were unlikely high-school sweethearts who stayed together for 17 years. She fell ill at a turning point in our lives, soon after being sworn in as an attorney (she practiced civil-rights law, her vocational dream, for mere months) and one week after buying our first house, where we planned to raise a family. Instead, she died there. This happened two years to the day after my mother succumbed to cancer at 55. Three of Mom's sisters died, also of cancer, during the same season of grief.

It was a devastating experience—two years that forced my first total life rethink. Bereavement was brutal; at times, I doubted I'd survive. I lost my footing and had to rebuild a foundation for my life. A detail of our final Christmas together haunts me. We spent it in the hospital, where she was delirious from dehydration. She'd been too ill to get me anything but managed to convey, despite her impairment, what she'd most wanted to give me: the recent rerelease of Smith's *Anthology of American Folk Music*.

I share all this not because I'm special; I'm not. I lost a partner and parent sooner than most and was a disoriented widower in my mid-thirties. The inevitable reality of life is the death of ourselves and everyone we love. But no experience in my life changed me more, and as I introduce this book about songs of death and loss, I'm mindful that my experience is both universal and unique to me. And if this particular life upheaval constitutes my own sudden reversal of fortune, this book is, in a way, my own tragic ballad.

The "conundrums for the compassionate" I mentioned refers to the ubiquity of tragedy and to misgivings I had over still grieving my wife two decades after her death:

17   "Final Days," www.facebook.com/sljonesart, 2018.

Who am I to carry a torch for someone long dead when surrounded by such suffering and injustice? The answer lies in the miraculous bond of shared experience: [Her] death links me to every other human being who watched helpless as a loved one perished, and awakening to this universality and attendant empathy is humanity's greatest hope.

I still believe that. It's among the myriad reasons I wrote this book. So, from here on, I'll step aside. There are other stories to tell, and I'll give their protagonists and interpreters my full attention. If, like me, you find the genealogies of songs fascinating, I hope the serpentine routes they take in these pages enthrall you. And if, like me, you value heart and brain equally, I hope these accounts move, enlighten, and even afford some closure to your own private pains.

STEVEN L. JONES, *LIFE DURING WARTIME (JOIE DE MORT)* (DETAIL), 2015

CHAPTER ONE: ANCIENT HISTORY:
ORIGINS OF THE MODERN MURDER BALLAD

DIGGING FOR CLUES IN THE FATAL FLOWER GARDEN

Just come in and stay with me. No harm will come to you.
—*Jacob and Wilhelm Grimm, "Hansel and Gretel," 1857*

"Fatal Flower Garden," recorded in 1929 by Nelstone's Hawaiians, is only the second of eighty-four songs on Harry Smith's epochal *Anthology of American Folk Music*—a collection justly celebrated in some macabre corners for its songs of dark, outré subject matter and tone (e.g., Clarence Ashley's "House Carpenter," G. B. Grayson's "Ommie Wise," Dock Boggs' "Sugar Baby"). But despite such robust competition from the remaining eighty-three, it may well be the darkest, most outré of them all.

Its provenance is unspectacular: one of eight known sides recorded by the obscure Alabama duo of Hubert Nelson and James D. Touchstone—their performing moniker a reference to their (then quite trendy) "Hawaiian" sound (basically hillbilly music plus lap steel guitar) combined with their hybridized surnames—and entirely unlike the comparatively up-tempo other seven (the best known of which, "Just Because," is a country standard famously covered by Elvis Presley). The song's surface eeriness arises from a discordant union of opposites—specifically, its incongruous blend of soothing "island" music and relaxed "folksy" singing with a lyric that describes (of all things) ritual child murder.

Harry Smith Archives

ANTHOLOGY OF AMERICAN FOLK MUSIC COVER ART, 1952.

Or, more accurately, almost describes.

It starts quietly, almost preternaturally so, and never varies in tempo or dynamics. Just a steady rhythm guitar strumming beats 2 and 3 in brisk but subdued waltz time while a steel guitar mutedly picks the song's tune. Then voices join in—two men in close harmony, Southerners, drawling its verses in an unhurried manner that might sound lazy or sleepy if not for the slight lilt they give to every other syllable.

It rained, it poured, it rained so hard
It rained so hard all day
That all the boys in our school
Came out to toss and play

They tossed their ball again so high
Then again so low
They tossed it into a flower garden
Where no one was allowed to go

The voices are gentle and childlike—grown men reciting a nursery rhyme. Appropriate, perhaps, for a nostalgic evocation of child's play on a rainy afternoon (and if you let it, the scratchy background noise of the 78 rpm source recording resembles rainfall). But as the verses get stranger, the voices remain unchanged and their sing-songy tone grows unsettling.

Up stepped this gypsy lady
All dressed in yellow and green
"Come in, come in, my pretty little boy
And get your ball again"

"I won't come in, I shan't come in
Without my playmates all
I'll go to my father and tell him about it
That'll cause tears to fall"

She first showed him an apple sweet
Then again a gold ring
Then she showed him a diamond
That enticed him in

Next, a short instrumental break: a "Hawaiian" retread of the verse's melody (the song's invariant structure—verse after verse without chorus, refrain, or change of tune, key, or rhythm—creates a hypnotic effect that complements the chant-like singing), the Pacific Island ambiance increasing the song's strangeness. Then, a sudden turn of the screw:

She took him by his lily-white hand
She led him through the hall
She put him into an upper room
Where no one could hear him call

Without elaboration or explanation, the narrative shifts from omniscient to first-person:

Oh, take these finger-rings off my fingers
Smoke them with your breath
If any of my friends should call for me
Tell them that I'm at rest

Bury the Bible at my head
The testament at my feet
If my dear mother should call for me
Tell her that I'm asleep

Bury the Bible at my feet
The testament at my head
If my dear father should call for me
Tell him that I am dead

The End. A tasteful glissando on the steel guitar and the song is over. The rain-like white noise ceases less than three minutes after it starts. And your neck hair is likely raised, your mind left swimming with the song's haunting, fragmented imagery.

While the song's clash of styles (pretty music with weird, ominous lyrics) explains its surface tension, much of the sense of unease in "Fatal Flower Garden" results from cognitive dissonance based on exclusion. It comes not from the story but from what's left out of it, and from the listener's attempts to fill in those narrative gaps. The song opens with a game of rainy-day pitch-and-catch and ends with a dying (or already dead?) boy dictating his final wishes (to whom—his killer?) for his parents and playmates. In between, a witchy temptress flashes fruit and jewelry at the boy until he succumbs, followed by a sudden jump-cut to his deathbed drama.

The key to the confusion is the song's origins in a centuries-old ballad and the peculiar process by which such songs mutated over time—acquiring and shedding verses, characters, and events as they passed among performers according to the whims, designs, and mnemonic imperfections of each. During that process, something critical was excised from "Fatal Flower Garden," leaving it without a center—specifically, without a murder, a killer, or a motive.

Each can be recovered. The song's historical source—the prosaic event that first inspired some anonymous songwriter to set it to music long ago—is known. One summer day in 1255, a nine-year-old English boy, Hugh of Lincoln, disappeared. Last seen at play with some neighbor children, his battered, bloodied corpse was later found at the bottom of a well. So, that's the murder—a heinous child-killing indeed. But who killed the boy and why? Here the record is equally clear (if no less reassuring): according to sordid accounts preserved for posterity by contemporary medieval scribes, Hugh—a pure-hearted gentile boy posthumously named a martyr and styled "Little Saint

Hugh"—was kidnapped and sadistically tortured to death in a Christ-defiling, sorcerous ritual . . . by evil Jews.

Sometimes lifting a stone reveals something foul and fetid underneath. Such blood-libel tales, offensive and preposterous as they seem today, were not uncommon once, and in medieval times they sprang up with deadly regularity, like buboes spreading plague. This one, in particular, had legs and, in the end, tragically made history.

Hugh of Lincoln's murder occurred after a flurry of deaths were blamed on Jews in twelfth- and thirteenth-century England, each followed by persecution, pogroms, and massacres. Lincoln had a sizable Jewish population, and a Jewish landowner named Copin (or Koppin or Jopin) was promptly accused of the slaying. He confessed—under torture—to killing the boy but also claimed that he died at the behest of an international cabal of Jewish necromancers dedicated to the kidnapping, torture, and ritual sacrifice (by crucifixion) of gentile children. In the madness and idiocy that followed, Copin was tied to a horse and dragged cross-town to the gallows. Eighteen "co-conspirators" were also hanged. The fallout from the hysteria was far-reaching: it played a significant role in the decision to expel all Jews from England in 1290 (they would not return until 1655).

Whatever the facts of Hugh's death, the rest of his story (and that of the song) shifts from the prosaic to the poetic. Presumably, his tale was told and retold by bards and balladeers for centuries, and, by the mid-1700s, a Scots-English folk song called "Sir Hugh" (Child 155) ("Sir" being a corruption of "Saint") had taken definite form. At some point during this gestation, the blame for the child's death became centered not on Copin, "a Jew," or "Jews," but on "a Jew's daughter," who beckons the boy after his ball breaks her window or lands in her yard. Francis James Child notes 15 versions of the song, with minor variations, in the third volume of *Ballads*. Unlike "Fatal Flower Garden," all but one (a curious Irish-American version wherein the killer isn't "the Jew's daughter" but "the Duke's daughter") describe the boy's murder and its aftermath.

A typical version, first published in 1806 but probably much older, fills in the "facts" missing from "Fatal Flower Garden" in lurid detail:

> *She's led him in through ae dark door*
> *And sae has she thro nine*
> *She's laid him on a dressing-table*
> *And stickit him like a swine*
>
> *And first came out the thick, thick blood*
> *And syne came out the thin*
> *And syne came out the bonny heart's blood*
> *There was nae mair within*

The boy dies; his body is weighted down with lead and callously tossed into a draw-well "fifty fathom deep." A postscript in most versions presents his funerary

Wellcome Collection/Creative Commons

BLOOD LIBEL: *MARTYRDOM OF SAINT WILLIAM OF NORWICH,* **INK DRAWING BY L. BEATRICE THOMPSON AFTER MICHAEL WOLGEMUT, 15TH CENTURY**

requests ("Bury the Bible at my feet, the testament at my head ...") as either his last words or a directive spoken by his spirit—usually to his mother—after death.

That this (seemingly) critical content should go missing in the song recorded by Nelstone's Hawaiians is probably no great mystery. Even in admittedly less enlightened times (i.e., 1929), such vicious anti-Semitism, not to mention explicit gore, was unlikely to find a sympathetic audience for performers who presumably desired commercial success as much as any rural musicians (and Nelson and Touchstone were savvy enough to go "Hawaiian" at the height of the fad's popularity). There is, in fact, no reason to assume the duo knew anything at all about the racist legacy of the song, which they likely encountered and "collected" A. P. Carter–style from musicians they knew or met while traveling. By then, it may have already lost all references to blood libel and explicit violence (more than one earthy ballad—"Pretty Polly," for instance—was trimmed of its most provocative content soon after arriving in the strait-laced States).

Child himself was repulsed by the ballad's racism and condemned the bigotry that inspired it. There is something deeply satisfying about reading his words (written decades before "Fatal Flower Garden" was recorded) after he dutifully spends seven pages reviewing the incendiary medieval record of Hugh's death and the murderous "Jewish conspiracy" that dispatched him: "[T]hese pretended child-murders, with their horrible consequences, are only a part of a persecution which, with all moderation, may be rubricated as the most disgraceful chapter in the history of the human race."[18]

What becomes of a song with such distasteful origins—is it rejected and abandoned, excised from the canon by people of tact and virtue? "Fatal Flower Garden" retains its place in the Smith collection, seemingly sans contention, and, though covered less often than cheerier *Anthology* fare like "Fishing Blues" or "King Kong Kitchie Kitchie Ki-Me-O," is still performed and occasionally recorded. ("Sir Hugh," on the other hand, courts controversy—long threads exist online debating whether to perform the song at all.)[19] Presumably, listeners understand that whatever despicable ideas inspired the song's progenitor can't justly be laid at its feet. Besides, "Fatal Flower Garden" is a song, not a tract—a work of poetry, not propaganda—and its absent center both obscures its hate-crime origins and inexorably alters its meaning.

So why does the song endure—what explains its dark powers of attraction and continued hold on the imagination? Part of its appeal is its sense of mystery. Just as what we don't know or can't see can make a scary film scarier, the missing middle of "Fatal Flower Garden" imbues an already eerie song with an additional layer of enigma and dread. But more is at work here, and internal evidence provides a key.

Note the substitution of the cringeworthy, racially charged "Jew" (in "Sir Hugh") with the blander, less ethno-specific "gypsy" (in "Fatal Flower Garden"). Today it's common to make a letter-case distinction between "Gypsy" and "gypsy," with a corresponding definition change. But in the past, the terms were interchangeable. The modern "Gypsy" always refers to a race of people: the dark-skinned, nomadic Romani. Like the Jews, they suffered centuries of persecution under Christendom (and were massacred en masse as part of Hitler's Final Solution). But the lowercase "gypsy" has (and had) a broader meaning—it too can mean Romani, but also (according to Merriam-Webster) "one that *resembles* [my italics] a Gypsy: especially, [a] wanderer."

In other words, in the parlance of the past, a gypsy needn't be Romani at all but possibly any nomadic outsider of unclear origin—especially one perceived as exotic or mysterious, who dwelt on or drifted through the fringes of society. These might include hobos, bohemians, and snake oil salesmen or, more fancifully, witches, spirits, and supernatural beings. This semantic shift is significant to the subject, because by the time of "Fatal Flower Garden," with Hugh of Lincoln's murder a fading or vanished memory, the song had taken on distinctly fanciful overtones.

---

18   Child, *The English and Scottish Popular Ballads*, vol. 3 (Mineola, N.Y.: Dover, 2003), pp. 240–241.

19   A rare modern version, styled "Little Sir Hugh," is a highlight of the British folk-rockers Steeleye Span's 1975 album *Commoners Crown*. Tune and lyrics are primarily the band's, but they retain the basic story, substituting "a lady gay . . . dressed in green" for the Jew's daughter. Hugh's funerary request becomes a recurring refrain, sweetly sung by the vocalist Maddy Prior: "Mother mother, make my bed / Make for me a winding sheet." But the description of the murder pulls no punches: "She lay him on a dressing board / and stabbed him like a sheep."

Students of "depth psychology" routinely analyze the underlying structures of dreams and cultural artifacts, locating recurring themes and motifs and elucidating their meanings. "Fatal Flower Garden" is rich with mythic resonances, and this archetypal quality likely explains the song's lasting power.

It also pinpoints its creepiest quality.

In an early scene from Val Lewton's *Curse of the Cat People* (1944)[20]—a haunting evocation of childhood with mythic and fairy-tale undercurrents disguised as a B-movie horror sequel—a lonely girl, rejected by her parents, wanders from home. A mysterious witch-like woman beckons her to leave the safety of the sidewalk and enter the unfamiliar yard of a spooky old house. She does so and, once within its gates, is rewarded with a white handkerchief, tossed by the woman from an upper-story window. It floats through the air, radiant against the grim grayscale of the film's photography and the child's melancholy life, and lands in her hand like a gift from Fairyland.

The handkerchief symbolizes her entrée to a psychological realm fraught with danger but pregnant with possibility. At this point, the film's plot truly begins, and its remainder movingly chronicles the girl's difficult passage from early childhood to prepubescence (notably with neither bloody violence nor people dressed as cats).

The scenario of a child tempted from the familiar path by an unknown entity or a mysterious dwelling place—most often in the woods—is ancient and ubiquitous. It occurs in fairy tales like Hansel and Gretel and Little Red Riding Hood, folk tales about the Russian Baba Yaga and the American Bloody Mary, and modern movies that draw from such sources like *The Blair Witch Project* (1999) and the *Evil Dead* trilogy (1981, 1987, and 1992). The motif also appears in paranormal lore (though not confined to child witnesses), as in the appearing and disappearing "ghost houses" sighted in remote or lonely locations (e.g., the woods beside south Chicago's decayed and supposedly haunted Bachelor's Grove Cemetery).[21] Typically, the child or young person in each sets off a life-threatening chain of events that, if confronted and resolved, offers insight and internal growth.

"Fatal Flower Garden," on the other hand, is conspicuous for its lack of resolution. In it, a boy at play—once Hugh of Lincoln, but now unmoored from any historical identity—is beckoned by a witch-like woman to leave the familiar path. She tempts him with gold, jewels, and (as in Snow White) "an apple sweet." He follows her into her mysterious house . . . and there the story ends—dismally, with his cold-blooded, off-screen murder. There's no triumphant outsmarting of the witch, no thrusting her into the oven, no cathartic struggle at all—only a doomed, dead boy and a disembodied voice.

---

20   Officially co-directed by Robert Wise and Gunther von Fritsch, though it's well known that Lewton was the primary auteur of his films.

21   There's even a curious case recorded by the UFO researcher John A. Keel of a mysterious "shed" that appeared early one morning on the familiar path of an elderly insomniac, only to vanish the following day. The man, who swore his experience was real, was frightened both by the structure's sudden appearance and a voice that called out to him, "Don't run . . . don't run." "I didn't 'sactly run," Keel quotes the man as saying, "but I walked pretty fast" (Keel, *The Mothman Prophecies*, Atlanta: IllumiNet Press, 1991, p. 149).

This is the evilest spell the song casts. It evokes the trappings of fairy tales but delivers nothing but death. Hansel, Gretel, and Little Red Riding Hood defeat their nemeses and (presumably) live to adulthood, wiser for their experience. The children and townspeople menaced by Baba Yaga or Bloody Mary escape or fight back. Even *Evil Dead*'s much-abused Ash, though never free of the demonic forces that plague him, wins a round or two before (inevitably) losing again. But, like the hapless twentysomethings of *The Blair Witch Project,* who never escape their own spooky house in the woods nor genuinely understand what they're up against, the boy in "Fatal Flower Garden" never has a chance: he perishes passively, terrified and alone.

In the end, despite its fairy-tale motifs, "Fatal Flower Garden" is a horror story in disguise. It's a narrated nightmare that neither instructs nor elevates but simply chills our blood and steals our sleep. This needn't be a worthless experience; good horror can offer insights into primal fears and a safe means for exploring them. But when the fears faced include sudden, cruel death at the hands of unimaginable evil, without hope or the possibility of meaning, it's probably best to bring along your Hawaiian guitar.

YOU CAN'T WIN A RACE WITH A CANNONBALL

I saw it. —Francisco Goya[22]

In the early nineteenth century, a topical folk song inspired by an imperial war radiated across the British Isles from an Irish epicenter. Shared by buskers and in mass-printed broadsheets, the song debunked notions of war as noble and glorious, instead offering a grunt's-eye view of its savage costs and deceitful motivations. It did so with a bare-bones scenario about a young man's ruinous injuries in the form of a rueful lament sung by his grieving mother.

My son John was tall and slim
And he had a leg for every limb
But now he's got no legs at all
They're both shot away with a cannonball

"Mrs. McGrath" (pronounced "McGraw"), or its shorter variant, "My Son John" (or "Ted"), is an anti-war song—a folk ballad generated by a specific conflict that transcends its particulars to denounce war in general. Inspired by the Peninsular War of 1807-1814—one of five campaigns constituting the Napoleonic Wars— the song uses the horrific outcome of violence to warn young men that military glory is a lie and a sham, that war is, at best, a rigged game wherein young men risk life and limb for dubious reasons. At the time, this was still a fairly radical

---

22   Title of an etching from the artist's *Los Desastres de la Guerre* series (1810-1820).

idea. The young man who goes to war and returns irremediably changed—his youth lost, innocence shattered, soul haunted—is a motif as old as war itself. But its use to question the whole enterprise of war was distinctly modern. While scattered anti-war traditions existed previously in the West, it took the post-Enlightenment era's willingness to challenge inherited truths to give the idea a broad voice.

First published in 1876, "Mrs. McGrath" dates from the Peninsular War and appeared as a Dublin broadside in 1815. Its narrative is straightforward, and lyrics vary little between versions. A British sergeant flatters Mrs. McGrath with images of her son in military garb ("… a scarlet coat with a big cocked cap / Mrs. McGrath, wouldn't you like that?"), then recruits him. Seven years pass without a word of his fate before a ship arrives and sets him ashore— alive but minus his legs. Mother and son lament his injuries in a darkly comic dialogue wherein she asserts that she'd rather have her son "as he used to be / Than the king of France and his whole navy." "My Son John" cuts the lyric in half, dispensing with all framing narrative and doubling the song's tension by reducing it to a terse first-person exchange about the boy's lost legs and ruined future and the folly of war. A sing-along chorus of nonsense syllables ("non-lexical vocables" is the musicological term) follows each verse in both variants.

> *Well, were you drunk or were you blind*
> *To leave your two fine legs behind?*
> *Or was it from sailing upon the sea*
> *That took your legs from the ground to the knee?*

The Napoleonic Wars were a fitting backdrop for such bitterness. In 1807, Napoleon launched a seven-year military campaign against Britain and Portugal to control the Iberian Peninsula. The following year he turned on his nominal ally, Spain. The Peninsular War was part of a broader program of European conquest that had netted the French Revolutionary hero turned tyrant control of over half the continent. But it also marked the beginning of the end for the *Empire française* and its supercilious commander. Compounding defeats culminated in the 1815 Waterloo disaster and his Atlantic island exile and death.

There was poetry, for some, in his comeuppance. While the egalitarian principles of the former Jacobin—who had transformed the French Republic into a dictatorship by political sleight-of-hand in 1799 and crowned himself Emperor in 1804—had always been less genuine than expedient, idealists of the era were still appalled by his brazenness. A disgusted Ludwig van Beethoven (whose original title for *Eroica*, his symphonic paean to the revolutionary zeitgeist, had been *Buonaparte*) famously excised the despot's name from the score when informed of his self-coronation. Others found poetry, however dark, in the tumult engendered by his hubris. In Spain, his Iberian land grab toppled the monarchy and plunged the nation into the internecine chaos of the War for Spanish Independence. While a more modern, democratic Spain eventually emerged, a storm cloud of disarray and violence enveloped the country for six miserable years. This was documented with harrowing intensity by the artist Francisco Goya in works like *Los Desastres de la Guerra* (1810-1820).

Goya's terrifying evocations of Mars run amok in *Desastres* questioned not merely the justness of the Peninsular War but, like "Mrs. McGrath," that of war itself. The artist's peculiar insider/outsider circumstances—official painter of the Spanish court before the monarchy's fall, firsthand witness to the atrocities of the invasion in its aftermath—informed his vision. Exposed equally to the ruthlessness of power and the retaliatory violence of its victims, he came to see civilization—two decades before Nietzsche's birth—as a fragile façade that masked inchoate brutality. In his work, he let the mask slip.

That "Mrs. McGrath" is an Irish song

George W. Hope/Library of Congress

DOUBLE AMPUTEE, AMERICAN CIVIL WAR, 1860S

highlights a startling fact. Among those fighting the French in the Peninsular War were nearly a hundred thousand Irishmen, representing a staggering forty percent of the British army. Britain had no military draft, so recruitment was aggressive and disproportionately aimed at the lower classes. This included much of the Emerald Isle, where economic strife made military life slightly more attractive than crushing poverty or debtors' prison. Inductees signed up for seven-year stints, their low yet reliable wages augmented by "beer money" allowances, but received little respect for their service. Though Anglo-Irish, Arthur Wellesley—1st Duke of Wellington, British field marshal, and nemesis of Napoleon (whom he trounced at Waterloo)—referred to the troops as bastards, drunks, and "the scum of the earth."

Many of these despised sons of Eire bore bayonet and musket against the French on May 3-5, 1811, when British-Portuguese forces routed an attempt by Napoleon to retake the town of Almeida at the Battle of Fuentes de Oñoro. Among their number may have been a soldier named John, or Ted, whose surname may have been McGrath and who may have returned from his seven years' service alive but missing his legs.

I wasn't drunk, and I wasn't blind
To leave my two fine legs behind
Was a cannonball on the fifth of May
Took my two fine legs away

Well known in Ireland (where it achieved anthemic status during the 1916 Easter Rebellion), "Mrs. McGrath" was rarely heard in America before the mid-century folk revival. Early recordings by the Weavers, Burl Ives, and Tommy Makem are lively but rather stiff and twee. Ives extolled the song's "use of wit to paint tragedy and make the telling bearable,"[23] but, to modern ears, the softened blow of these renditions packs little punch. Makem's version is expertly performed but too mannered (e.g., the *ritardando* that accompanies Mrs. McGrath's closing lament—a bitter or keening cry in better versions) to raise much emotion.[24]

Newer versions—by Bruce Springsteen, Fiddler's Green, and the Stanfields—fare better by jettisoning the ballad's pub-song qualities and darkening its ambiance. Springsteen slows his to a dirge and sings in a quiet, gruff voice over martial percussion and Irish instruments, while the latter two bands—a generation younger—speed the song up and raise its rock quotient with distorted guitars. All three return some bite to the song but also weigh it down with self-consciousness. Springsteen's version, in particular, feels like an art piece—its dramatic effects well-orchestrated and intended but contrived.

"My Son John" is perhaps better suited for modern times. Its less-is-more reductionism is akin, in its way, to both Ramones-style minimalism and Beckett-esque existential bleakness. Tim Hart and Maddy Prior's 1976 version (on *Folk Songs of Old England, Vol. 2*) models the song's strengths with nothing but guitar and their resonant voices in close harmony. The pair (ironically best known for their band Steeleye Span's ornate arrangements of traditional material) let the words and tune speak for themselves. The result is mesmerizing—a pared-down blend of both that stays with the listener long after the song's minute-and-a-half duration.

More recent renditions—by Lew Bear, the Imagined Village (who updated the song for the "War on Terror"), even the actor and singer John C. Reilly—make the song new in ways worth hearing, but none so boldly as the 1989 interpretation by Boiled in Lead. No other treatment updates the song so skillfully while simultaneously staying true to its centuries-old roots—reviving the passion and political sting that must have animated the song over a century ago by restoring some of its underlying rage and terror.

Formed in Minneapolis in 1983, Boiled in Lead (the name derives from the Scots murder ballad "The Twa Sisters") applied a post-punk, Celtic-by-way-of-the-American-Midwest sensibility to the British folk-rock model of *Liege and Lief*–era Fairport Convention. Their 1989 album *From the Ladle to the Grave* was a career highlight—a nearly seamless set of fourteen songs, played with irreverent humor and punk vim and vigor by the band's best lineup.

23 "Mrs. McGrath," *The Contemplator*, www.contemplator.com/ireland/mcgrath.html

24 Makem more than redeems himself on a gripping version of a related song, the traditional "Johnny, I Hardly Knew Ye" (Roud 3137), recorded with the Clancy Brothers in 1961. It tells a similar tale of a young man returning from war, battered and limbless, set to a martial melody derived from "When Johnny Comes Marching Home" (ironically, a song about bringing the boys back with honor rather than never sending them in the first place). Widely covered, "Johnny, I Hardly Knew Ye" is also frequently excerpted or interpolated in other songs (e.g., the Clash's "English Civil War").

Ladle adds Eastern European, African, and Middle Eastern strains to the multicultural mix and incorporates political themes—liberal, feminist, anti-war—smoothly and without sanctimony. Their version of "My Son John," developed from live jams and perfected in the studio, closes the album with fitting *Sturm und Drang.*

It begins with a brisk, bodhran-like rhythm so ominous you don't notice, at first, that it's the Bo Diddley beat—sped up and drained of all joy and sex. Scratchy rhythm guitar joins in, bass follows, and soon Todd Menton sings the familiar, 200-year-old words. He does so with such lucidity he almost over-articulates them, spitting out each syllable with vehemence bordering on contempt. Especially those "non-lexical vocables": his is the only version where the song's genial "whack-fol-de-riddle" nonsense chorus conveys as much menace—maybe more—as the proper words.[25] Menton's tenor voice neither booms nor shrieks; it tells his tale with focused intensity. It's a riveting performance that seems to channel the wraith-like voices of every soldier ever sent to war who realized too late he was cannon fodder.

> *And all foreign wars I'll now denounce*
> *Twixt this king of England or that king of France*
> *I'd rather my legs as they used to be*
> *Than the king of Spain and his whole navy*

Images of war blur together in the mind's eye—a montage of interchangeable flags, uniforms, and anonymous falling and fallen men. Menton runs out of verses, and the band fills the void with a cacophonous instrumental mid-section—a scorching evocation of battle built around Drew Miller's growling bass and David Stenshoel's screeching reeds. When the atonal assault ends—as if by ceasefire, with feedback lingering in the air like smoke—the doomy drums begin anew, and Menton says his piece one last time, quietly now, almost whispering the words:

> *For I was tall, and I was slim*
> *And I had a leg for every limb*
> *But now I've got no legs at all*
> *You can't win a race with a cannonball*

A clarion power chord sounds off in four sets of three, the last of which explodes like a final bomb before slowly fading in the still-charged air. An absurdist touch closes the song with eerie poetry: a lone Irish fiddle is faintly heard sawing mournfully (mindlessly?) away, then abruptly ceases, like the last animated skeleton returning to its grave before daybreak on Halloween night.

---

25   Menton compares his vocal approach to the staccato patterns of the Irish frame-drum. "I'm actually a bodhran instructor now," he told me. "I tell people to attack. Literally, it's the whacking thing, it has some punch to it. After you state your case, 'I was tall and I was slim,' then unconsciously using the whack—literally saying, 'Are you listening to me? Do I have your attention now?'" (Interview by the author, 2015).

Prado Museum/Creative Commons

FRANCISCO GOYA, *THIRD OF MAY 1808*, 1814

Stenshoel described the song's "chaotic center" to me as a "kind of aural *Guernica* . . . intended to call to mind the suffering inflicted by war."[26] It's an apt touchstone. Pablo Picasso's iconic anti-war painting—prompted by the 1937 fascist bombing of a Basque village during the Spanish Civil War—was, in a sense, a reinvention of Goya, a reaching back in time by one Spanish genius to another, the latter a formerly apolitical artist, suddenly galvanized to create a didactic work. The dark wartime art of Goya suffuses Picasso's masterpiece— especially his 1814 painting *Third of May 1808*, made when the artist was sixty-eight (but must have felt 100).

The painting shows a firing squad of French soldiers coldly executing Spanish peasants who resisted Napoleon's invasion of Madrid—summarily, at night, by stark lamplight. Goya freezes the action before the guns fire, showing the expressions of panic, terror, and despair of the doomed men whose only crime was the spontaneous defense of their homes and city. They stand in a mound of corpses—the shooters' previous victims—like beasts in a slaughterhouse assembly line. A central figure lifts his arms in shock and stares at his killers: "Where is your humanity?" he seems to say. But Goya gives the soldiers neither expressions nor faces, portraying them as a phalanx of sheer military force—a killing machine forged from dehumanized groupthink.

A previous artist would have organized these figures into a contrived tableau, minimizing bloodshed and giving each a distinct, symbolic pose and expression. Goya's image is composed but lacks all neoclassical stiffness, and his rendering— earthy, gory, loosely painted—pulls no punches in the name of "taste." Similarly,

---

26   Interview by the author, 2015.

John Skerce, *Blood on the Tracks: The Life and Times of S. Brian Willson*/PM Press

S. BRIAN WILLSON AFTER BEING RUN OVER BY A TRAIN, 1989

while his sympathies lie with the condemned men, he refuses to construct a simple allegory with clear-cut heroes and villains and, by doing so, rejects the inherent nobility (or at least inevitability) of war. In *Third of May 1808*, war is the enemy. In the end, Goya's soulless executioners are victims of state power equal to the ordinary folk they murder so mercilessly because under their uniforms they, too, are ordinary folk, debased by militarization and played as pawns in a tyrant's game.

Picasso applied all he learned from Goya to *Guernica*, recasting the old master's innovations for the Age of Anxiety. A jeremiad against an act of war, its somber deathscape ultimately condemns war itself by reminding us with each viewing that war always kills innocent people—an intolerable incongruity in a civilized society. *Guernica* also presciently delineates the most horrific quality of modern warfare— its utter detachment. If Goya's peasants stare pleadingly into their killers' eyes, Picasso's villagers never even see them. The bombs that take their lives issue from hidden assassins, insulated by technology from face-to-face reckoning.

Boiled in Lead dedicated their searing version of "My Son John" to an anti-war activist named S. Brian Willson. Willson had volunteered for service in Vietnam but returned disillusioned with the war and his country, a hawk-turned-dove. His response was admirably proactive. He earned a law degree, joined forces with other veterans, and committed to challenging official narratives of U.S. military actions.[27]

In the '80s, this meant policing the Reagan administration's aggressive policies in Central America—especially in Nicaragua, where the president had cast the former military police of the brutal dictator (and U.S. ally) Anastasio

---

27   Willson's best-known quote evokes his Vietnam epiphany and anti-war activism: "We are not worth more. They are not worth less" (S. Brian Willson, *Blood on the Tracks: The Life and Times of S. Brian Willson*, Oakland, Calif.: PM Press, 2011, pp. xviii–xix).

Somoza in the unlikely role of "freedom fighters." Reagan also condemned the popular movement that deposed Somoza as dangerous subversives "in America's backyard," tweaking paranoia to justify proxy war.

On September 1, 1987, Willson and other activists gathered at a California naval base to peacefully protest the shipment via train of munitions to Reagan's right-wing allies in Central America. They did so by blocking the tracks in an act of civil disobedience. A train failed to stop and plowed through the protestors, most of whom managed to avoid being hit. Willson was not so lucky. Critically injured, the naval base refused to transport him to a hospital, so his wife and friends struggled to keep him alive while waiting fifteen to twenty minutes for an ambulance. It was later learned that the FBI had declared Willson a suspected domestic "terrorist" and that the train that nearly killed him had been instructed not to stop. Willson's skull was fractured and the right lobe of his brain was damaged, but he survived.

He did, however, lose both legs below the knee.

THE TRIPLETT TRAGEDY

Truly old Watauga is making for herself a dark and bloody record.
—Watauga Democrat, *January 6, 1910*

In the early 1960s, late in life, an Appalachian woman bestowed a singular gift on the world—a song, spare but stirring, that related the grim events of a long-ago winter, half a century after they occurred.

A horrible sight I'll now relate
On Yadkin Elk it did take place
On Christmas morning at nine o'clock
The people met an awful shock

"The Triplett Tragedy" is a broadside-style ballad.[28] It documents with minimal poetic license how Columbus "Lum" Triplett killed his brother Marshall Triplett in a booze-fueled brawl, only to, in turn, be mortally wounded by Marshall's son, Granville Triplett. This occurred in 1909 in rural Elk Township in Watauga County, North Carolina, near the source of the Yadkin River. While a fact-based account, "The Triplett Tragedy" leaves myriad questions unanswered, including the cause of the lethal quarrel. The song was virtually unknown until an *a cappella* rendition, sung by the elderly Elk native Sophronie Miller Greer, appeared on a Smithsonian/Folkways LP in 1963. The singer's link to the tragedy transcended geography: twenty-six years old when Lum Triplett died, Sophronie was his widow.

She was also kin to one of American folk music's "first families." Her daughter by a second husband, Hazel Mae Greer, was married to the brother of the iconic

---

28   Credited to an obscure North Carolina postman/balladeer named Ed Miller.

old-time musician (and fellow Watauga native) Arthel "Doc" Watson. Sophronie's plaintive recitation of "The Triplett Tragedy" was included in a collection of musical performances by Watson and various relatives, compiled from field recordings by the archivist Ralph Rinzler and released at the height of the early '60s folk revival as *The Watson Family*. If Harry Smith's *Anthology of American Folk Music* was that movement's bible, Rinzler's set—recorded in North Carolina from 1960 to 1963—was a worthy adjunct to the canon. Rarely has such rich and varied traditional music been captured for posterity *in situ*—novelty tunes, instrumentals, ballads, and spirituals, performed by Watson and his family with skill and striking un-self-consciousness.

Even in this august context, "The Triplett Tragedy" stands out. The song is the only unaccompanied performance on *The Watson Family* and, for its duration, a hush beyond silence seems to surround Sophronie's solo voice. Sung when she was seventy-six and her sole recording, it's the only murder ballad known to have been recorded by a central participant in the events it describes. And, for five and a half minutes, it seems to stop time.

> *At Marshall Triplett's this begun*
> *The brothers met it seemed in fun*
> *They drank together all as one*
> *And then this trouble it begun*

The sound is stark, raw. The song lacks all aural niceties and demands full attention in an age of mass distraction. Its simple tune recalls both "Nottamun Town" (Roud 1044), the eerie medieval melody Bob Dylan borrowed for "Masters of War," and Buell Kazee's mournful reading of "The Butcher Boy" (Laws P24, Roud 409)—only sparer, more stripped down. For fourteen verses, its four-line structure, AABB rhyme scheme, and deliberate tempo never vary. The hypnotic result draws you deeper into the song's gradually unfolding narrative, line by line, fact by fact. Lyrics are similarly plain and direct—descriptive and utilitarian with just a dollop of pro-temperance sentiment and eschatological drama.

The voice is riveting. Aged and unlovely, it lacks the pleasant tone of similarly affectless but easier-on-the-ear primitives like Jean Ritchie or Ralph Stanley. Because she lived the events she recounts, the performance radiates authenticity. Despite the ballad's outside authorship, conceptual distinctions between singer and "singer" collapse—vocalist and narrator merge. Strength and vulnerability fuse into stoic dignity, with pain just below the surface. It sounds like she has waited all her life for this moment—to tell her story and share her truth with the world, suggesting that the song has been her companion for fifty years of remembering, grieving, and coping.[29]

---

29   Given the particulars of its best-known performance, it's unsurprising that covers of "The Triplett Tragedy" are rare. Indeed, there seems to be only one–a moody rendering by a contemporary Portland, Maine-based septet called the Ghosts of Johnson City, who rework the song in a reverent old-time arrangement with a gothic Americana gloss.

**SOPHRONIE MILLER GREER (FAR LEFT) ON HER PORCH WITH FAMILY
AND MUSICIAN HAZEL DICKEN, C. 1960**

*The reports of the fearful tragedy are so diversified that it is indeed hard
to get the straight of it.* —Watauga Democrat, *January 6, 1910*

On Christmas Day, 1909, violence ripped a family apart in North Carolina's
remote High Country. A drunken altercation between brothers—both middle-
aged family men—was quelled but re-erupted, causing death by exsanguination
when one brother stabbed the other. Blood seeped into ancestral soil and, like
the Bible story of the first murder, left one man dead and another doomed. The
slayer was apprehended by a deputy sheriff who also happened to be his dead
brother's son. Severely beaten by his nephew, he succumbed to his injuries days
later and died in jail. Brother killed brother, nephew killed uncle, and, as with
all such traumas, those left behind nursed psychic wounds as best they could,
then carried on. Poor farmers in early-twentieth-century Appalachia lacked the
luxury of prolonged introspection: life was hard, and grief and rage, like violence,
had to be quickly contained lest they threaten survival.

> *Then Marshall seemed to stand in the rear*
> *And struck Columbus with a chair*
> *"There is one thing that I do know*
> *You drink only to save your own"*

Tamer Sophronia "Sophronie" Miller was born in 1884 to a farmer–preacher
and his wife. Her paternal grandfather had been a fifer in the Confederate army.
Thirty-one years younger than Lum Triplett, she was his second wife. Lum
had half a dozen grown children from his first marriage. Widowed in 1904, he
married Sophronie soon after. It's unclear whether the couple had children: four
months after her husband's death, census records list Sophronie as the mother
of one child, but no child lives with her.

Facts are slippery things, often inspiring as many questions as they answer.
"The Triplett Tragedy" is based on relatively recent events, documented in print

and public records. Yet chasms open when one tries to flesh out its skeletal narrative or better comprehend its players' actions. Both brothers died, so there was no trial or attendant investigation. Consequently, journalistic accounts from regional newspapers are critical sources of information.

> *Marshall Triplett was killed in a drunken row on Christmas night at Elk, this county, by his brother Columbus. Both parties were drinking and got into a controversy about some subject. Hot words were passed but friends interfered and the parties separated. Later they met and a pitched battle followed which resulted in Marshall Triplett's death.* —Lexington Dispatch, *January 5, 1910*

This seems to be the earliest published account, prompted by Lum's arrest and internment in the county jail the same day. Yet it's already eleven days from the actual event, and the first discrepancy between press and song occurs almost immediately: the former places the killing at night, the latter in the morning. An article in the local Watauga paper offers a more detailed account the next day:

> *One report is that Columbus Triplett, drinking heavily went to the home of his brother, Marshall, and over some offense, not known to us, began to curse and abuse him in a violent manner. The brother resented the bitter language, but no blows were passed, a daughter of deceased persuading her enraged uncle out of the house and some distance away, but his blood running high he soon returned, and Marshall hearing him in the yard, went out, and a general rough and tumble fight ensued ...* —Watauga Democrat, *January 6, 1910*

Questions proliferate: What caused the fight? What "controversy" or "offense" could drive a man to commit murder, let alone fratricide? Was the visit planned—a Christmas celebration? Where was Sophronie—did she accompany Lum to Marshall's house?

Press and song agree that the fraternal fracas was initially disrupted by family or friends. But the fire soon reignited:

> *They met in combat by the barn*
> *Mrs. Triplett went to stop this wrong*
> *Columbus stabbed Marshall in the thigh*
> *And left him on the ground to die*

Marshall Triplett and his first wife divorced (unusual for the era; was he a violent man? a drunk?). He remarried and, between his two wives, fathered a large brood. His eldest that Christmas was Granville, twenty-nine; his youngest, a ten-month-old. His second wife Ida ("Mrs. Triplett") was heavily pregnant with their last child, who would be born six weeks after her father's death.

The fatal thigh injury—a quick and ghastly death ("within three minutes," wrote the *Democrat*) caused by severing the femoral artery—is consistent in all accounts. It may have extra-medical significance: because who tries to kill a man by stabbing him in the leg? It seems probable that the blow was defensive in nature—meant to wound, not to kill. In which case, Lum may never have intended his brother's death at all, further compounding the tragedy.

> *Then Marshall's wife in great distress*
> *Stayed by her husband while in death*
> *The children's screams was heard around*
> *Which did produce a solemn sound*

Solemn. One tries with difficulty to imagine the scene—the mix of shock and despair, stillness and pandemonium, that must have accompanied Marshall's death after the frenzied fight. His body prone, his wife and children around him, his lifeblood spilling rhythmically onto the hardened ground, staining winter snow crimson red.

Where was Lum? Did he stay behind or flee the scene? The most glaring narrative gap in both press and song is that, from December 25th (after Marshall's death) until his arrest on January 5th, Lum Triplett is unaccounted for. Was he in hiding, roughing it somewhere in the region's dense woods and rocky crags? No manhunt, let alone lynch mob, seems to have been organized. Marshall would have been buried within days of his death. Was there a funeral? Did Lum attend?

> *The deputy sheriff undertook to arrest Columbus Triplett after he had killed his brother but he resisted. The officer succeeded in making the arrest after beating Triplett dreadfully. He was lodged in jail here today about 10 o'clock.*
> —Lexington Dispatch, *January 5, 1910*

"Here" is Boone, the location of the Watauga County jail. The deputy sheriff is Lum's nephew, Granville Triplett, and his apprehension of his uncle is the most contested portion of the tale. Note that the familial relationship is unmentioned in this account, possibly unknown, and that Lum didn't go peacefully. "The Triplett Tragedy" says otherwise:

> *Then Lum went off to go away*
> *And met Gran Triplett on his way*
> *At Leroy Triplett's this was said*
> *Lum said to Gran, "Your father's dead"*
>
> *Lum said to Gran, "I'll let you know*
> *I've killed your father at his home*
> *I'll now surrender up to thee*
> *You treat me kindly if you please"*

Here, the deputy sheriff is unaware that his father is dead until told by Lum at a relative's home. The wording is vague ("Lum went off to go away") and time truncated ("And met Gran Triplett on his way")—presumably for dramatic effect and narrative concision. The arrest, in fact, occurred eleven days after the killing. But here everything happens in swift succession, seemingly within twenty-four hours. Lum meets Granville by chance, confesses his crime, and offers no resistance. (A January 13th article in the *Democrat* agrees that Lum "surrendered" to his nephew.) Regardless, Granville would not be appeased:

Gran said to Lum, "One thing I'll do
If you killed Father I'll kill you"
He then beat Lum at a dreadful rate
And made bad bruises on his face

"He was so badly beaten up that he had to be helped to his cell," wrote the *Dispatch*, noting this was Lum's second violent melee in less than two weeks. But it was a kick to the torso administered by his nephew that proved his undoing, causing "intense suffering" (the *Democrat*) and leaving him "in a dangerous condition" (the *Almanace Gleaner*, January 20).

Gran then took Lum to Watauga jail
He went behind the bars to stay
Those beats and bruises they inflamed
Which brought Columbus to his grave

Lum died nine days later, on January 14th. A postmortem implicated Granville: his kick had triggered a slow death from internal injuries, and a warrant was issued for his arrest. Lum's demise mirrored his brother's, only in reverse. Weakened by fighting, single blows ultimately slew both—Marshall in a painful instant, Lum over agonizing days.

Press accounts are uniformly sympathetic to Lum's fate, despite the homicidal transgression that set it in motion:

Columbus Triplett died here behind prison bars on the evening of the 14th inst.,
after days of indescribable anguish. This was the last scene in the fearful tragedy
begun by the two Triplett brothers on Christmas day ...

The kind family who keeps the jail, Mr. and Mrs. Robbins, together with the
county physician did all they could for his comfort much to their credit. A fellow
prisoner also stood by him night and day until the end came.
                                        —North Wilkesboro Hustler, *January 28, 1910*

Marshall and his family are barely mentioned. Perhaps he was less liked in the community, or perhaps Granville's cruelty tarnished the family in the public eye. Lum's prolonged misery clearly aroused compassion. But it must also have triggered powerful Christian archetypes among the predominantly Baptist citizenry—of the crucified Christ, awaiting delivery from the prison-like tomb, of the repentant sinner, the "wretch like me" saved by "amazing grace," suffering now but bound for glory. The anecdote about the fellow prisoner provides a Biblical narrative. It is redolent of both the penitent thief ("Remember me when thou comest into thy kingdom") and the centurion at Calvary ("Truly this man was the Son of God")—a comforting New Testament end to an Old Testament tale of brother killing brother.

> *Those brothers sleep in the same graveyard*
> *Their wives and children's troubled hard*
> *Their resting place there sure must be*
> *Till they shall rise at Judgement Day*

> *Summing it all up it was one of the saddest things that has ever occurred in our county.* —North Wilkesboro Hustler, *January 28, 1910*

After Lum's death, Granville Triplett went into hiding. Apprehended by the sheriff in mid-February, he was held in the same jail where his uncle died. His murder trial began on March 29th and ended a day later when he pleaded guilty to the reduced charge of assault with a deadly weapon (his shoe or boot). Sentenced to eighteen months' hard labor ("on the roads"— *Democrat*, April 14, 1910), he may have served only three. Lum's survivors were likely bitter over the reduced charge, enraged if he walked with fifteen months unserved. After release, Granville returned to his family, but the former deputy sheriff would have other brushes with the law. He died of tuberculosis at age fifty-one in 1933. Sophronie long outlived him, passing away in 1978, eighteen years after she sang "The Triplett Tragedy" for Ralph Rinzler's microphone.

A notable detail in press accounts of the affair appears in a homily-like epilogue printed in several papers after Lum's death. Its purple prose prompts yet another question:

> *A man* [Lum] *in middle life, who had reared a family of six children ... to die in a prison cell without a relative to stand by him in the dark hour, and even after Death had set its seals upon him, no one to claim the lifeless body, certainly paints a picture that makes a dark blot on the civilization of our fair county ...*
> —North Wilkesboro Hustler, *January 28, 1910*

Without a relative to stand by him. Lum's grown children lived in Texas— this may have precluded their coming or delayed their arrival. But where was Sophronie? Is the underlying pain when she sings partly from guilt over not being at his side? Various scenarios could explain her absence: perhaps she was barred from the jail, had a breakdown and was recovering with family, or felt unsafe traveling to see him. Or did she turn temporarily against him—condemning him as a drunken murderer and brother-killer? These scenarios resonate with another Christian archetype: Peter's denial of Christ.

Just weeks after Lum's death, Sophronie conceived a son born on October 28, 1910. The father may have been Jasper Greer, her second husband, though it's unclear when they married. A daughter—Doc Watson's future sister-in-law—followed in 1914. Sophronie and Jasper separated soon after her birth. They seem to have lived apart until he died in 1943, yet they never divorced.

Confusion over parentage, relationship status, and marriage dates is common when researching families of this era. Then as now, children were born out of wedlock and marriages failed or faltered. But in less accepting times, under the sway of old-time religion, fear of stigma and scandal increased obfuscation. Such infractions could, of course, result in violence, even murder, and it's possible they played a role in the Triplett drama. Truth, like human behavior, is rarely simple, and the precise motivations of its actors will never be known.

A final anecdote: in a book about another infamous North Carolina murder—the slaying of Charles Silver by his wife Frankie in 1831—the folklorist and historian Daniel W. Patterson mentions "The Triplett Tragedy" in a passage about community responses to songs about local crimes. According to Patterson, Granville Triplett knew and loathed the song:

> [It] outraged him, and he threatened to kill anyone who sang it. The only person in the community who dared to defy him was Lum's widow, Sophronie Miller Greer. She took her revenge upon Granville by standing on her porch and singing the ballad as he stalked past her house, with his face stony and his fists clinched ...[30]

There's something profoundly satisfying about the image of Sophronie standing tall and fearless on her porch, delivering this devout rejoinder to her hostile nephew as he crosses her property. Having been through a hell only she could fathom, the song afforded her a powerful reckoning: first with her husband's killer and later with the world.

30   Daniel W. Patterson, *A Tree Accurst: Bobby McMillon and Stories of Frankie Silver* (Chapel Hill: University of North Carolina Press, 2000), pp. 117-118.

PAT HARE MURDERS HIS BABY

O, beware, my lord, of jealousy;
It is the green-ey'd monster, which doth mock
The meat it feeds on.
—*Shakespeare,* Othello

In 1954, a Memphis bluesman cut two solo sides for a 45 rpm single. They remained unreleased for years but generated substantial buzz among those who heard them—especially the intended A-side, a monstrously grim dose of barrelhouse piano, fuzz-tone guitar, and straining vocal called "I'm Gonna Murder My Baby." The song proved prescient in two remarkable ways. Its distorted guitar sound prefigured the jagged riffs and power chords of the next decade's heavy rock, two months before Elvis Presley launched the rock and roll era with "That's All Right (Mama)." But the song's lyric—a dark-humored account of blind jealousy driving a man to murder—was a forecast of doom for the man who made it. In one of the ultimate ironies of the blues, the singer foretold a crime he later committed.

Good morning, Judge
And your jury too
I've got a few things that I'd like to
Say to you

I'm gonna murder my baby
Yes, I'm gonna murder my baby
Yes, I'm gonna murder my baby
Don't do nothin' but cheat and lie

On December 15, 1963, Minneapolis police apprehended an intoxicated thirty-three-year-old man involved in a domestic dispute that left his married girlfriend and a responding police officer shot and mortally wounded. The officer died in an ambulance en route to a hospital, but the woman lingered for nearly a month, succumbing to her injuries the following January. Though injured in the gunfire, the suspect lived to stand trial and was hastily convicted and sentenced to life imprisonment that February. His name was Pat Hare, and he was a musician of some note—a sideman to some of the biggest names in blues—but virtually unemployable by the time of his arrest, due to worsening alcoholism.

The tragedy that ended his career that winter afternoon—precipitated by a lethal mix of jealousy, booze, and firearms and ending with pools of blood and lost or broken lives—was a predictable finale to a saga writ large in the blues itself, but also curiously prefigured in his own music. It was an old story that had been brewing for years, decades, or since the dawn of man.

Auburn "Pat" Hare was born poor on an Arkansas farm in 1930. His birth name alone might have led him to the blues, but whatever his motivation, he started playing guitar at ten and was schooled in his teens on the instrument by Joe Willie Wilkins of Sonny Boy (Rice Miller) Williamson's band. A quick study, he was soon gigging with Sonny Boy on the *King Biscuit Time* radio show and with Howlin' Wolf onstage as *Pat Hare*—a nickname mercifully given to him by his grandmother.

PAT HARE RECORD SLEEVE, 1954

Anecdotes are hard to source and sometimes contradictory, but from an early age he seems to have been amiable when sober but fraught and unpredictable when drunk. He was stable enough to marry and support three children. Yet, possibly tall tales describe alcohol-fueled scuffles with other musicians (including the imposing Wolf, whom Hare is supposed to have taken a shot at) and a brawl involving a farm rake that left him with a permanently bent finger. Less sensationally, he also played minor-league baseball. Throughout the '40s and '50s, he was an in-demand accompanist to a roster of blues greats, including—in addition to Sonny Boy and Wolf—James Cotton, Bobby "Blue" Bland, and Junior Parker.

Relocated to Memphis in 1952, he came onto the radar of the musical Midas Sam Phillips—best known as the discoverer of Elvis and a pantheon of founding rock and roll demigods, but also a prodigious scout for blues talent. That same year he seems to have been fired from Wolf's band but settled into a steady gig as a session player for Phillips' Sun label. The association led to Hare's first (and last) recordings under his own name—a pair of sides recorded for a single in 1954 but ultimately rejected for release by Phillips for unclear reasons (they would remain officially unissued for decades).

Listening to the incendiary would-be A-side proffers a guess: more than half a century later, "I'm Gonna Murder My Baby" still shocks for its aggressive sound and homicidal humor.

Yes, she left home in the mornin'
She didn't get back 'til night
She swears before her maker
That she's treatin' me right

I'm gonna murder my baby
Yes, I'm gonna murder my baby
Yes, I'm gonna murder my baby
Don't do nothin' but cheat and lie

Fourteen years later, a London session player named Jimmy Page would forge a similar sound of intricate guitar runs and distorted chords atop heavy blues with Led Zeppelin—but with three equally shrill fellow musicians and a stack of Marshall amps. Hare's backup on "I'm Gonna Murder My Baby" is just that—backup. And his bombastic guitar sound was achieved by "turning the volume knob of his Sears & Roebuck cereal-box-sized amp all the way to the right until the speaker was screaming" (in the writer and musician Cub Koda's memorable words).[31] Zeppelin would also mine the blues for lyrics (often without attribution), and Page penned some comparably nasty verses about women ("Lots of people talkin', few of them know / Soul of a woman was created below"). But the singer Robert Plant's hammer-of-the-gods delivery obliterated the sly humor that often characterizes such utterances in the blues. Regardless, with such volatile sounds on wax at 706 Union Avenue, it's perhaps understandable that—in that *Billboard* Top 10 year of "Secret Love" and "Oh! My Pa-Pa"—even the risk-taker who gave Elvis and Jerry Lee Lewis to the world balked, in the end, at releasing the track.

Not that the sentiment or scenario in "I'm Gonna Murder My Baby" was unique. Hare's song is an extreme example, but blues singers have been threatening to kill their "babies" since the genre's birth, and in songs as diverse in tone as Pink Anderson and Simmie Dooley's hokum "Papa's 'Bout to Get Mad" (1928) ("You gonna keep on messin' 'round, honey / Until you get my goat / Remember, I got a razor / And you got a great big throat") to Lightnin' Hopkins' doomy "Bring Me My Shotgun" (1960) ("The only reason I don't shoot you, little woman / My double-barrel shotgun, it won't fire"). Hillbilly and country analogs abound, from Clarence Ashley shooting Little Sadie down (1930) to Johnny Cash dispatching Delia with his "sub-mo-chine" (1994).[32] Rock and roll—blues and country's unruly child—follows suit. Harsh, even hateful, these songs might be. Yet despite periodic misapprehension from well-meaning zealots (both left and right), they remain songs: cultural constructs that express intense emotions through music and fictive narratives (even when based on fact).

Blues is shadow music—"shadow" in the Jungian sense, meaning it expresses facets of the psyche generally kept hidden from polite company and the easily offended.[33] Its Southern spawning ground was a psychic landscape scarred by the whip and countless lynchings and a physical locale of back-breaking labor with little hope of escape. In this intolerable setting, blues gave voice to the Delta's id, expressing dark impulses and repressed thoughts. It also rested uneasily beside

---

31   Vladimir Bogdanov et al., eds., *All Music Guide to the Blues* (San Francisco: Miller Freeman Books, 1999), p. 170.

32   In "Delia's Gone," a folk song inspired by the real-life murder of fourteen-year-old Delia Green by her fifteen-year-old beau, Mose Houston, in Georgia on Christmas Eve, 1900. Cash cut a mild version in 1962 but recast the song in grittier form on *American Recordings*, the first of his Rick Rubin–produced late-career comeback records.

33   Jung felt that most people had little awareness of their shadows and that this ignorance caused volatile disjuncture, à la Jekyll and Hyde. Integration of opposites was the remedy, but this required an unflinching confrontation with the unconscious. Dream analysis was a fruitful approach, but creativity could also be curative. Blues singers seemed to instinctively understand this and expressed their hidden turbulent sides through music.

the indigenous sacred music that was its counterpart. If the blues was Saturday night, reckless and raw, gospel was Sunday morning, righteous and repentant. A strident dualism defined the two in the prewar era, with blues musicians seen as disreputable, if not downright demonic.

Carl Jung notably rejected such schemas: to assert the light while denying the shadow risked turbulent inner imbalance. Rather, such poles were complementary, and, over time, blues and gospel achieved a kind of yin-yang stasis in the popular imagination. At times, as in the gloriously sensual blues gospel of the Staple Singers, they even merged. But, Robert Johnson legends aside, many modern listeners—affluent fans of "smooth" blues like Robert Cray, Keb' Mo', or *Clapton Unplugged*—seem to have little real sense of the form's dark and desperate origins. The night might belong to Michelob, but the blues—ultimately—belongs to the night.

A recurring motif in blues is the woman (or man—lest we forget, the earliest recorded blues singers were formidable, outspoken women) who's done a lover wrong. A common adjunct involves fantasies of revenge ranging from retaliatory infidelity to physical violence. This can get ugly: denying misogyny in the blues is as wrong-headed as generalizing the blues (or country, or rock, or rap) as misogynistic. But context is instructive. In a culture broken by slavery and still bleeding under Jim Crow, it's unsurprising that men with little power would cling to whatever power they had and be enraged if their minimal dominion felt threatened. Thus the marriage or lover's vow took on disproportionate weight, and if that bond was broken, it could trigger volatile rage. This dynamic is hardly unique to Black men in the early twentieth century; masculine dominance rooted in insecurity is a pernicious and widespread evil. But men of lowly status with little means to redress grievances are, perhaps, more vulnerable to it. "Me and the devil / Were walking side by side," sang Robert Johnson in 1937, having answered a sepulchral knock that many of his contemporaries no doubt also heard. "I'm going to beat my woman / Until I get satisfied."

Johnson's sinister image and haunting vocal in "Me and the Devil Blues" are atypical: blues is rarely so earnest, even when its subject matter is dire, and humor—often dark, sometimes deathly so—tends to dull its sharpest barbs and broadsides. "I'm Gonna Murder My Baby" is no different. When Hare announces his homicidal intentions in court, casually interjecting asides like "I just thought you'd like to know, jury," he hilariously preempts not only his arrest, trial, and conviction but his own (then uncommitted) *crime*. It's boastful insolence worthy of the most over-the-top bluesman (or rapper, reggae toaster, or calypso singer) and riotously funny. Only the real-life outcome tempers the levity. The primary difference between his song and a score of others like it is that, blind drunk and tormented by who knows what devils of his own, he made good on his threat.

My baby used to help her man
Treat me right!

But then she goes out
And stay all night long

I'm gonna murder my baby
Yes, I'm gonna murder my baby
Yes, I'm gonna murder my baby
Don't do nothin' but cheat and lie

The prestige of Hare's final employer obscures his personal disintegration. In 1957, Muddy Waters hired him to replace guitarist Jimmy Rogers in his band, and for the next six years Hare gigged and recorded with the iconic bluesman (he's heard on both *At Newport 1960* and the same year's *Muddy Waters Sings "Big Bill"*). By the end of their collaboration, Hare was passing out drunk on the bandstand. Now divorced, he had a tempestuous relationship with a Chicago woman he suspected of infidelity.

Unable to raise her by phone one night (and no doubt deep in his cups), he fired a rifle through her window. No one was hurt, but a warrant was issued for his arrest. Hare dodged it, hiding out in the city before returning to the family farm in Arkansas. Waters sent scouts to find and recruit him for a new band he was forming in Minneapolis (despite his decline, he remained a solid guitarist). Hare joined, but his drinking worsened, and a pay dispute ended with him threatening a fellow musician with a gun. Had homicide not intervened, Hare's last stint with Waters would likely have still been short-lived.

In 1963, Hare was living with a married woman named Agnes Winje. Paranoid that she was going to return to her estranged husband, on December 15th he drank all day, fought with and took potshots at his frightened paramour, and told a friend on the phone, "That woman is going to make me kill her."[34] Alas, no one but Hare pulled the fatal trigger. The first responder, Officer James E. Hendricks, was killed at the scene. Hare later stated he had no memory of the shooting (though police claimed he confessed)—plausibly saying he was in an alcoholic blackout. While serving life for first- and third-degree murder, he quit drinking, attended Alcoholics Anonymous meetings, and joined the Stillwater Prison band (Sounds Incarcerated). Sober, Hare was more even-keeled and seemed destined for eventual parole. At times, he was allowed to leave prison to play music—including at a reunion gig with Waters. He died of cancer in 1980, at age fifty.

Hare wrote the verses of "I'm Gonna Murder My Baby," but the song's tune and half its chorus derive from a 1941 blues by Peter Joe "Doctor" Clayton called "Cheating and Lying Blues." A St. Louis-by-way-of-Georgia singer-songwriter, Clayton recorded for the Bluebird label in the '30s and '40s, then migrated to Chicago in 1950 (with the guitarist Robert Lockwood Jr., the stepson of Robert Johnson) after a house fire killed his family. The tragedy freed him to pursue music full-time but also drove him to drink. Little remembered today due to a modest recorded output (he also died young, at forty-eight),

---

34   Kevin Hahn, "Pat Hare: A Blues Guitarist," *Juke Blues*, Summer 1991.

Clayton wore floppy hats and oversized glasses—a comic look that mirrored the tone of the composition Hare released as "I'm Gonna Murder My Baby."

> *I work like a bee*
> *And come straight home with my pay*
> *My baby either clowns it up*
> *Or give it all away*
> *I'm gonna murder my baby*
> *If she don't stop cheatin' and lyin'*
> *Well, I'd rather be in the penitentiary*
> *Than to be worried out of my mind*

If Hare's version is darkly sardonic and aurally aggressive, Clayton's is easy on the ears and mainly played for laughs, his woe-is-me vocal (atop affable piano backing) and indignant rube act congruent with his clownish hat and specs. A clever lyricist, known for the story-song "Pearl Harbor Blues" as well as vaudeville-ish hokum like "Moonshine Woman Blues" (both 1942—the latter replete with "drunken" tuba accompaniment), it's hard to hear Clayton's song, with its goofy references to Superman and Hitler, and imagine him hurting—let alone murdering—anybody. Even with the "green-ey'd monster" ascendant in the final verse, Clayton's song remains cuckold humor of the stag-antlers-hat variety:

> *Four o'clock this mornin'*
> *When I stagger in the block*
> *The little moonshine joint in the rear*
> *Has just started to rock*
>
> *I sneaked inside*
> *To get a better view*
> *I caught my woman*
> *Doin' the boogie too*

A less burlesque version of "I'm Gonna Murder My Baby," featuring Clayton's "penitentiary" chorus but an otherwise fresh set of lyrics, was recorded in 1963 by the bluesman Robert Nighthawk (*né* McCullom). Here, Hare's hot reading and pungent sarcasm yield to a cooler, soulful but sly, delivery.

> *I went down to Eli*
> *To get my pistol out of pawn*
> *When I got back home*
> *My woman had gone*
>
> *Yes, gonna murder my baby*
> *If she don't stop cheatin' and lyin'*

Well, I'd rather be in the penitentiary
Than to be worried out of my mind

Like Hare, he was better known as a sideman than as a solo player. Nighthawk's *nom de* blues (sometimes preceded with the appellation "Prowling") jibed with the transient, under-the-radar nature of his career. Born in Arkansas (also like Hare), the singer-guitarist left home young and wandered the country, busking and gigging, for most of his life. He cut occasional solo sides but more often accompanied better-known artists like Henry Townsend, Big Joe Turner, and the original Sonny Boy Williamson (John Lee Curtis). A fine slide guitarist and underrated singer, he performed on '40s radio as Robert Lee McCoy. Around the time Hare ended two lives and his career, Nighthawk emerged in Chicago and performed in clubs and on the street off and on for the rest of his life. He died in 1967 at age fifty-seven, in Arkansas.

Nighthawk brings an understated but remarkable authority to his Chicago blues version of Clayton's "Cheating" (sometimes called "Goin' Down to Eli"). His expressive slide and spare-but-forceful small band backing (minimal drums, a second guitar) forge a down-and-dirty, hip-swaying foundation for his resonant baritone. If Hare's "I'm Gonna Murder My Baby" feels a little too real for comfort and Clayton's "Cheating" lacks bite, Nighthawk's variation balances urgency with calm and—critically—injects sex into the mix. Dark and lustful elements commingle in his rendition (in a sense, Nighthawk rediscovers the erotic side of jealousy) in a sweaty equilibrium redolent of *film noir*. This extends to the song's humor: "Goin' Down to Eli" ends, like Clayton's "Cheating and Lying Blues," with the singer-voyeur peeping at his lover through a window of the nip joint "in the rear," which has "just begin to rock":

I kinda ease upside
To get a better view
I saw my woman
Doin' the monkey too

The implication of "doin' the monkey" ("the boogie" in Clayton's version) is clear. Still, the dance-as-sex euphemism is funny, not edgy, suggesting the genial carnality of Rufus Thomas—the Memphis rhythm and blues pioneer whose songbook bulges with zoological references ripe with sexual innuendo (e.g., "The Dog," "Walkin' the Dog," "Can Your Monkey Do the Dog," and "Somebody Stole My Dog"). If Clayton's "Cheating and Lying Blues" is cartoon cuckoldry, Nighthawk's "Goin' Down to Eli"—murder threats notwithstanding—is bluesy erotica. Early rock and roll, like blues, delights in paradox: in finding links between sex and violence, flirtation and threat, sacred and profane, and gleefully exploding the boundaries between binaries.

This subversive, sexy brew features explicitly in a film clip that's also the best way to experience Nighthawk's song. In 1964, the experimental filmmaker Mike

ARCHIBALD MOTLEY, JR., *BLUES*, 1929

Shea completed a fifty-minute, no-narration, black-and-white documentary about Chicago's Maxwell Street Market—a near-century-old outdoor meeting and mercantile space that, until urban renewal and the University of Illinois at Chicago finally cannibalized it in 1994 (a feeble remnant, relocated to a spot less visible to passing traffic, remains)—was one of the city's most vital off-the-grid cultural institutions. A vast, funky, American-style bazaar, Maxwell Street was packed each Sunday with sundry goods (clothing, folk art, a vacant lot's worth of hubcaps) and unforgettable characters (hawkers, soapbox preachers, a man who hypnotized chickens). Shea's documentary *And This Is Free* captures the market's boisterous, postwar incarnation in all its diverse racial, ethnic, and economic glory.

Maxwell Street was also a mecca for roots music—a place where Southern-style white gospel singers in crewcuts and ties bumped physical and stylistic elbows with nattily dressed blues musicians. Every Sunday, they busked through lo-fi amplifiers to entertain traders and their marks. Shea's camera captures it all, including an unforgettable sequence in which Nighthawk and a small band play "Goin' Down to Eli" for an enthused crowd of primarily Black listeners.

It's a stellar performance, ably augmented by Shea's gritty, black-and-white visuals: Nighthawk, ruggedly handsome, singing seated beside a second guitarist with a dangling cigarette ... dancers swaying sensually, then lewdly, grinding their hips front-to-back in pairs—then *trios*—feigning fornication ... slickly dressed men laughing, slapping backs, sharing pulls of hooch from a brown-bagged bottle.

The lack of self-consciousness of these men and women is striking and underscores personal and political realities. Each is wringing every possible bit of pleasure from their day of no work, far from the city's (white) power centers, in the historic year that the 88th Congress literally replaced Jim Crow with Civil Rights. The lusty song and dance, juxtaposed with Black and white gospel singing, also serves as a symbolic rejoinder to priggishness, or perhaps—to revive Jung's paradigm—a reassertion of shadow as the essential flip side of light. That the literal subject of the song they're celebrating is infidelity and the threat of homicide is a paradox worthy of the things murder ballads are made of.

STEVEN L. JONES, *CORNUCOPIA (VICTROLA AND WAGON)* (DETAIL), 2013

CHAPTER TWO:
HARDLY GETTING OVER IT:
CONTEMPORARY RECKONINGS
WITH TRAGEDY

SUFFER LITTLE CHILDREN

But Jesus said, Suffer little children, and forbid them not, to come unto me;
for of such is the kingdom of heaven. —Matthew 19:14

In 1984, the Smiths' star was ascendant. New darlings of the English music press, the Manchester band's well-crafted, riff-heavy singles updated mid-'60s British rock with post-punk snarl and a coy queerness that drew a legion of young

Morrissey/my scan

fans unmoved by hardcore or hair metal. They also made inroads in America via the burgeoning "college" radio format. When their first LP, *The Smiths*, hit stores that February, adventurous rock fans on both sides of the Atlantic were listening. The unlikely blend of the guitarist Johnny Marr's layered melodicism with the single-name singer Morrissey's baritone-*cum*-falsetto croon was ear-catching, and closer listening revealed ambitiously literate introspective lyrics.

THE SMITHS COVER ART, 1984 (WITH CROPPED FILM STILL FROM ANDY WARHOL'S FLESH, 1968). DESIGN BY MORRISSEY

Yet, for a debut album, *The Smiths* was a rather gloomy affair. Beneath its surface sprightliness, themes of dread, alienation, and sexual confusion festered—predilections underscored both by murky sound and by the LP's eye-catching but somber Andy Warhol–Joe Dallesandro cover art. Originally titled *The Hand That Rocks the Cradle* (after one of its most unsettling songs), childhood innocence lost and violated is a persistent subtext and the explicit subject of its most beautiful song.

Over the moor, take me to the moor
Dig a shallow grave and I'll lay me down
Over the moor, take me to the moor
Dig a shallow grave and I'll lay me down

"Suffer Little Children" closes the album. A gentle ballad, part lullaby, part prayer, part Keats ode, the song was inspired by a ghastly series of murders that made headlines when Morrissey, the lyricist, was a boy. Haunted by youthful memories of the crimes, he evoked their desolate facts and iconography in a musical tribute to the victims.[35]

Between 1963 and 1965, a pair of sadistic lovers murdered five children in Greater Manchester, burying four of their corpses in shallow graves on Saddleworth Moor. The killers sexually assaulted four of the victims and photographed and tape-recorded the youngest (age ten) as she was tortured. Arrested, charged with, and convicted of the crimes were Ian Brady (twenty-eight years old when tried), a misanthropic, Scots-born stock clerk, and Myra Hindley (twenty-three), his masochistic typist girlfriend. Both came from broken homes, and Hindley was abused as a child. In a familiar trope, something in their troubled backgrounds and insecure social statuses drew them together and, once a couple, sparked an explosive mix of eroticism and rage that soon erupted into serial murder. The killings became tokens of their bond. Before their apprehension, they ritually revisited the lonely graves for romantic interludes and picnics, taking scores of black-and-white photos, which they jealously guarded.

Lost forever to their homicidal coupling were Pauline Reade (sixteen years old), John Kilbride (twelve), Keith Bennett (twelve), Lesley Ann Downey (ten), and Edward Evans (seventeen). Most were lured by Hindley into the couple's car, kidnapped, and later killed. All but Evans ended up on the moor; Bennett's body, though presumed buried there, has never been found. The callousness of the murders stunned Britain. For the rest of their lives, Brady (who died at seventy-nine) and Hindley (who died at sixty) remained newsworthy, mostly tabloid figures—social pariahs mythologized to national boogeyman status with name recognition comparable to Bundy or Dahmer in the States.

Anyone growing up in the U.K., let alone Manchester, during the mid-'60s knew of the Moors Murders—heard adults discussing the crimes (if only in hushed tones), saw the stark mugshots of the sinister couple on television or the gray newspaper photos of police digging up the countryside. One such child, seven years old at the time of the arrests and trial, was Steven Patrick Morrissey.

Edward, see those alluring lights?
Tonight will be your very last night
A woman said, "I know my son is dead
I'll never rest my hands on his sacred head"

"Suffer Little Children" was one of the first songs written by Morrissey and Marr for the Smiths. Understated and unsensational, its music is suffused with echo like the landscape it describes, its lyrics spare and delicate despite the gloomy subject matter ("But fresh lilaced moorland fields / Cannot hide

---

35   The fixation endured: in 2009, the singer published "The Bleak Moor Lies"–an account of a ghostly figure he says he encountered on the Yorkshire moors in 1989, later incorporated into his memoirs (*Autobiography*, London: Penguin Classics, 2013).

the stolid stench of death"). Victims are mentioned by name ("Lesley Ann and your pretty white beads / Oh, John, you'll never be a man"), but the crimes are never described. Point of view shifts fluidly from a singer-narrator (presumably Morrissey) to the ghostly voices of the children to a still-living (as she was in 1984) Myra Hindley. The latter confesses her primary role in the slayings despite her (alleged) brutalization by Brady ("Oh, whatever he has done, I have done").

Both killers proclaimed their innocence at trial. But by 1987, two decades into life sentences, each had confessed to all five murders. Brady remained largely aloof and remorseless, but Hindley increasingly expressed sorrow and regret for her actions. Cynics suggested there was integrity, at least, in Brady's consistent psychopathology and accused Hindley of shedding crocodile tears in hopes of reducing her sentence. Hindley confirmed her desire for release but insisted her remorse was real. She admitted her complicity but insisted that Brady had terrorized, threatened, and raped her into submitting to his deviant desires.

By the '90s, her confession seemed unequivocal: "I ought to have been hanged," she told her attorney. "My crime was worse than Brady's because I enticed the children, and they would never have entered the car without my role."[36] But "Suffer Little Children" was written when she was still defiant, and in the song's most chilling turn, the victims themselves pledge to haunt her forever—

We may be dead and we may be gone
But we will be, we will be
We will be forever by your side
Until the day you die
This is no easy ride

—and condemn her to a life of dreamless sleep:

We will haunt you when you laugh
Yes, you could say we're a team
You might sleep, you might sleep
You might sleep
But, oh, you will never dream

Hindley died in prison in 2002. Brady was officially diagnosed a psychopath in 1985 and, per British law, transferred from prison to a hospital for the criminally insane. He said he never wanted to be released and repeatedly begged to be allowed to die. In 2017 he died of natural causes.

Five decades' worth of books, articles, and TV programs—some good, some bad, some awful—have chronicled the Moors Murders, creating a composite portrait of the killers that's compelling but incomplete. In it, Brady is the surface weirdo: an illegitimate loner and Nazi obsessive—domineering, alcoholic,

---

36   Simon Edge, "Evil of the Lady Killers," *The Express*, 11 October 2008.

Parrot of Doom/Creative Commons

BURIAL SITE: SADDLEWORTH MOOR VIEWED FROM HOLLIN BROWN KNOLL, 2009

sexually sadistic—inspired by a misreading of Nietzsche to commit a series of Leopold and Loeb–style "perfect murders." Hindley is, by comparison, a cipher: outwardly "normal"—gregarious, socially adept, well-liked—yet ineluctably drawn by some inner pathology to Brady, for whom she was soon donning fetish boots and miniskirts and dying her bouffant-styled hair "Aryan" blonde. Beaten and terrorized as a child by her alcoholic father, the trauma seems to have left her acutely vulnerable to brutal nihilists like Brady, her psyche an impossibly confused nexus of alternately cruel and compliant psychosexual urges. An earnest Catholic convert at seventeen, "within months" of meeting him (at eighteen), she later wrote, "he had convinced me that there was no God at all."[37]

No sane or reasonable person would contest that infanticide and the sexual assault of children are monstrous crimes. To document such activity for personal posterity—as sadistic souvenir or abhorrent conceptual art—tests the limits of human depravity. But the inevitable public transformation of Brady and Hindley into monsters by the public and media—subhuman loci for the venting of collective rage and terror—diminished any chance of truly understanding what molded and motivated them. Howls for Hammurabi-style retribution were legion during and after the trial, with Hindley, especially, pilloried in print as "the most evil woman in Britain."

Women who kill children violate primal psychological and entrenched societal taboos that can force normally repressed misogynistic vitriol to the surface. Hindley's union with Brady—illicit at best and likely non-consensual—led not to childbirth but child murder. Like the Hindu goddess Kali, whose procreative powers are inseparable from destruction and death, Hindley, though childless, became an archetypal anti-mother—outside the safety net of myth, in a dualistic culture with little tolerance for Eastern yin-yang.[38]

37   Kay Carmichael, *Sin and Forgiveness: New Responses in a Changing World* (London: Routledge, 2003), p. 6.
38   "In her depiction as grotesque," wrote the author Claire Valler, "Hindley's mugshot becomes suffused with the horror of

God save Myra Hindley
God save Ian Brady
Even though he's horrible
And she ain't what you'd call a lady
—The Sex Pistols and "Great Train Robber" Ronnie Biggs: "No One Is
Innocent (A Punk Prayer)" (1978)

Painting Brady and Hindley with so broad a brush of revulsion guaranteed an eventual backlash from less reverent corners of the pop world. By the late '70s, Britain's punk subculture was especially given to rattling the cages of the self-righteous with intentionally offensive evocations of the murders and of Hindley-as-anti-mother. "God Save Myra Hindley," read one of the Sex Pistols' manager Malcolm McLaren and fashion designer Vivian Westwood's iconoclastic T-shirts, complete with stark, Warhol-esque portrait (designed by the Situationist artist Jamie Reid) and sold at their outré London boutique, Sex. (The shop was one of punk's formative stomping grounds.)

Indeed, McLaren seemed semi-obsessed with Hindley as dark pop icon, S&M figure, and harbinger of another mythic anti-mother, the rising right-wing stalwart Margaret Thatcher—the Iron Lady whose social-Darwinist policies transformed the British welfare state into a bastion of neoliberal economics. In McLaren's self-serving but entertaining film *The Great Rock 'n' Roll Swindle* (released in 1980, a year after Thatcher became prime minister), the subversive impresario dances Classic Hollywood–style with the punk mascot (and little person) Helen Wellington-Lloyd while warbling the British singer Max Bygrave's maternal-themed "You Need Hands" and cheerily pasting Hindley posters on the façades of burnt-out buildings.

Hated by leftists (including McLaren and most punks), Thatcher was fodder for a generation of artistic upstarts who caricatured the politician as a dominatrix, often explicitly linking her with Hindley. This confluence peaked with a pair of high-profile portraits by the punk-inspired artist Marcus Harvey. Large-scale and confrontational, each created mosaic-like images from myriad small marks or objects in the style of Chuck Close. The first, *Myra* (1995), eerily recreates Hindley's mugshot with innumerable children's palm prints; the second, *Maggie* (2009), portrays the ex–prime minister with cast sculptural objects, including vegetables, skulls, and dildos. Both artworks caused entirely predictable scandals *du jour* in Britain's tabloid press.[39]

A brief tempest also formed around "Suffer Little Children" after its release. With post-punk iconoclasm in the air, some journalists—who seemed either to have not listened or to have wholly misunderstood the song—derided it as ghoulish and profit-driven, resulting in negative publicity and a few chain-store bans. Morrissey passionately defended the song as a respectful rumination on evil and grief, inspired by his childhood memories. Later he befriended Ann

---

perverted femininity" (*Crime and Punishment in Contemporary Culture*, e-book, London: Routledge, 2005, p. 137).
39   "Myra Hindley is to be hung in the Royal Academy," read an editorial in *The Sun* (26 July 1997). "Sadly it is only a painting of her."

West, mother of the Moors victim Lesley Ann Downey. Despite the Smiths' punk roots (and their singer's often combative relationship with the press), a single listen reveals the song's utter sincerity. Unsettling it may be; disrespectful it's not. In the case of "Suffer Little Children," Morrissey was just another born-in-the-'50s Manc, still haunted by the pall that settled over his birthplace when Ian Brady's spade first struck soil on that "sullen, misty" moor.[40]

The Moors Murders inspired another song by a British musician youthfully affected by the crimes—this one a Londoner and son of a policeman. "I wrote the song after reading books on criminology," wrote the folk-rock pioneer Richard Thompson in 2008. "My father had a good collection, being a detective and all. Hindley and Brady were inescapable at the time, all over the news, something you couldn't ignore, even as a 15-year-old ..."[41] "Love in a Faithless Country," from Thompson's 1985 album *Across a Crowded Room*, isn't "about" the murders; unlike "Suffer Little Children," the song contains no outright references to the killings. But it does trade on a related theme: that of the homicidal couple on the run, unrepentant and bonded by their crimes, a subversive whiff of erotic charge in the air. Had Thompson not acknowledged the murders' chief inspiration, no listener would likely make the connection. Yet it's there. And, once the link is made, the already ominous track gains chilling intensity.

Always move in pairs and travel light
A loose friend is an enemy, keep it tight
Always leave a job the way you found it
Look for trouble coming and move around it

Such couples on the run have a history: Brady and Hindley were not unique. Difficult as it is to assimilate, romantically linked pairs sometimes kill for fun, and their victims have included children, whom they sometimes sexually abuse. Such behavior violates all social codes, and though several theories exist, none seems sufficient to explain it. Often the power dynamic in such relationships is tilted toward an older, dominant male—an obvious psychopath seeking a sexual-partner-in-crime with whom to share his perverse proclivities. The more passive partner is typically driven by some elusive combination of lust and fear and, after capture, leans heavily on the latter to explain their actions.

---

40   Alas, time has done Morrissey's reputation few favors. By the 2020s, the ex-Smith had transformed from an outspoken, politically inconsistent but roughly left-ish champion of outcasts and the highly sensitive to a full-blown reactionary–a supporter of the U.K.'s nativist far-right party For Britain who regularly makes headlines over questionable quotes (e.g., "You can't help but feel that the Chinese are a subspecies" and "Everyone ultimately prefers their own race"). Billy Bragg, a former fan, spoke for many when he said, "As an activist, I'm appalled by this transformation, but as a Smiths fan, I'm heartbroken" (Roison O'Connor, "Billy Bragg Says He's 'Heartbroken' for Fans of the Smiths after Latest Morrissey Outburst," *Independent*, 28 June 2019).

41   Richard Thompson, "Catch of the Day," *BeesWeb* website, 2008, archive.richardthompson-music.com/catch_of_the_day. asp?id=952. (This was Thompson's official website and is no longer online.)

Tony Rees/Creative Commons

RICHARD THOMPSON, 1982

In America, this motif first emerged in 1958, when the drifter Charles Starkweather (twenty years old) and his underage girlfriend, Caril Ann Fugate (fifteen), went on a killing spree that left eleven people dead, including Fugate's mother, stepfather, and baby half-sister. Their nihilistic crimes inspired both music (Bruce Springsteen's 1980 song "Nebraska") and films (Terrence Malick's restrained 1973 *Badlands* and Oliver Stone's hysterical 1994 *Natural Born Killers*). Starkweather and Fugate didn't sexually abuse their victims, but later murderous pairs upped the transgressive ante with sex crimes sufficiently horrendous to steal one's sleep. In the 1970s and '80s, the British couple Fred and Rosemary West raped, tortured, and murdered numerous women and girls, including their own children. In the '90s, the Canadians Paul Bernardo and Karla Homolka committed similar sex murders; among their victims was Homolka's teenage sister.

> *Always make your best moves late at night*
> *Always keep your tools well out of sight*
> *It never pays to work the same town twice*
> *It never hurts to be a little nice*

"Love in a Faithless Country" is driven less by words than by music. "Suffer Little Children" lulls the listener with steady, tonal accompaniment; the only musical clue to its dismal theme is a minor-key modulation toward the end of its repeated chord progression. But Thompson's song jars with dramatic pauses, dynamics shifts, and outright dissonance. Like other sprawling tunes that close Thompson LP sides ("Sloth," "Night Comes In," "Pharaoh"), it uses contrasting elements and flexible space to create a moody soundscape—here redolent of the vast, lonely moors. Interestingly, a woman's voice is used to haunting effect in both songs: as "Suffer Little Children" fades, female laughter is heard in the background (evoking

Hindley, carefree and predatory), while "Love in a Faithless Country" is punctuated with shrill, startling vocal interjections from the background singer Christine Collister (as if Hindley's façade has fallen, revealing her shattered interior).

> *Learn the way to melt into a crowd*
> *Never catch an eye or dress too loud*

Three full verses consist of such elliptical advice, blandly expressed vocational directives for . . . whom, exactly? These mildly sinister pronouncements— ostensibly shared between lovers—could apply equally to thieves, spies, mercenaries, or cutthroats. And perhaps that's the point: to conjure all of the above and, by doing so, reveal kinships among activities that involve furtively sneaking around to violate innate rights of privacy, property, and personhood. In places, it's possible to ascribe a specific line to the Moors Murders ("Always keep your tools well out of sight" might refer to Brady, the gravedigger; "It never hurts to be a little nice" could be Hindley, coaxing her trusting prey). But overall, the lyrics and associations remain oblique. The true textual clue to the horror at the heart of the song is one of juxtaposition—the repeated refrain that falls between each banal, cloak-and-dagger verse:

> *That's the way we make love*
> *That's the way we make love*
> *That's the way we make love*

Thompson makes the point explicit in the final lines of the last verse: "You've got to be invisible, my friend / To find the joy on which we must depend." Because *… that's the way we make love*. The unfathomable link between sexual arousal and child murder is the song's hellish center, and Thompson twists the knife again, as it were, by using the euphemism traditionally reserved for romantic love to describe the couple's aberrant bond. Thompson's lyric also implies an awareness on the part of his shadowy protagonists that they already exist in a hell of their own making because, while joy is indeed something in life we "find," to "depend" on it—to "must" have it—suggests not joy but addiction—a Faustian bargain that, left unaltered, will lead to one's doom.

> *The concept of hell and endless torment is popular with those who believe*
> *that they aren't headed there. —Ian Brady* [42]

> *You couldn't hate me more than I hate myself. —Myra Hindley* [43]

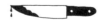

42   Ian Brady, *The Gates of Janus: An Analysis of Serial Murder by England's Most Hated Criminal* (Port Townsend, Wash.: Feral House, 2015), p. 92.

43   Letter from Myra Hindley to Ann West, 1987, quoted in Arthur Martin, "They Call Me Evil Myra . . . I Find It Deeply Upsetting," *Daily Mail*, 25 July 2013.

GETTING HOME ALIVE

Stars, hide your fires,
Let not light see my black and deep desires.
—*Shakespeare,* Macbeth

The song starts with one of the most ominous intros of its era—dull, almost plodding drums in funerary time, soon joined by a mournful A minor/F/G bass line in a simple eighth-note pattern. These speed up almost imperceptibly until a shimmering burst of distorted guitar properly launches the song. The tempo nearly doubles as Coltrane-like sheets of sound—despairing, not transcendent—rain on the listener like howls of pain. The effect is a powerful sonic simile. It captures in sound the sudden shift from near-narcotic numbness in the face of grief to wincing despair.

The style is '80s hardcore—that formally rigid strain of post-punk associated with speed and intensity—only looser and more tuneful. When the guitar pulls back and a voice emerges, the words are comparatively subdued—delivered with reportage-like restraint as if imbuing them with more emotion might cheapen their chilling directness.

Hey little girl, do you need a ride?
I've got room in my wagon, why don't you hop inside?
We could cruise down Robert Street all night long
But I think I'll just rape you and kill you instead

Chords and rhythms never vary. The barrage of feedback, bass, and drums eases slightly for each verse, then re-erupts. A chorus built on a single word repeats loop-like throughout the song's four and a half minutes, stranding the listener in a spiral of despair as if caught irrevocably between denial and death.

Diane, Diane, Di-ane
Diane, Diane, Di-ane
Diane, Diane, Di-ane
Diane, Diane, Di-ane

It's difficult to convey on the page the experience of hearing these words sung. It's just a woman's name, sung in groups of three, drawn out slightly every third iteration. But the rhythmic repetition of its two syllables—24 times per chorus, atop the maelstrom of sound—becomes a dirge-like wail that confuses the ear. "Diane" becomes "Die Anne" becomes "Dying," seemingly all sung at once. A background voice adds a call-and-response descant that preempts the main melody, starting a beat before the lead vocal like a prescient Greek chorus. It's all weirdly catchy, and this amiable quality makes the song more unnerving.

The singer returns for the second of three verses. He maintains the same conversational composure, then begins to crack. On the final line, his low-key delivery gives way to a ragged shriek.

I heard there's a party down at Lake Cove
It would be so much easier if I drove
We could check it out, we could go and see
Oh, won't you come and TAKE A RIDE WITH ME?

Ten more "Diane"s follow—a relentless wraith-like chant. Then a guitar break built entirely on rising and falling chords that teeter like a keening cry. Part of the song's power comes from the singer's decision to vocalize the killer's point of view. Yet it clearly *isn't* the killer's point of view. Rather, he sings the killer's words but emotes from his own perspective, like an outside observer forced to watch what unfolds. By listening, we share his experience.

In the final verse, the singer loses it again. His terminal scream in the last line is a harrowing cry of pain.

We could lay in the weeds for a little while
I'll put your clothes in a nice, neat little pile
You're the cutest girl I've ever seen in my life
It's all over now, AND WITH MY KNIFE ...

The ellipsis is implied, the sentence unfinished. The deed is done but the camera, as it were, pulls away. If the cinematic convention of sparing the viewer comes to mind, so does the killer's-eye-view shot used in slasher films—a controversial device that forces (or encourages—therein lies the controversy) movie watchers to identify with the stalking, homicidal behaviors of psychopaths. But only a tin-eared fool could mistake the song for exploitation. It's one of the most compassionate songs in this book—an unflinching attempt to channel unbearable emotion through words and music so direct it's as if the musicians are literal transducers of agony.

For Hüsker Dü, such cathartic expression was the band's bread and butter. Formed in St. Paul, Minnesota, in 1979 by the drummer Grant Hart, the bassist Greg Norton, and the guitarist Bob Mould (Hart and Mould both sang and wrote most of the songs), they began as one of countless bands inspired by punk that sprang up in the Midwest at the dawn of the '80s. They developed a blistering, high-velocity wall of sound as hardcore took hold and angry kids blasted through jingoistic screeds in suburban basements across the country. Hüsker Dü admired hardcore's aggression and stripped-down dynamics but were skeptical of its stylistic conformity and political naïvety.[44] Impressive as the band's aural

---

44 This skepticism extended to their inscrutable name–a Danish/Norwegian phrase and board game moniker meaning "Do you remember?" with added heavy-metal umlauts. Meant to distance the band from their more ideologically-named brethren (Agent Orange, Social Distortion, et al.), it also jokingly alluded to their refusal to dismiss the '60s music they

Daniel Corrigan/Creative Commons

HÜSKER DÜ: GREG NORTON, GRANT HART, AND BOB MOULD, 1986

onslaught was, their early records meandered, bereft of purpose or personality. That began to change with the 1983 release of *Metal Circus*—a nineteen-minute, seven-song mini-album that enriched their sound with more personal lyrics and stronger melodies. It marked the point when the band rejected hardcore orthodoxy and developed a unique voice of their own.

With nary a weak track, *Metal Circus* climaxed with its penultimate song— oddly the record's longest, slowest track among fleeting bursts of amphetamine punk ("Deadly Skies" clocks in at 1:49). Mould's incendiary "Out on a Limb," a sonic panic attack built around detonations of buzz-saw guitar, closed the record. But Hart's "Diane" lingered in the ear like a memory trace. Inspired by the 1981 murder of a nineteen-year-old St. Paul waitress, Diane Edwards, it's the record's *ballad*—the softer, more leisurely-paced track meant to give the listener a break from thornier songs about helplessness ("Real World"), self-abuse ("First of the Last Calls"), and desperation ("Lifeline").

Such contradictions typified the band. As their music matured, Hüsker Dü increasingly blended abrasive noise with tender tunes and traded political screeds for personal statements—candid and vulnerable but, like punk, direct and unsentimental. They also rejected punk's knee-jerk aversion to All Things Hippie. Though born too late for the '60s, that era was still the band's prime musical and political reference point, and over time, Beatles, Byrds, and Donovan influences came to the fore in their less strident but still left-leaning music. The band's fusion of catchy tunes with caustic accompaniment opened new expressive possibilities for the band and for post-punk more generally.[45] But

grew up with and to their temperamental kinship with the stoic Scandinavians of the Twin Cities, whose no-nonsense introversion mirrored their own.

45   A dark/light style vividly captured in the title of Scots fellow travelers the Jesus and Mary Chain's debut album

there were political overtones as well. By melding '60s melodicism and post-punk noise, the band cannily evoked the perceived failure of counterculture politics in the Reagan '80s. They did so with bitterness but also sympathy. Rather than mock their forebears, as college campuses bred not radicals but Young Republicans, Hüsker Dü mourned the rightward trend.

Hart personified this generational crossroads more than Mould. A yin figure to Mould's yang, the two began as collaborators, became competitors, and ended as adversaries. Hart's temperament was less severe than Mould's. The latter, tall and menacing, carried himself onstage with a no-nonsense glare. But Hart, shaggy-haired and chubby, wore hippie beads and drummed barefoot. Hart described his working-class upbringing as dysfunctional but "not *very* [my italics] abusive."[46] At age ten, he lost an older brother, a budding drummer and music fan, in a car wreck. He acquired his brother's drum kit, and music became a passion and a refuge. He learned drums, guitar, and keyboards and played in various garage bands. Hart preferred '50s and '60s pop to the metal and prog of the FM radio era—an influence that affected Hüsker Dü's sound. When he befriended Mould at a St. Paul record store, both were rock fanatics newly galvanized by punk.

Hart and Mould shared more than musical tastes and ambition. Both were closeted about their sexuality, Mould as gay and Hart as bisexual, and, as Hüsker Dü became a viable band, they kept their sexualities quiet and used booze and speed as a bulwark against insecurity. While the hardcore scene was ostensibly left-wing and tolerant, it was also hyper-masculine, and anti-gay rhetoric and violence were part of the scene. Hart later turned to heroin, and his addiction was a factor in the band's acrimonious 1988 breakup.[47] Characteristically, when Mould stopped drinking the same year, he did so without slips or relapses—he just quit.[48] Hart would never fully shake dependence and died at fifty-six of liver cancer.

Diane Elizabeth Edwards was a seemingly average girl with an average teenage job waiting tables at a Perkins Pancake House in West St. Paul. The circumstances of her death lack the poignant or provocative details that sell true crime books. Her slaying, when mentioned at all, is generally listed as a link in a series of events that led to the downfall of her murderer. According to Mould, Hart vaguely knew her. In 1980, the year of her death, Hart and Edwards were both nineteen, and his embryonic band was less than a year old.

Joseph Donald Ture (pronounced "Tuh-ree") was born in St. Paul in 1951. His childhood was unstable: his parents divorced when he was ten, and he spent time in institutions. He disliked his stepmother and called his birth mother an unfit parent. A detective later described him as a "very mixed-up character"

Psychocandy (1985).

46   Daniel Kreps, "Grant Hart, Hüsker Dü Drummer and Singer, Dead at 56," *Rolling Stone*, 14 September 2017.

47   All three members agreed it was only a factor. Others included tensions over the band's lack of major-label success (they had signed with Warner Brothers in 1985 with much fanfare but modest sales) and the suicide of their manager.

48   When *Spin* magazine essentially outed him in the early '90s, his response was similarly unequivocal–he buffed up his body, DJ-ed electronica in clubs, and resided for a time as a hirsute bear in San Francisco's Castro district.

JOSEPH TURE, JR., MUGSHOT, 1979

with a "bad bringing-up [*sic*]. Life was not easy for him. I don't feel sorry for him. But I can see why he kind of didn't like women."[49] Youthful trauma and resentment festered with adolescent attraction to the opposite sex. He asked girls out and grew enraged when turned down. A pathological aversion to rejection took hold, alongside a collateral need for vengeance. As a teenager, he joined the Marines but washed out before completing training. He became a drifter—an habitué of diners and chain restaurants where he'd jot down names and descriptions of female workers he fancied in journals and notebooks.[50] A stalker and misogynist ("I had a lot of problems with some women because I tell them where it's at … [and] if I don't like someone, I don't beat around the bush"), he sometimes traced women's addresses via their car tags.[51] Sandy-haired with modish sideburns in adulthood, he was not conventionally unattractive but seemed to repulse women.

In 1978, Ture broke into a home in a remote area of St. Cloud, Minnesota, seeking retaliation against sixteen-year-old Susan Huling. Susan was a waitress pursued by Ture. She rebuffed him and told her mother Alice about the incident, and Alice confronted the twenty-seven-year-old Ture, calling him a "pervert." He invaded their house and felled Alice, Susan, and her two siblings with a shotgun. Huling's eleven-year-old brother survived the attack by playing dead. In 1979, Ture bludgeoned to death eighteen-year-old Marlys Wohlenhaus, also a waitress, in her family home. That same year, he killed Joan Bierschbach, age twenty, yet another waitress, whom he abducted and held captive in a cabin outside St. Cloud for three or four days. He later told a cellmate that she recited the Lord's Prayer each time he attacked her. Interspersed with these crimes were more rapes and attempted rapes.

On Friday, September 26, 1980, Diane Edwards was walking home from work. Unable to get a ride that night, she decided to make the seven-block trek on foot. Ture was waiting for her. He had been watching her in the restaurant, and police

---

49   Retired Stearns County Police Detective Lou Leland, quoted in Madeleine Baran and Jennifer Vogel, "Joseph Ture, Jr.," *APM Reports*, 11 October 2016, www.apmreports.org/story/2016/10/11/joseph-ture-jr

50   "That's how I get most of my dates," Ture said in a prison interview, "is [*sic*] with waitresses" (Baran and Vogel, "Joseph Ture, Jr.")

51   Ibid.

later found her name in one of his journals. At 9:05 p.m., a group of teenaged girls saw Ture force Edwards into a '74 Ford Galaxie and drive away. Two weeks later, her nude body was found in a ditch in rural Sherburne County. According to a confession which he later recanted, Ture raped her in the car, stabbed her, then drove to the dump site, where he raped her once more. She may have already been dead. He left her clothes in a pile and fled.

In 1981, Ture was imprisoned for a different rape and, while incarcerated, was convicted of the Edwards murder. A circuitous, decades-long legal soap opera ensued with written confessions, retractions, and eventual convictions for the unsolved Huling and Wohlenhaus killings (but not the Bierschbach slaying, for which he nonetheless remains the chief suspect). Sadly, the notoriety of those crimes overshadowed what happened to Edwards, consigning her murder to a kind of footnote status. In a 2012 interview, Hart said a book he read about the Ture murders[52] made him "physically sick." He also lamented that "[t]here was not as much info about the Edwards murder as the other girls."[53]

Ture's predilection for diner and chain-restaurant servers aligned with his modest means and transient lifestyle. But it also squared with his pathology. Anyone who's waited tables, tended bar, or worked behind a counter will tell you that the worst thing about these jobs is the sense of being trapped—forced to interact with obnoxious, sometimes malignant individuals from a subservient position, often physically unable to move. A server, by definition, serves and, at its worst, this arrangement gives predators free rein to ogle and harass. That women working low-wage jobs are compelled to fulfill dominance fantasies for bullies and creeps in order to survive highlights a sadistic side of capitalism. But for Ture, this dynamic must have been a dream come true. It allowed him to scrutinize women who couldn't avoid his gaze, catalogue them in his notebooks, and solicit their attention in an unequal power relationship. This likely mollified his insecurity but also ensured that rejection left him doubly enraged.

If the most startling thing about "Diane" is its composer's personification of the killer, its most salient quality in the context of this book is how aptly it mirrors traditional murder ballads—down to its skeletal narrative and unclear motive. "Pretty Polly," that darkest of dead-girl songs, comes to mind. It describes the treacherous slaying of a naïve girl by a sniggering suitor, Willie, who lures her into the woods with vague promises of pleasure or gifts. Once there, he shows her a grave he's dug the night before. Terrified, she pleads for her life, but he stabs her to death, then buries her in the grave. As an Appalachian ballad, first popularized on record by both B. F. Shelton and Dock Boggs (both in 1927), the story is patchy: Polly is killed for no discernible reason. Perhaps to ameliorate this fact, some performers add a "reassuring" denouement in which Willie, haunted by his crime, turns himself in and awaits eternal damnation. Forebears of "Pretty Polly" are less fuzzy on details. In one of the song's

52   John S. Munday, *Justice for Marlys: A Family's Twenty Year Search for a Killer* (Minneapolis: University of Minnesota Press, 2006).
53   MacDara Conroy, "Grant Hart–All of My Old Friends Are Assholes," *Thumped*, 2 December 2012.

progenitors ("Pretty Polly" has a complex lineage, exhaustively traced by other researchers),[54] "The Gosport Tragedy" (Laws P36, Roud 15), the killer is a ship's carpenter who murders his fiancée when he discovers that she's pregnant. "The Gosport Tragedy" ends not with conventional justice but with supernatural vengeance meted out by the victim's ghost.[55] None of these details survives in "Pretty Polly," and the result is dreamlike and disturbing.

Unlike "Diane," "Pretty Polly" alternates points of view between the killer, the victim, and an omniscient narrator. But both songs portray the sadism of an unhinged psycho who informs both victim and listener of his homicidal intentions early on. In "Pretty Polly," the girl grows uneasy as she's led deeper into the woods and asks Willie if he means her harm. He answers: "Pretty Polly, Pretty Polly, you're guessing about right / I dug on your grave six long hours last night." In "Diane," the singer follows the reassuring "We could cruise down Robert Street all night long" with the jarring "But I think I'll just rape you and kill you instead."[56] In both cases, the premature announcement inspires dread in the listener, who must sit through the rest of the song knowing its outcome, aware of the victim's doom.

Such fatalism, redolent of Protestant predestination, is typical in tragic ballads, which found a broad audience among people of limited means and power—as did the country music the ballads inspired. But a similar sense of existential gloom imbues much of post-punk. Punk had found release in sheer snotty exuberance—however pessimistic its stance or subject, volume, speed, and irreverence gave the music joy. But the style that followed was more deliberate, introspective, and philosophical. From Public Image Ltd to Joy Division, an icier sheen linked it to the despondence of hillbilly and country.[57]

Hart's own despondence ultimately overwhelmed him. If writing and performing "Diane" with his old band was an act of courage and exorcism in fiery youth—a means of processing unspeakable horror and protesting brutality through art—then, over time, the feat lost its luster. Dense listeners asked him if the song was "pro-rape." Zealous fans sang along to the chorus with incongruous arena-rock enthusiasm. Hart found himself torn between defending the song from the sanctimonious woke and admonishing unruly audiences at solo gigs

54 E.g., Rennie Sparks' previously referenced essay, "Pretty Polly," in Willentz and Marcus, *The Rose and the Briar*. See also Paul Slade's fine synopsis in *Unprepared to Die: America's Greatest Murder Ballads and the True Crime Stories That Inspired Them* (London: Soundcheck Books, 2015).
55 Another source, "Lady Isabel and the Elf Knight" (Child 4, Roud 21), features a wily protagonist who outsmarts her assailant, killing him instead—by magical means, in some versions.
56 A similar revelation occurs in another "Polly"–Nirvana's bleak ballad from their 1991 breakthrough album *Nevermind* (which incidentally owed much to the cathartic pop-punk of their predecessors, Hüsker Dü). Inspired by the 1987 torture and rape of a Tacoma teenager abducted on her way home from a rock concert, "Polly" is a spare folk blues amidst noisy anti-anthems. It opens with the chilling couplet, "Polly wants a cracker / I think I should get off her first." The writer and singer, Kurt Cobain, was later appalled to learn that a pair of miscreants played the song as background music during a sexual assault.
57 Such self-consciousness could also backfire, as in the overwrought cover of "Diane" by the Irish alt-metal band Therapy? that transforms Hüsker Dü's raw immediacy into a glacial chamber piece for strings and choir-like chorus. A ham-fisted video for the song features a writhing, water-soaked model who cradles the singer's naked body and lip-syncs his dire vocal in a pretentious gender switch.

to remember it was a true story about a real person. "The most significant thing about her life," he told a Serbian crowd in 2010 with deadly irony, "was her death." Eventually, he dropped "Diane" from live performance.[58]

One last late-night walk. Another woman alone, menaced by shadows, never makes it home.

On July 7, 1993, twenty-seven-year-old Mia Zapata, a punk singer whose band the Gits were part of the burgeoning Seattle grunge scene, left a popular dive bar at midnight. It was the anniversary of a close friend's death—Stefanie Sargent, founding guitarist with the punk/grunge fellow travelers 7 Year Bitch. The two bands were friendly and helped inspire the politically provocative riot grrrl movement of the '90s. Sargent had died of an overdose the previous year, and Zapata and members of both bands had been drinking to her memory. The Gits singer had sworn off alcohol during a recent tour but relapsed during the sad commemoration. After visiting nearby friends, she was walking home, blasting music on a Sony Walkman. At 3:20 a.m., her body was found on a dead-end street a mile and a half away from where she had last been seen. She had been beaten, raped, and strangled. The murder remained unsolved until 2003, when DNA evidence implicated Jesus Mezquia, a lifelong criminal who came to the U.S. from a Cuban prison during the 1980 Mariel boatlift. Mezquia was convicted of the Zapata slaying in 2004. He neither testified nor confessed, but authorities believe he stalked her that night and eventually forced her into his car.[59]

Zapata's murder devastated the close-knit Seattle music community, inspiring musical tributes and a self-defense group called Home Alive.[60] Of the elegies-in-song, the most powerful was "M.I.A."—a riveting track from ¡Viva Zapata! (1994), 7 Year Bitch's sophomore album. (The title alludes to Mia by way of leftist revolutionary Emiliano Zapata, linking the slain singer's Mexican-American heritage and instinctive feminism to the assassinated peasant-turned-guerrilla leader and his unschooled socialism.)[61] "M.I.A." rages against male-on-female violence to growling bass, syncopated drums, and bursts of jagged guitar like a riot-grrrl take on post-punk minimalists such as Pylon or Gang of Four. As with Hüsker Dü's "Diane," the song melds heartbreak with fury. But "M.I.A." was written when Zapata's murder remained unsolved, and the singer Selene Vigil's anguished lyric and alternating wails of "I'll see ya" and "I can't see" convey this lack of closure like an open wound.

It's dark here
No direction
Just aggravation

---

58   In 2012, Hart said, "I stopped playing 'Diane' because I could no longer stand putting on the mask of a monster" (Conroy, "Grant Hart–All of My Old Friends Are Assholes"). See the Serbian concert video at www.youtube.com/watch?v=Nvow6s9Ee28.
59   Mezquia died in prison in 2021.
60   See www.teachhomealive.org
61   The link may have been familial as well. In the Gits drummer Steve Moriarty's 2024 biography *Mia Zapata and The Gits: A True Story of Art, Rock, and Revolution* (Port Townsend, Wash.: Feral House), he notes that Mia's father claimed to be a grandson of Emiliano Zapata.

Aggravation over losing you
To who?
No justice
No clue

"Diane" and "M.I.A." document young lives cut short by after-hours walks on lonely streets. Zapata grew up in Louisville before following her muse and relocating, first to Ohio, then to Washington. In each locale, she immersed herself in the local punk scene. Anyone familiar with such milieus knows that sympathetic meeting places—in those days, primarily bars and clubs—were few and far between. Once a fledgling community found a watering hole that welcomed creative outcasts, it became prized turf for an underground scene. Such venues helped subcultures grow and thrive, but there were concomitant risks. Youth, hormones, and rebellion bred overindulgence, and passionate swagger often masked psychic frailties. Yet, for all the mythologizing of self-destruction and debauchery in rock, a simple fact is often overlooked: all those young, horny, frequently impaired musicians, fans, bartenders, and servers had to get home at night. And that necessity didn't always augur a safe outcome.

Taverns, clubs, practice spaces, communal housing, and crash-pads—all accommodated and nurtured talent, however run-down the building or forbidding the neighborhood. But sketchy environs and vampire-hour ventures put teens and twenty-somethings at risk, especially in laxer, pre-helicopter-parent times. It's a reality that haunts "Diane," even though Edwards wasn't walking home from a rock club. It must have also haunted Hart, a working musician in an underground band used to late hours and lousy locales, always wondering if those fresh young faces in the crowd—their vulnerability shielded by a façade of spiky-haired bravado—would make it home unmolested.

How tragic that a list of names confirms the danger.

LIKE A GOD WITH A THUNDERBOLT

War is a motor for art. —Futurist slogan, 1915

"Drone Operator" by Jon Langford is a biting critique of modern warfare by an aging punk rocker—a self-identified "working-class socialist" who's never shied from using the alt-country genre he partly invented to confront degradations of empire and capital. The song—a first-person account of a military drone pilot's musings—disturbs due to its slow-burn portrait of a detached but sane killer, shielded from all harm and (short-term) consequences of his actions. His physical isolation and high-tech weaponry capture the remote character of mechanized combat and provide a chilling update of both the murder ballad and the anti-war song.

I'm not really a soldier
I'm more likely to die
By car wreck or cancer
Than an eye in the sky
That follows them home
Right in through their window
They'll never know
They'll never know

Langford's song is a twenty-first-century broadside by a lifelong anti-war activist. It documents the latest leap in a two-century trend that's seen ever more lethal weapons developed with attendant disconnection from the human cost of mass killing. This shift from battlefield engagement to long-distance assault is rarely acknowledged—at least critically—in mainstream discourse but has preoccupied artists, writers, and musicians since the Industrial Revolution. An early modern work by a vanguard artist—part of a movement that exalted high-tech machinery with messianic fervor—is a trenchant touchstone and ancestor. Like "Drone Operator," the painting freeze-frames an instant in this troubling evolution with disquieting results—but from a very different perspective.

In 1915, Gino Severini painted a prophetic picture. *Armored Train in Action* shows a sleek, metal military train with massive swiveling gun turret and a line of soldiers firing rifles from a reinforced railcar at an unseen enemy. It's an example of Italian Futurism—an art movement that used fractured forms and intense color to celebrate the dynamism and speed of the Machine Age. The multiple perspectives and overlapping planes in Futurist painting derived from Cubism. But unlike Cubism, with its subdued palettes and mild, bohemian subject matter (guitars, nudes, café-table still lifes), *Armored Train* uses festive colors for its literally gray theme and lovingly renders violent imagery (gunfire, smoke, explosions) like the idyllic trees, clouds, and ladies' parasols of a tableau by Georges Seurat.

The painting startles in two ways, both of which inform its prescience. First, it's unabashedly pro-war—both specifically supporting the Great War, the global conflict then underway (which Italy had just joined)[62] and pro-war more generally. Second, it disturbingly documents the distance and detachment of modern warfare—its gradual shift from face-to-face combat to impersonal assault mediated by machines. Modern art is typically left-leaning and skeptical of war. But Severini and the Futurists embraced war as "the world's only hygiene"[63]—a means to level an *ancien régime* they loathed, casualties be damned, and launch a glorious new world of machine technology and authoritarian rule. Their bombastic leader, the poet Filippo Marinetti (Futurism wasn't strictly visual; it incorporated all the arts), urged Severini in a 1914 letter to "[t]ry to live the war pictorially, studying it in all its mechanical forms (military trains, fortifications, wounded men, ambulances,

---

62   Despite nominal allegiance to Germany and Austria-Hungary, Italy declared war on the latter in May 1915 and joined the Allies (Britain, France, Russia).

63   Filippo Marinetti, "The First Futurist Manifesto," *Le Figaro*, 20 February 1909.

Museum of Modern Art/Creative Commons

GINO SEVERINI, *ARMORED TRAIN IN ACTION*, 1915

hospitals, parades, etc.)"[64] Severini did so, crafting in *Armored Train* a dehumanized masterpiece that exalts war, war machines, and the War Machine.

This dehumanization extends to both shooters and victims: the former are portrayed as uniform figures of no individuality, obedient cogs in a murderous machine, while the latter remain offstage and invisible. Missing is any sense of tragedy or loss because there are no full human beings to pity or mourn. In Goya's seminal anti-war painting *The Third of May, 1808* (1814),[65] the Romantic artist unflinchingly portrays the summary execution by firing squad of Spanish peasants who defended their homes from Napoleonic invasion. Goya depicts the defenders as human, with distinct emotions, but the soldiers as a faceless, machine-like mass. A century later, Severini essentially cuts and pastes Goya's killers into *Armored Train*—an Industrial Age analogue of anonymous slaughter. But there's a chilling difference: in *Third of May*, Goya condemns this orderly barbarism; in *Armored Train*, Severini celebrates it.

A century after Severini, the shift from close combat to remote assault reached a new peak (or low, depending on one's point of view). A cutting-edge technology removed soldiers from battle completely, allowing them to target and kill in safety and comfort, with no direct reckoning with their victims. The faceless shooters in *Armored Train* fire on others long-distance, through slits in a mobile metal bulwark that envelops them. But the protagonist in Langford's "Drone Operator"—"not really a soldier" in any traditional sense of the word—sits in an air-conditioned room half a world away from the human beings he obliterates, watching screens and manipulating a joystick like a lethal video game.

Gamers, in fact, with their strong hand-eye coordination and ability to stare at screens for hours, are heavily recruited for the job.[66] Langford's "pilot" is distinctly

---

64   Caroline Tisdall and Angelo Bozzolla, *Futurism* (New York: Oxford University Press, 1978), p. 177.

65   Discussed in connection with "You Can't Win a Race with a Cannonball" in chapter 1.

66   Another qualification is their experience of danger as fantasy. A 2017 study by the forensic psychologist Jacqueline Wheatcroft found that gamers matched or outperformed airline and military pilots as drone operators because they had no authentic sense of the risks associated with flight. "When asked how gamers could do so well considering they had never experienced the kind of fear that often accompanies actual flight, Wheatcroft said that may work in their favor, since *emotions sometimes get in the way of good decision-making*" (my italics) (Tim Wright, "Do Gamers Make Better Drone Operators Than Pilots?", *Smithsonian* Magazine, 29 August 2017).

adolescent—his statements shortsighted, defensive, and petty. He resembles the stereotypical basement nerd, a man-child still living with his parents, yet this slacker has found work at a real-life PlayStation that blows up real-life bad guys.

When I was a young boy
I played all the games
Straight out of grad school
Someone gave them my name
So I drifted into
A job with good pay
Through traffic and construction
I drive in every day

Unmanned Aerial Vehicles (UAVs) were first used under George W. Bush in the early years of the post-9/11 "War on Terror." But drone warfare increased dramatically under his successor, Barack Obama, who lauded the technology as a safe-for-our-troops alternative to boots-on-the-ground combat, capable of precision targeting with minimal collateral damage. While the latter claim proved dubious,[67] the former was undeniable. Removing troops from battle certainly put them in less (immediate) danger, and public support for drones was robust in the U.S. across the media-sanctioned spectrum of opinion, from the hawks of Fox News to the cruise-missile liberals of MSNBC. Concerns about lack of due process, targeted assassination, and—eventually—the extrajudicial killing of American citizens overseas were mostly steamrolled by fever-pitch "never again" propaganda.[68] Larger issues—the questionable necessity, legality, and morality of such attacks, the fact that killing non-combatants creates more, not fewer, terrorists—were marginalized.[69] Big-picture debate was nonexistent. Claims that war itself is immoral, unsustainable, a crime, and a racket weren't even humored. War was affirmed a necessary evil by the powers that be—made

---

67   Estimates of civilian deaths caused by U.S. drone strikes vary wildly. A study by the non-profit U.K.-based Bureau of Investigative Journalism of 14,040 strikes between 2002 and 2022 lists these statistics: overall casualties, 8,858-16,901; civilian casualties, 910-2,200; children killed, 283-454.

68   Anwar al-Awlaki, an American expatriate living in Yemen, was killed by an Obama-ordered drone strike in September 2011. His sixteen-year-old son, Abdulrahman, was killed two weeks later. Both were U.S. citizens, the former an imam and suspected al-Qaeda leader. Rather than bring him to trial, he was placed on Obama's "kill list" and executed by drone. Al-Awlaki's son was collateral damage—a bystander killed in a botched drone attack on another U.S.-targeted man. Since the boy couldn't credibly be accused of terrorism, the White House press secretary, Robert Gibbs, passed the buck, telling reporters he wouldn't have died if "he'd had a more responsible father." In a cruel book-end to the affair, Awlaki's eight-year-old daughter, Nawar, was shot and killed in a 2017 commando raid launched by Obama's successor, Donald Trump. (Gibbs is quoted in Conor Friedersdorf, "How Team Obama Justifies Killing a 16-Year-Old American," *Atlantic*, October 2012.)

69   But slipped through here and there. "These power-damaged people," wrote the activist George Monbiot in a *Guardian* op-ed, "have been granted the chance to fulfill one of humankind's abiding fantasies: to vaporize their enemies, as if with a curse or a prayer, effortlessly and from a safe distance" ("With Its Deadly Drones, the U.S. Is Fighting a Coward's War," 30 January 2012). The dissident intellectual Noam Chomsky, in a rare CNN piece, condemned the drone program as "the most extreme terrorist campaign of modern times"–a natural extension of the Bush Doctrine of "preventative" war that targets "people suspected of perhaps intending to harm us some day, and any unfortunates who happen to be nearby" ("Chomsky: Paris Attacks Show Hypocrisy of West's Outrage," 20 January 2015, https://www.cnn.com/2015/01/19/opinion/charlie-hebdo-noam-chomsky/index.html).

so by the world's bad actors, who must be confronted by the world's good actors, invariably America and its allies.

None of this sat well with Langford. The Welsh-born Chicago transplant, inspired by American culture but repulsed by its imperial arrogance, had spent nearly forty years confronting power through music when he wrote "Drone Operator." He did so in ramshackle outfits like the post-punk Mekons (which he co-founded in 1976) and the roots-rock Waco Brothers—bands that consistently challenged mainstream political dogmas—but also with Skull Orchard, an alt-rock aggregation that performs his more personal but still outwardly engaged material. "Drone Operator" is a standout track from *Here Be Monsters* (2014)—a Skull Orchard set about early-twenty-first-century dislocation and despair, essayed with mordant wit but creeping weariness. Langford's never-say-die principles—pro-labor, anti-capital-punishment, anti-war—still inspire, but you can't rant for decades to little tangible change without some spiritual fatigue.

"'Drone Operator' is politics with a capital *P*," he told *Vice* when *Here Be Monsters* was released. "I knew as I was writing the song that this [drone warfare] was really fucking wrong ..."[70] So he purged his venom in a song—a tense, bluesy ballad in swaying 6/8 time, built on rising-and-falling E/F# minor chords and short, caustic verses. Its oscillating structure perpetuates for five and a half minutes, but there's no cathartic release, only a fadeout. Instead, the song circles, patient and dreadful, like a Predator drone over a dusty village.

> *So don't call me a coward*
> *I know what is allowed*
> *I'm like a god with a thunderbolt*
> *Sitting on a big white cloud*
> *I'm a drone operator*
> *I've got targets to scan*
> *I sit drinking coffee*
> *With one eye on the ground*
> *In the tribal lands*

"It seems like the most cowardly form of warfare you could imagine," said Langford, like a modern-day Goya denouncing *Armored Train*. "God knows what people living in dirt and poverty in Yemen and Pakistan and Afghanistan think of somebody who would even do that."

Today, Futurism is hard to stomach. Yesterday's avant-garde always bears its share of embarrassments—gross overstatements, fatuous gestures, impenetrable theories—usually rooted in youthful exuberance or ideological rigidity. Such fumbles inevitably accompany efforts to radically rethink norms. But Futurism's bloodlust for mayhem and authoritarianism gets no easy pass. While the movement's rhetoric was always grotesque ("We will glorify war . . . militarism,

---

70   Matthew Caron, "Jon Langford on Drone Warfare, Alternative Astronomy, and Honky-Tonk," *Vice*, 26 February 2014.

patriotism, the destructive gesture of freedom-bringers, beautiful ideas worth dying for, and scorn for woman," reads its Marinetti-composed Manifesto of 1909)[71], early Futurist art focused not on annihilation but exhilaration in an age of rapid change. Works like Umberto Boccioni's *The City Rises* (1910)—a blurred-color tableau of a skyscraper under construction—or Giacomo Balla's reverent study of a lightbulb, *Street Light* (1909), are utopian in nature and lack militaristic overtones. Such restraint wouldn't last. Marinetti's ceaseless demands for "hygienic" mass destruction drew increasingly strident responses from Futurist artists (like Severini's *Armored Train*).[72] When Europe, then a tinderbox of chauvinistic nationalisms vying for dominance, broke out in war, he was elated: "The red holidays of genius have begun! There is nothing for us to admire today but the dreadful symphonies of the shrapnels and the mad sculptures that our inspired artillery molds among the masses of the enemy."[73]

Marinetti got what he wanted. World War I was a catastrophe of previously unimaginable scale that killed 20 million, wounded 21 million more, and leveled much of Europe. Widespread misery and economic collapse ensued, paving the way for ascendant fascism. A generation of young men was nearly wiped out for unclear reasons—because, in the words of the philosopher Bertrand Russell, "a set of official gentlemen, living luxurious lives, mostly stupid, and all without imagination or heart, have chosen that it should occur rather than that any one of them should suffer some infinitesimal rebuff to his country's pride."[74] Among the dead were many artists, including the Futurist Boccioni. It was also the first fully mechanized war—a dystopian nightmare of technology, mass production, and the assembly line in the service not of humankind but of human slaughter. Battlefield combat devolved into trench warfare as troops fought over dismal patches of muddy earth strewn with corpses and rife with rats and disease. Men were blown apart by bombs, ripped open by machine guns, poisoned with mustard gas, driven mad by shelling, and crippled for life. The war caused a breach in the social fabric, and the era's remaining art is full of rage and pain.

The antidote to Futurism—the movement that rejected its reactionary zeal and wiped it off the Western stage—was Dada. True to its nonsensical name, the style embraced nonsense, but its aims were sophisticated and corrective. Dada held the twin doctrines of reason and progress—foundational creeds

---

71   See www.italianfuturism.org/manifestos

72   Severini's pre-war art was mostly concerned with the motion of dancers and cabaret crowds. After the war, he abandoned Futurism and embraced neoclassicism.

73   Filippo Marinetti, "War, the World's Only Hygiene," Sergio Reggi '900 Collection, APICE Center, University of Milan, 1915.

74   Whole libraries document the events that led to the conflagration, but a fatal intermingling of three ideologies lit the match: imperialism, nationalism, and racism. The U.S. and Europe had spent the previous century amassing colonial empires, and colonialism was competitive and nationalistic, just as imperialism was expansionist and claimed a "missionary" function—to bring civilization to ignorant non-whites. Bickering and brinkmanship fed the fire, which erupted in 1914. Men were conscripted or volunteered, many of them swayed by propaganda that appealed to their honor and national pride. In the words of Ernest Hemingway (a Red Cross ambulance driver during the war): "[It] was the most colossal, murderous, mismanaged butchery that has ever taken place on earth. Any writer who said otherwise lied. So the writers either wrote propaganda, shut up, or fought." (The Russell quote is from a letter to the London *Nation*, 15 August 1914, the Hemingway one from "Introduction," *Men at War*, New York: Bramhall House, 1955, p xiii.)

of the post-Renaissance world—responsible for the cataclysm and rejected both. "Revolted by the butchery of the 1914 World War," wrote Jean Arp, one of its founders (unlike Futurism, Dada had no Marinetti-like leader), "we sang, painted, made collages and wrote poems *with all our might* [my italics].[75] We were seeking an art based on fundamentals, to cure the madness of the age ..."[76] So the Dadaists reveled in the irrational, made work from trash, and celebrated the untrained art of children, "primitives," and the insane. The movement began in a Zurich café, then spread across Europe. But it was not an art of dandies and dilettantes: many Dadaists had fought in the trenches, and their trauma and disillusionment fed their work, especially in devastated Germany.

One such artist was Max Ernst, an ex-infantryman who said he died when drafted in 1914 and was "resurrected" when demobilized four years later. Ernst created one of Dada's most haunting works: a tiny collage of a dreamlike vista called *Murdering Airplane* (1920). Its central image is a monstrous human/warplane hybrid—an absurd construction of machine parts and human limbs that hovers menacingly over a barren battlefield as two soldiers, dwarfed by the behemoth, struggle to carry a wounded comrade to safety. Like the Futurists, the Dadaists were obsessed with the interface between man and machine, but they had no utopian vision of merging the two. When this nexus occurs in Dada, it's always unsettling, as in the recurring motif of the war cripple—the fragmented man reassembled by prosthesis, a literalization of Marinetti's repellent call for "the mad sculptures that our mad artillery molds." But Ernst's *Airplane* goes beyond cyborg to something darkly mythic: the bare arms of his nightmare contraption are female—elegant and sensual—implying a mantis-like death for those seduced by war.

Dada was too shrill to last long as a movement, and over time it morphed into a less uncompromising style: Surrealism. But its legacy was far-reaching, and one of the latter-day moments when its anti-art, anti-establishment creed reasserted itself was 1970s punk.

Jon Langford is a painter as well as a musician. His illustrative art—photo-derived images festooned with words and phrases on colorful distressed-wood panels—decorates albums and hangs in galleries. His art, like his music, is accessible but deeply thoughtful and largely ignores high-vs.-low hierarchies. Song and painting reflect each other: he makes art based on music and music based on art. This complementary paradigm evolved over time. "For years I didn't paint at all," he writes in his 2006 illustrated memoir *Nashville Radio*. "An artist needs a subject and for a long time I didn't have one."[77] A self-described "hick" when he left Wales in 1976 for the University of Leeds, he underwent the classic art-school trial by fire—immersed in art history, theory, and radical politics, he grew overwhelmed and lost his footing. The impasse led to the Mekons, at first

---

75   Such idealism–hard to fathom in more cynical, defeatist times–was characteristic of the modern avant-garde, which believed that art could and should change the world.

76   Hans Richter, *Dada: Art and Anti-Art* (London: Thames & Hudson, 2016), p. 25.

77   Jon Langford, *Nashville Radio: Art, Words and Music* (Portland, Ore.: Verse Chorus Press, 2006), p. 19.

less a band than an art project, inspired by the provocation and defiant amateurism of punk. It started as "a joke, a one-liner," he recalls, "a bunch of drunken art students scribbling daft songs ... on beer-mats at the pub."[78] Over time, a still scrappy but proper band emerged—principled and intellectual, yet anarchic and raw. Simultaneously, Langford's art bloomed as he applied punk principles to painting, trading esoteric theory for exoteric picture-making and working with what he knew—mostly music and growing up in working-class Wales.

JON LANGFORD, *DRONE OPERATOR,* 2014

Jon Langford/Yard Dog Gallery

For *Here Be Monsters*, he created both cover art and a painting for each song, reproduced on square card-stock inserts. The "Drone Operator" painting is a flat, sigil-like rendering in teal and gold of a silhouetted figure seated before a computer monitor, ludicrously mounted on a classical plinth like a victorious general on a triumphal arch. A Predator drone hovers overhead, and heraldic letters pompously declare job description (and song title) on the stone base. The image captures the song's theme in simple strokes—the elevation of this remote-control warrior, a twenty-something Walter Mitty with his old-school PC, to heroic status in our era of little-debated endless war. But it misses the song's tone, its claustrophobic build-up (without release), and the personality of its protagonist, whose blasé attitude darkens the song with each successive verse.

> *I'm a drone operator*
> *I am part of a team*
> *I study my monitor*
> *Wipe some dust from the screen*
> *It didn't look like a wedding*
> *It really wasn't my call*
> *When it all was over*
> *We went to a bar*
> *We drank beer*
> *And watched basketball*

Here Langford mocks military claims of unerring accuracy. In an earlier song, the furious Gulf War–era "Funeral" by the Mekons (*Curse of the Mekons,* 1991),

---

78   Ibid., p. 20.

he takes the opposite tack—assuming the precision capabilities of modern arsenals—but finds the result no less craven:

Smart bombs replace the dumb bombs
We can aim right into someone's kitchen
Hard rice sprays from the cooking pot
Into the eye's delicate jelly

In 2014, *The Intercept* published an exposé of the U.S. drone program based on interviews with two former pilots.[79] Unlike the character in Langford's song—smug, defensive, steadfastly loyal to the military—these ex-soldiers were troubled by their actions and went rogue. The first, who remained anonymous (though NSA documents leaked by the whistleblower Edward Snowden verified his claims), detailed severe flaws in the surveillance tactics used to track targets—particularly, unreliable tracing of mobile phones. "We're not going after people, we're going after their phones," he said. "Once the bomb lands or a night raid happens, you know that phone is there. But we don't know who's behind it, who's holding it." He also described participating in strikes that killed bystanders. "They might have been terrorists. Or they could have been family members who [had] nothing to do with the target's activities."[80] This contradicted claims by the Obama administration, amplified by compliant media, that every conceivable precaution was taken to avoid killing innocent people.

A brief perusal of mainstream liberal commentary reveals a reflexive approval of aggressive acts committed by Democrats that are condemned as atrocities when committed by Republicans. The lead-up to the Iraq War, for instance, under George W. Bush saw massive anti-war protests; by contrast, his successor's incursions into Pakistan, Libya, Yemen, Syria, and Somalia were far less controversial. Langford condemns the hypocrisy. "That's absolutely true," he told me in 2022, "and the escalation of the drone campaign under Obama was largely influenced by Joe Biden . . . who realized you could fight foreign wars quite happily if there weren't a lot of embarrassing body bags coming home. So drone warfare was perfect for a nice bit of neocon liberal imperialism. . . . Then Trump comes along and suddenly liberals think the FBI and the CIA are their chums..."[81]

The second pilot in the *Intercept* exposé gave his name. Brandon Bryant served six years as a "stick monkey" in an Air Force drone squadron that killed 1,626 people. Bryant confirmed the faulty intelligence and the killing of bystanders and elaborated on both. He also said he confronted his superiors with his concerns but was ignored. "The system continues to work because, like most things in the military, the people who use it trust it unconditionally," he told *The Intercept*. "They make rushed decisions and are often wrong in their assessments. They

79   Jeremy Scahill and Glenn Greenwald, "The NSA's Secret Role in the US Assassination Program," *The Intercept*, 9 February 2014.

80   Ibid.

81   Interview by the author, 2022.

jump to conclusions and there is no going back to correct mistakes." Anguished by his actions, Bryant left the Air Force in 2011. The killings of Anwar al-Awlaki and his son were a turning point: "I was party to the violations of constitutional rights of an American citizen who should have been tried under a jury."[82] He became a whistleblower and anti-drone activist.[83]

Can I buy you a drink?
Yeah, I'd do it all again
To stem the flow of body bags
The politicians find so hard to explain
So please don't complain
There's no pain, no pain
And when this bar is closed
I'll follow you home
I'll follow you home
In through your window
You'll never know
You'll never know

When Langford wrote "Drone Operator," he said he was "trying to work out what it might be like to be [one]." He guessed that "someone who did that might have some serious issues in their personal life."[84] Bryant and the anonymous pilot confirm his suspicion. But for every soldier whose conscience cracks, who recovers some autonomy and rethinks their assumptions about war, there's a slew of others who live with their deeds. Some do so callously, even belligerently, others uneasily or with creeping doubt. Most troubling are those who remain passive, unquestioning, and just follow orders.

"Just following orders" is, of course, also known as the Nuremberg defense. The phrase made headlines in 1945-46 when Nazis accused of war crimes used it to justify their actions in World War II. But Nuremberg Principle IV, codified by the United Nations, is unequivocal: "The fact that a person acted pursuant to order of his Government or of a superior does not relieve him from responsibility under international law, provided a moral choice was in fact possible to him." Prominent Nazis who used the defense were hanged. It resurfaced in 1961 when Adolf Eichmann—an escaped Nazi official and major planner of the Holocaust— was captured and tried in Jerusalem. The mild, bespectacled Eichmann belied stereotypes of maniacal Nazis—he seemed less a fascist enabler of genocide than a typical bourgeois bureaucrat. He described himself as left-leaning, denied being an anti-Semite, and said, "My heart was light and joyful in my work, because

---

82   Scahill and Greenwald, "The NSA's Secret Role in the U.S. Assassination Program."

83   In a chilling interview for *GQ* (Matthew Powers, "Confessions of a Drone Warrior," October 2013), he described the aftermath of a strike: "The smoke clears, and there's pieces of the two guys around the crater. And there's this guy over here, and he's missing his right leg above his knee. He's holding it, and he's rolling around, and the blood is squirting out of his leg … It took him a long time to die. I just watched him." The raid was Bryant's first ever "hit." He was nineteen years old.

84   Caron, "Jon Langford on Drone Warfare, Alternative Astronomy, and Honky-Tonk."

the decisions were not mine."[85] A court-appointed psychiatrist found him sane. The philosopher (and Holocaust survivor) Hannah Arendt attended his trial and coined the phrase "banality of evil" in response to his mild, detached manner. After his execution, she argued that ambition and "thoughtlessness" motivated him more than ideology or hatred—that he was an unreflective, eager-to-please "joiner," blindly obedient to his superiors.[86]

The Trappist monk and activist Thomas Merton was deeply troubled by Eichmann's sanity diagnosis and, by extension, those who uncritically green-light war or excuse or participate in war crimes. "I am beginning to realize that 'sanity' is no longer a value or an end in itself," he wrote in a 1966 essay. "If [man] were a little less sane, a little more doubtful, a little more aware of his absurdities and contradictions, perhaps there might be a possibility of his survival."[87] In a chilling poem, he personified the genocidal civil servant and closed with a reference to remote mass-killing:

You smile at my career but you would do as I did if you knew yourself and dared In my days we worked hard we saw what we did our self sacrifice was conscientious and complete our work was faultless and detailed

Do not think yourself better because you burn up friends and enemies with long-range missiles without ever seeing what you have done[88]

"Without ever seeing ..." Clearly, this is both the crux of "Drone Operator" and a modern moral dilemma. If war is a necessary evil—a questionable but widespread assumption—surely a corresponding principle is that those who wage it must have the integrity to face unflinchingly its human cost.

---

85   Alan Rosenthal, "Eichmann, Revisited," *Jerusalem Post*, 20 April 2011.

86   In a series of *New Yorker* articles, later collected in book form as *Eichmann in Jerusalem: A Report on the Banality of Evil* (New York: Viking Press, 1963).

87   Thomas Merton, "A Devout Meditation in Memory of Adolf Eichmann," *Raids on the Unspeakable* (New York: New Directions, 1966), p. 49.

88   Thomas Merton, "Chant to Be Used in Processions around a Site with Furnaces," originally published in Lawrence Ferlinghetti's *Journal for the Protection of All Beings*, no. 1, 1961 (text reproduced here: thehealingprojectwebcast.blogspot. com/2012/03/thomas-merton-chant-to-be-used-in.html). The subversive comedian Lenny Bruce used to recite and riff on Merton's poem in his sprawling, socially conscious monologues–often under a dramatic spotlight, like an interrogated prisoner.

AND EVERYBODY CRIED

My favorite memories of being a parent involve the days when nothing happens.
When we're just laying around doing nothing but basking in each other's joy
and love. —Patterson Hood[89]

"Two Daughters and a Beautiful Wife" is the opening track of Drive-By
Truckers' acclaimed seventh album, *Brighter Than Creation's Dark* (2008). A
low-key, up-tempo ballad, it seems almost out of place on a set of often high-
volume, at times incendiary, songs about the struggles of everyday people in the
waning, post-9/11 days of the American Dream. Written by the band's co-leader,
Patterson Hood, the song sets the confused, wistful thoughts of a man who's
either just died or awakened from a dream to spare guitar, banjo, and brushed
drum accompaniment, augmented by mournful pedal steel and delicate piano.

> *When he reached the gates of heaven*
> *He didn't understand*
> *He knew that friends were coming over*
> *Or was it all a dream?*
> *Was it all a crazy dream?*

The song's placement was predetermined: "I put great care into the pacing
and sequencing of our albums," Hood told me, "[and] from the moment of its
inception, it was always the first song for *Brighter Than Creation's Dark*." As a
prelude to what follows, it resembles a prayer offered before a storm.

> *He saw them playing there before him*
> *What were they doing there?*
> *It felt like home, it must be all right*
> *Or was it all a dream?*
> *Was it all a crazy dream?*

Inspired by the brutal murder of a family, "Two Daughters and a Beautiful
Wife" never explicitly mentions the crime. Instead, its death-or-a-dream
narrative device distracts us from the unclear source of the singer's confusion
and shifts our focus to the comforting image of an early-morning family idyll.
We don't fully understand what's happened but are reassured by its vision of a
playful bedroom sprawl of kids and parents in PJs.

Hallmark cards and feel-good films, of course, trade in similar imagery.
And it's a credit to the band's artistry that neither this kinship nor the song's
use of the hoary voice-from-heaven motif (one of country music's corniest
clichés) sentimentalizes "Two Daughters and a Beautiful Wife" or muddles
its melancholy tone. Partly it's the music: the E minor chord that completes
each verse's three-chord sequence is ominous, seeming to warn us that any

89   All Hood quotes are from a 2015 interview by the author.

Jason Thrasher

DRIVE-BY TRUCKERS WITH PATTERSON HOOD, CENTER, 2008

reassurance the song offers will come at a price. But "Two Daughters and a Beautiful Wife" also throws down a gauntlet with its tender central image, asking us to choose between sincerity and snark, between loving sentiment and reflexive cynicism, before we move on.

> *Memories replay before him*
> *All the tiny moments of his life*
> *Laying 'round in bed on Saturday morning*
> *Two daughters and a wife*
> *Two daughters and a beautiful wife*

Such unequivocal humanism is admirable. It also helps explain the song's placement as the lead track on an album that chronicles the struggles of everyday people—not without satire, sarcasm, or biting humor, but always with compassion and a sense of inherent worth. Embracing the honest sentiment of the song allows us to savor its bittersweet evocation of a man who realizes that paradise was his all along—not in any kingdom in the sky but in those "tiny moments" of comfort and togetherness shared with his loved ones, before he left (or was forced to leave) this sweet old world.

In the early afternoon of January 1, 2006, firefighters were called to a two-story home in a quiet neighborhood in Richmond, Virginia. A friend of the family that lived there—a couple and their two small children—had arrived early for a planned New Year's Day party and, finding the house filling with smoke, frantically called 911. Christmas trees and lights still decorated surrounding homes, and neighbors, enjoying the holiday, were moving slowly or sleeping in when the trucks arrived, sirens blaring. First responders hurried inside and discovered a fire burning in the smoke-filled basement. They also found four bodies—two adults and two children—unmoving and prone on the floor. Immediately they started shifting the still forms toward the clean air outdoors in hopes of reviving them. But in the process, they made a horrific discovery: all four had been bound and gagged and were already lifeless. A tragic holiday house fire turned out to be a brutal act of arson and murder.

All day, across the city, people were jarred by the terrible news. The victims had been well-known residents, universally liked by all who knew them. Bryan Harvey, forty-nine years old, was a musician of some renown—the former singer-guitarist for the post-punk Americana duo House of Freaks (whose other member, drummer Johnny Hott, had made the 911 call that afternoon). In recent years, Bryan's musical career had taken a back seat to raising a family. His wife Kathryn, thirty-nine, owned and operated World of Mirth, a popular toy and novelty shop that she maintained like an immersive, campy art installation. Their daughters, Stella and Ruby, were nine and four. They had met their deaths, it was soon discovered, due to an oversight emblematic of both the couple's trusting nature and their neighborhood's peaceful reputation: Bryan had inadvertently left the door ajar that morning after fetching his newspaper, giving whoever murdered him and his family access to their home.

The facts of the crime that emerged were callous and horrible. The family had been held hostage in the basement—muzzled, restrained, and unable to comfort one another—while their home was ransacked. The killings occurred some time afterward and were abrupt and savage, clumsily committed with the Harveys' own kitchen knife and claw hammer. So pitiful and appalling was the state of the bodies that hardened cops and firefighters reportedly cried at the scene. The motive for the massacre remained elusive: the Harveys had been robbed, but of very little—a laptop, some cash, Bryan's wedding ring. To wipe out an entire family for such paltry plunder seemed either deranged or unimaginably cruel.

In the days that followed, police gathered evidence, local media expressed shock and disbelief, and spontaneous shrines of cards, candles, and other mementos accumulated outside the house and Kathryn's shop. At a packed memorial at the local Byrd movie theater, musician friends numb with grief played a tearful version of George Harrison's "All Things Must Pass." It was a dreadful end to the holiday season and a chilling start to the New Year. And the violence wasn't over: within days of the tragedy, another family was found slain in a different part of town—further evidence of a binge of assault and murder so brutal and unfocused it would haunt the city for years to come.

Meanwhile on Earth, his friends came over
Shocked and horrified
Dolls and flowers by the storefront
And everybody cried
Everybody cried and cried

This is as close as the song gets to the terror and anguish it mostly obscures. When Hood and bassist Shonna Tucker sing "shocked and horrified," it jolts and nearly transports us where we, the singer, and Hood least want to go: to where a father watches helplessly as his wife and children die, and all the weeping in the world won't bring them back or wipe from our minds how they were killed. Faced with such facts and the barely tolerable emotions they provoke, even the gentlest soul might feel the urge to strike out at someone or something with previously unimagined viciousness. In the days after the Harvey murders, many who knew them (and shared their liberal humanist values) admitted to an old-school desire for blood revenge. Some surprised themselves by embracing the death penalty.

Is there vengeance up in heaven?
Or are those things left behind?
Maybe every day is Saturday morning
Two daughters and a wife
Two daughters and a beautiful wife

Hood still opposes an eye for an eye. He also says he's "not at all religious." But he is a father whose first child happened to be born shortly before the Harveys' daughter Stella. He also personally knew the Harveys. "Bryan and Kathryn usually came to Drive-By Truckers shows and at least once brought the girls to an all-ages show we played one afternoon. When I saw their pictures [on the news], my heart nearly stopped." The crime so disturbed him that he sought peace and resolution in his craft (songwriting) and the iconography of his cultural heritage (Christianity). "I just couldn't make any sense or find any kind of closure to the horror of it all . . . the image of them frolicking leisurely in heaven was about as comforting an image as I could find." Yet he worried that the gesture might cause further harm: "I was very concerned about putting the song out, as I really didn't want it to hurt anyone or cause anyone who knew and loved the Harveys to be hurt by it . . . [So] I played the song for my Richmond friends in private, and almost everyone told me they found the song to be comforting and beautiful."

Hood and Bryan Harvey were linked by more than fatherhood. Both were artistically ambitious Southerners who formed bands that sought to merge the grit of American roots music with punk DIY and a socially conscious take on their heritage. Hood, from Muscle Shoals, Alabama, co-founded Drive-By Truckers in 1996 (with his fellow songwriter Mike Cooley) as an updated Southern rock band in the Lynyrd Skynyrd mode that set rich storytelling to fiery redneck stomp. Prolific touring and recording earned them critical acclaim and a large cult following. Bryan, a Richmond native, formed House of Freaks (with Johnny Hott) in 1986 in a then-novel guitar-and-drums format. Their ragged folk/blues/rockabilly hybrid garnered enough under-the-radar acclaim that they relocated to Los Angeles and signed with a major label. Both bands set literate lyrics to raw, sweaty music with an earnest but world-weary vibe. "Remember Me Well," the closing track on House of Freaks' 1991 album *Cakewalk*, captures this sincere yet sardonic tone in a rueful ballad that backs Bryan's unvarnished voice with waltz-time guitar and funerary brass.

> *In a hundred years spent*
> *With the worms that will dwell*
> *When I'm gone from this world*
> *Please remember me well*
>
> *You can dance on my grave*
> *You can ring out the bell*
> *You can drink to my health*
> *But remember me well*

Over time, Bryan grew tired of touring and life in L.A. He disbanded House of Freaks in 1995 and moved back to Richmond. By then, he'd married the former Kathryn Grabinsky—an ex–art student he met at a Richmond café where she waited tables.[90] In 1996, their daughter Stella was born. Ruby followed in 2001. Bryan took a computer job with a local school district, and Kathryn opened her shop. The couple bought a roomy brick house on a tree-lined street in an old trolley neighborhood in south Richmond. Bryan still played music but as a hobby, not a vocation, gradually trading rock and roll for family life. The shift suited him. He mellowed and, with children under his care, exchanged world-weariness for cautious optimism. "I think you have to be hopeful about life when you have a child," he told a fan website after Stella's birth. "I think you owe it to them."[91]

In September of 2006, two twenty-eight-year-old ex-cons—Ray Joseph Dandridge and Ricky Javon Gray—were convicted of the murders of the Harvey family. Poor, uneducated, and recently released from prison, the two had linked up in late 2005 and decided to pursue a vaguely defined criminal path to Easy Street. On the morning of January 1, 2006, they had been cruising neighborhoods looking for a house to rob, when they spotted the door that Bryan Harvey had left ajar.[92] Their accounts of what transpired next answered questions about the crime but did little to satisfy anyone's need to know, at a human level, why

---

90   Voted "most beautiful" in her 1984 Virginia Beach high school yearbook.

91   Gary A. Harki and Joanne Kimberlin, "A Man Set for Execution, and the Unforgotten Murders That Could Have Happened to Anyone," *Virginian-Pilot*, 14 January 2017.

92   A third accomplice, twenty-one-year-old Ashley Baskerville, stayed in the killers' parked car as a lookout. Days later, she and her mother, Mary Baskerville-Tucker, and stepfather, Percyell Tucker, were also slain by Dandridge and Gray.

Sue Zechini

THE HARVEY FAMILY: RUBY, STELLA, KATHRYN, AND PAUL, C. 2006

the slayings occurred. The simple truth was that Dandridge and Gray might have picked any house that morning. They didn't know the Harveys and had no vendetta against them—they were simply obstacles in the way of what they wanted. "I don't believe sorry is strong enough," Gray told police after confessing to the Harvey murders. "None of this was necessary."[93]

There can be grim satisfaction in learning the motive behind a terrible crime. Traumatized by a senseless act, it's only human to seek sense in it. Crimes of passion, conspiracy, or insanity provide bleak comfort to survivors because they imply someone died for a cause, as part of a plot, or at the hands of a maniac. There was no such comfort for those grieving the Harveys: everything about their killers seemed haphazard, almost arbitrary. By the time they were apprehended, they had murdered nine people (including Gray's wife) by gun, knife, battery, strangulation, or suffocation and nearly killed a tenth (who survived the assault but lost use of an arm)—all during simple burglaries. Neither was insane by any common or clinical standard, just profoundly cold-hearted. At some point in both men's lives, normal responses of empathy and compassion withered and gave way to a deadening flatness.[94] How and why that loss of humanity occurs, what crushes the spirit and warps the souls of once-full human beings, is a vast question beyond the scope of this essay (as are complex but critical issues of economics and race). After conviction, Dandridge was sentenced to life in prison; Gray was sentenced to death.[95]

93   Paige Akin Mudd, "Ricky Javon Gray's Chilling Confession Is Read to the Jury," *Richmond Times-Dispatch*, 17 August 2006.

94   "There's folks out there so dead to the world they'd slit your throat for a quarter," a street person once said to me when I was a social worker in Chicago.

95   On January 18, 2017, Gray was executed at Greenville Correctional Center. In 2021, the death penalty was abolished

A final image: Gray showed little emotion during his trial until his mother testified during its penalty phase. Frail and in tears, she described a childhood of neglect and abuse for her son, much mocked by some observers and media.[96] As she spoke, she held a photo of him as a boy dressed in a sailor suit. Gray wept during her testimony. It was a haunting moment and hard to shake, because everyone starts as the equivalent of that boy in a sailor suit—innocent, unspoiled, brimming with potential, needing only love, nurturing, and opportunity to grow into something worthwhile. When that process is corrupted, when those basic needs aren't met, and something monstrous is produced instead, it's a tragedy almost always compounded by further tragedies.

---

in Virginia.

96   But corroborated by psychiatrists and witnesses. The abuse included severe beatings and multiple rapes, starting at age seven. Before he was a teenager, Gray was drinking heavily and using PCP.

STEVEN L. JONES, *OPEN HYMNAL #3*, 2019

CHAPTER THREE:
GAME-CHANGERS, OUTLAWS, AND FOLK HEROES

A WALKIN' CHUNK A MEAN-MAD

I love a good man outside the law just as much as I hate a bad man inside the law.
—Woody Guthrie, "Pretty Boy Floyd" lyric sheet notation, 1940s[97]

In 1939, an infamous hold-up man and killer was immortalized in a broadside-style ballad penned and performed by the populist singer Woody Guthrie. "Pretty Boy Floyd" paints a compelling poetic-license portrait of the notorious armed robber as a modern-day Robin Hood. Like many folk songs, it uses factual material as a springboard for fantasy, collecting anecdotes and ascribing motivations to its subject that are impossible to verify. As with other once-historical, now-mythic figures (including Sherwood's merry archer), Floyd becomes—in Guthrie's hands—less a flesh-and-blood man than a larger-than-life metaphor. The difference is that Floyd was no King Arthur or Honest Abe Lincoln, evoked from the mists of time or at least a previous century, but a man who lived and died within (then) recent memory. Guthrie's choice to consciously mythologize him was thus risky and bold.

Well, gather 'round me, children
A story I will tell
'Bout Pretty Boy Floyd, the outlaw
Oklahoma knew him well

On October 22, 1934, Charles Arthur "Pretty Boy" Floyd—a bank robber suspected by the FBI as a gunman in a 1933 Kansas City shootout that killed four lawmen and a criminal fugitive in their custody—died in a hail of bullets in a cornfield in rural Ohio. Named Public Enemy No. 1 the previous July (after John Dillinger lost the title in a pool of blood in a Chicago alleyway), Floyd was perhaps the most enigmatic of the legendary, non-Mob criminals who thrilled newspaper readers and led cops and G-men on serpentine chases throughout the American Midwest during the bleak years of the Great Depression and Dust Bowl.

An unassuming, Georgia-born Oklahoman who liked to bake pies when he wasn't masterminding robberies, Floyd seemed ill cast in the role of loathsome evildoer. Mug shots consistently show a man uncomfortable with the camera—tousle-haired but snappily dressed, with a broad, sad face. Unlike Dillinger, or Bonnie and Clyde, he took no exhibitionistic delight in his notoriety, nor did he rage wild-eyed at authority like the sociopathic George "Baby Face"

---

97   Quoted at the *Woody Guthrie* website, woodyguthrie.org/biography/woodysez.htm

Nelson. His path from hayseed to federal pariah seemed less pre-ordained than accidental: the hard-luck story of a country boy who, thwarted by poverty and limited life options, turned to crime incrementally—from teenaged petty thief to repentant ex-con to bootlegger's hired gun to bank heist adept blamed for all manner of atrocities he did and didn't commit. To the end, he denied participating in the most serious crime he was charged with—the so-called Kansas City Massacre. And, with fitting ambiguity, there's evidence that both supports and refutes his claim.

Such inscrutability invites myth-making—the grafting of a focused identity onto an indistinct figure—and, more than any other outlaw of his era, the disenfranchised farmers and laborers hit hardest by the hard times of the '30s held Floyd up as a hero. With reason: tales of "Pretty Boy" (a press nickname he despised) shredding mortgage documents during hold-ups to free farmers from debt, unlikely as they sounded, were, in fact, true. And these and other acts of insurrectionist wealth-redistribution elicited sympathy from a rural working class that blamed banks and big business (also with reason) for their miseries. From such class disparities, legends are born.

"Pretty Boy Floyd" has been covered by everyone from the traditional folkie Ramblin' Jack Elliott to the new-wave *noirists* Wall of Voodoo. But versions by Guthrie (1940) and the Byrds (1968) capture the song's homespun charm and subversive spirit in thematic song collections that enrich the ballad's meaning by contextualizing it within larger wholes: Guthrie on *Dust Bowl Ballads* (1940), the Byrds on *Sweetheart of the Rodeo* (1968).[98]

Only one episode in the song seems invented from whole cloth, and Guthrie dispenses with it in the first three verses.

It was in the town of Shawnee
A Saturday afternoon
His wife beside him in his wagon
As into town they rode

There, a deputy sheriff approached him
In a manner rather rude
Using vulgar words of anger
And his wife she overheard

Pretty Boy grabbed a log chain
And the deputy grabbed his gun
In the fight that followed
He laid that deputy down

Floyd was a suspect in at least five homicides before the Kansas City slayings. After the Massacre, an FBI agent and a retired sheriff-turned-mercenary both

---

98   Since lyrics differ only slightly between the two versions, song quotes derive from both.

died at his hands or those of his accomplices while trying to apprehend him. None of these killings seemed unnecessarily cruel or vicious to a public predisposed to give "Pretty Boy" the benefit of the doubt (and unlike other figures in the '30s crime wave, Floyd seems to have taken no pleasure in killing). But Guthrie's oddly Victorian account of a duel to defend the honor of his lady fair appears to have no factual basis—it merely serves to establish his (anti-)hero's innocence from the start, the better to portray him as a victimized class warrior.

> *He ran through the trees and bushes*
> *And lived a life of shame*
> *Every crime in Oklahoma*
> *Was added to his name*

> *He ran through the trees and bushes*
> *On the Canadian River shore*
> *And many a starving farmer*
> *Opened up his door*

The truth behind Floyd's unraveling is comparatively prosaic, if far more tragic. Convicted of a St. Louis payroll robbery in his early twenties, he served three years of a five-year prison sentence, during which time his wife divorced him. Paroled in 1929, he vowed to go straight, but lack of work, the failure of his family's farm, and numerous brushes with the law left him feeling bitter and persecuted. In November, his beloved father was shot and killed during a quarrel with a local shopkeeper. When the shooter was acquitted (on grounds of self-defense), the already overwrought Floyd seems to have snapped. Soon after, his father's killer disappeared. The son is widely assumed to have avenged his father. And "Pretty Boy" (nicknamed for his boyish, innocent-looking face) returned to robbery—this time hitting banks in a spree so brazen it guaranteed he'd spend the rest of his life a wanted man.

Through it all, despite official demonization and a sensationalist but condemning press, the "Robin Hood of the Cookson Hills" received moral and practical support from sympathetic farmers who hid, sheltered, clothed, and fed the outlaw. Whenever possible, Floyd showed his gratitude.

> *But many a starving farmer*
> *The same old story told*
> *How the outlaw paid their mortgage*
> *And saved their little home*

> *Others tell you 'bout a stranger*
> *That come to beg a meal*
> *And underneath his napkin*
> *Left a thousand-dollar bill*

"Pretty Boy Floyd" debuted as a recording on *Dust Bowl Ballads*, Guthrie's 1940 concept album of sepia-toned songs about the Okie catastrophe. Sequenced in the record's middle, after "Dust Can't Kill Me" and "Dust Pneumonia Blues," it provides a respite from accounts of crushing poverty and respiratory illness (thousands died from exposure to the apocalyptic "black blizzards" that menaced the drought-ravaged Plains states from 1934 to 1940). A tale of action, and therefore hope, amid songs of ineluctable but deadening passivity, "Pretty Boy Floyd" glows like a righteous beacon in an end-times fog. Its placement and relative gleam imply that its narrative of a

THIS MACHINE KILLS FASCISTS: WOODY GUTHRIE, 1943

"good man outside the law" might hold the key to combating the selfishness and greed of those "inside the law"—i.e., by *breaking* the law in a spirit of radical solidarity and sharing. As if to underline the point, Guthrie next sings "Blowin' Down This Road (I Ain't Going to Be Treated This Way)"—the most unequivocally defiant tune on *Dust Bowl Ballads*.

Another legendary figure, this one entirely fictional, appears on *Dust Bowl Ballads* in an eponymous two-part story-song: Tom Joad, the migrant worker hero of the nation's most read book of 1939, John Steinbeck's Dust Bowl chronicle *The Grapes of Wrath* ("as pitiful and angry a novel ever to be written about America," said the *New York Times*).[99] Steinbeck, who shared Guthrie's sympathies with the uprooted poor and his antagonism toward the system that displaced them, had given "Pretty Boy" a brief but significant mention in a speech by the matriarch of the "crackered out by the cats" clan—Ma Joad:

> *I knowed Purty Boy Floyd. I knowed his ma. They was good folks . . . He done a little bad thing an' they hurt 'im, caught 'im an' hurt him so he was mad . . . an' purty soon he was mean-mad. They shot at him like a varmint, an' he shot back, an' then they run him like a coyote, an' him a-snappin' an' a-snarlin', mean as a lobo. An' he was mad. He wasn't no boy or no man no more, he was jus' a walkin' chunk a mean-mad . . . Finally they run him down an' killed 'im.*[100]

99   Peter Monro Jack, "John Steinbeck's New Novel Brims with Anger and Pity," *New York Times*, 16 April 1939.
100   John Steinbeck, *The Grapes of Wrath* (New York: Penguin Books, 1976), p. 98.

Ironically, the same bastion of law and order whose agents shot Floyd dead in an Ohio cornfield—the FBI director-for-life and compulsive scandalmonger J. Edgar Hoover—for years used the IRS to harass Steinbeck for his leftish politics. The much-audited Pulitzer- and Nobel Prize–winning author wrote the U.S. Attorney General's office in 1942 in frustration: "Do you suppose you could ask Edgar's boys to stop stepping on my heels? They think I am an enemy alien. It is getting tiresome."[101] Hoover had successfully used the '30s crime wave—which resulted partly from the sudden widespread availability of Thompson submachine guns at a time when agents weren't even armed—as an impetus to build the FBI into an investigatory and fighting force to reckon with. He did so, in part, by consciously exaggerating the facts of the wave's most notorious participants. One can imagine his chagrin at the likes of Guthrie and Steinbeck exalting one of his vanquished supervillains as a proletarian hero.

It was in Oklahoma City
It was on a Christmas Day
A whole carload of groceries
And a letter that did say

"You say that I'm an outlaw
You say that I'm a thief
Well, here's a Christmas dinner
For the families on relief"

If the sunniness of "Pretty Boy Floyd" downplays its dissident message on *Dust Bowl Ballads*, the Byrds' rendition on *Sweetheart of the Rodeo* (1968) dashes by so breezily—in a jaunty bluegrass arrangement—that it's even easier to miss the song's essential radicalism. A seminal country-rock album, *Sweetheart of the Rodeo* was part of a late-'60s return-to-roots trend that included Bob Dylan's *John Wesley Harding* and the Band's *Music from Big Pink* (both 1968). These records looked to country music—the seeming antithesis of all that was revolutionary and new—for inspiration at the height of the youth-centered rock and roll counterculture. This seeming rearguard gesture by cutting-edge artists reminded listeners that rock was part of a legacy that emerged from country and blues. It also suggested there was something to be learned by embracing, not rejecting, the music of the past and the culture that produced it.

In the case of "Pretty Boy Floyd," this was that principled lawlessness was neither new in this country nor "un-American." Rather, it was part of a continuum of popular revolt against institutional tyranny that regularly arose during times of social and economic unrest—from the labor movement of the Gilded Age to the unabashed pseudo-socialism of the nation's pre-war FDR period.

Guthrie saves his best lines for last, and rarely was his "simple man of the people" persona more effective at winning hearts and minds with a wink:

101　Herbert Mitgang, "Policing America's Writers," *New Yorker*, 28 September 1987.

Now as through this world I ramble
I see lots of funny men
Some will rob you with a six gun
And some with a fountain pen

But as through your life you travel
As through your life you roam
You won't never see an outlaw
Drive a family from their home

Guthrie's romanticized take on Pretty Boy's life of crime was neither the first nor last iteration of the theme. A feature in the *Oklahoma News*, published days after Floyd's death, captured the outlaw's mythic legacy and evoked his archetypal forebear:

> *Like the famed marauder of the English forests, he took money from those who had it—the banks—and divided the proceeds of his raids with the poor. The penniless tenant farmers kept their mouths shut; they had no scruples about taking contraband wrested from bankers.*   —Oklahoma News, *Oct. 26, 1934*

Heroic outlaw narratives remain a staple of folklore and pop culture, and tales of Robin Hood–like figures are at least as old as their namesake—an obscure sylvan bandit who first captured the public imagination in medieval Britain. Child records nearly forty ballads about his exploits, as old as the fifteenth century, and the earliest say nothing about his origin or motivations. His portrayal as a peasant revolt leader during the absentee reign of Richard Coeur de Lion dates from the sixteenth century. From that point on, he evolves into the familiar image of a roguish champion of the righteous poor against the rapacious rich—family-friendly and suitable for Disney movies.

This cheery assimilation is striking because, even stripped of violence and safely ensconced in a fairy-tale past, such narratives violate deeply entrenched social norms. By celebrating criminals as virtuous, they presume that redress of grievances is no longer (or never was) possible and posit lawlessness as the remedy to a corrupt or broken system. In such a "world turned upside-down," hierarchies collapse and dogs may turn on their masters.

A vivid example (in film, not music) of this anarchic spirit exploding in the pop world was Arthur Penn's *Bonnie and Clyde* (1967)—an edgy essay in outlaw heroics, controversial but wildly popular, that played a crucial role in updating the theme for the '60s generation. Gangsters had been glamorized in American movies before, but never with the erotic charge and moral ambivalence Penn gave his felonious lovers—on the run in a landscape of migrant families and foreclosed farms. Bearing little resemblance to their real-life counterparts (a homely and, by biographical consensus, disagreeable pair), Faye Dunaway and Warren Beatty make armed robbery seem thrilling and justifiable. A pivotal scene features an itinerant farmer borrowing Clyde's sidearm—with his permission and encouragement—to shoot holes through a sign declaring that the bank has repossessed his farm.

Pop musicians have also glorified gangsters—in manners both crass (there's an '80s hair band called Pretty Boy Floyd) and thoughtful. In the latter case, they often claim symbolic kinship with criminals perceived as living honest lives in a crooked society—echoing organized crime's perennial complaint that the only real difference between the underworld and its aboveground counterpart is that the Mob is honest about what they do, while the government and big business are shameless liars. In some subcultures—Jamaican reggae, for instance, with its long line of songs romanticizing gangsters (e.g., Prince Buster's "Al Capone") and its street-urchin class of "rude boys"—harsh social realities give this stance more bite. In the West, the trope perhaps peaked with '70s punk and '80s hip-hop.

Probably no punk band mined American crime for signifiers with more style and intelligence than the Clash, whose class-conscious co-leader, Joe Strummer, was that movement's Woody Guthrie. Born John Mellor—son of a crofter's daughter and a British diplomat—Strummer rejected his middle-class background in his teens, trading a life of posh schools and privilege for a scruffy life on the margins, playing in bands and squatting in hovels. He admired Guthrie, even going by the nickname "Woody" for a time. In 1979, with Thatcher in office, Reagan in the wings, and the U.K. and the U.S. veering rightward, the staunchly leftist Clash released *London Calling*—a brilliant, ragged blend of rock, jazzy blues, and reggae that celebrated gangsters and rude boys alongside Spanish Republican anti-fascists. They followed the LP with a single—the infectious "Bankrobber"—about a Floyd-like hood that "never hurt nobody," whose philosophy is articulated early in the song:

Some is rich, and some is poor
That's the way the world is
But I don't believe in lyin' back
Sayin' how bad your luck is

Outlaw motifs permeated hip-hop long before "gangsta" was a designated genre. In 1982, the pioneering South Bronx rappers Grandmaster Flash and the Furious Five unleashed "The Message" on a public conditioned to think of rap as mere novelty music. A spine-tingling mid-tempo meditation on being trapped in ghetto life, "The Message" took its template from contemplative '70s soul hits like Sly and the Family Stone's "Family Affair" (1971) and the Temptations' "Papa Was a Rolling Stone" (1972). But the seminal hip-hop sextet adapted the claustrophobic, pull-no-punches tone of those socially conscious singles to the new street style. Doing so paved the way for the politically engaged rap of '80s bands like Public Enemy, led by Chuck D, a Clash fan.

The repeated refrain in "The Message"—*It's like a jungle sometimes, it makes me wonder how I keep from goin' under*—grows tenser with each utterance as the song's protagonist sinks deeper into hopelessness and crime. Toward the end, our (anti-)hero makes a surprise appearance:

> *Now you're unemployed, all non-void*
> *Walkin' around like you're Pretty Boy Floyd*
> *Turned stick-up kid, but look what you done did*
> *Got sent up for an eight-year bid*

But unlike Floyd, who at least died a fugitive and some kind of hero, this rude boy's run ends not with a bang but a whimper: consigned to a prison cell and unable to take it anymore, he hangs himself.

The street tough in "The Message" is no Robin Hood–style subversive. His self-destructive path is grounded in socio-economic reality ("You'll grow in the ghetto, livin' second rate / And your eyes will sing a song of deep hate"). But unlike "Pretty Boy Floyd," his crime spree has no redeeming communal spirit. Blinded by the injustices of his life, he looks admiringly toward the "thugs, pimps, and pushers" and other petty hoods for a way out. The Furious Five's portrait is compassionate but critical—they portray him as nihilistic but condemn his nihilism.

What's missing from "The Message" that animates "Pretty Boy Floyd" is a sense of radical consciousness—the idea that, once freed of delusions about systemic fairness, one can fight for something greater than self-interest. Those who do so don't necessarily fare better than those who don't, but at least they keep one set of transformative myths—and therefore hope—alive.

POSTCARDS OF THE HANGING

> *The way to right wrongs is to turn the light of truth upon them.*
> —Ida B. Wells, A Red Record, *1894*

In 1956, Ella Fitzgerald made an achingly beautiful recording of a standard ballad. To restrained accompaniment by the pianist Paul Smith, the then-thirty-nine-year-old "First Lady of Song" reinterpreted a tragic tune—a song usually played, at least in part, for laughs—imbuing it with quiet dignity and an edge of heartbreak. Her version also challenged assumptions about her artistry. Widely considered the greatest of all female jazz singers for her superb technique and mastery of swing—Billie Holiday is her only true competition—her fragile rendition belied conventional wisdom that her emotional tenor went no deeper than simple joy. After an opening flourish of plaintive piano chords, she sings with her trademark exquisite tone, phrasing, and diction. The song is satirical, but Fitzgerald sings it straight, and her sincerity and natural warmth, coupled with her sublime vocal skill, make for a riveting three minutes.

Miss Otis regrets she's unable to lunch today
Madam
Miss Otis regrets she's unable to lunch today
She is sorry to be delayed
But last evening down in Lover's Lane she strayed
Madam
Miss Otis regrets she's unable to lunch today

Carl Van Vechten/Library of Congress

"Miss Otis Regrets" is a lynching ballad. It's a story of murder and vigilante justice, set to a stolid but graceful tune, that ends with its protagonist dragged to her extrajudicial doom. What makes such a disagreeable notion palatable is the song's satiric edge—it takes the form of an RSVP penned by a lady of manners, Miss Otis, who remains stoic and polite to the bitter end, responsibly elucidating her luncheon-date absence while being fitted for the noose.[102] Earlier versions are typically arch and camp—cognizant of the song's troubling themes but content to delve no deeper than its surface ironies. Fitzgerald mines the song's underlying despair, injecting it with a plainspoken vulnerability that's an extension of her own sunny nature. The song's lyrical absurdity and fussy but lovely melody make "Miss Otis Regrets" impervious to humorless or self-righteous readings.[103]

ELLA FITZGERALD, 1940

But Fitzgerald maximizes emotion in a weirdly subversive way. We expect weighty despair from the likes of Holiday—her melancholic, at times strident counterpart. But to hear the effervescent singer of "A-Tisket A-Tasket" express dejection and betrayal so unguardedly, even in the context of black comedy, is a forlorn experience.[104]

---

102 The song is ostensibly voiced by a house-servant of Miss Otis, but clearly expresses her point of view, sympathetically delivered by a loyal retainer. Thus, the song's perspective shifts easily from servant to Miss Otis, especially in less comical versions like Fitzgerald's.

103 Especially lovely is the staggered rubato phrase that highlights the third line of each verse, i.e., "She is sorry to be delayed / But last eve–ning–down–in–Love–er's–Lane–she–stray–ay–ayed." This switch to clipped speech and half-tempo mimics the process of writing a note and proofing it aloud, syllable by syllable. It also emphasizes poignant plot points: in the following verses, it occurs in the lines, "She drew a gun and shot her lover down" and "She lifted up her lovely head and cried." The descending melody is mournful, but emotion is supplanted each time by the composure-restoring "Madam" and a pause. The best readings, like Fitzgerald's, break your heart with each iteration.

104 Fitzgerald sang "Miss Otis" countless times and made two studio recordings: the piano and vocal version on *Ella Fitzgerald Sings the Cole Porter Songbook* (1956) and a full-band revisit on *Hello Dolly!* (1964). Her singing is flawless on both,

Not that Fitzgerald's life was roses and rainbows. Just as we expect Holiday's harrowing history of childhood trauma, professional exploitation, and addiction to affect her blues-drenched artistry, corresponding logic assumes that Fitzgerald's lighter, less anguished work reflects a more carefree background. In fact, Ladies Ella and Day were both products of broken homes, worked in bordellos (but not as prostitutes), and endured physical and sexual abuse. Her mother died after a car wreck when Fitzgerald was fifteen, and she fled an abusive, alcoholic stepfather. She ran errands for mobsters, was sent to reform school, and, by her late teens, was homeless in Depression-ravaged New York. Music became a refuge and abiding dream: like Holiday, a means to numb pain, process emotion, and—crucially—escape poverty. But not racism. Both singers were scarred by bigotry, even at the heights of their careers. And Fitzgerald—like another jovial jazz genius whose surface cheer masked unplumbed pain, Louis Armstrong—became a civil rights activist.[105]

How all this affected her music can't be quantified. But the grace and gravitas that make her "Miss Otis Regrets"—performed in reflective middle age—so moving must have resonated with her circumstances.

> *When she woke up and found that her dream of love was gone*
> *Madam*
> *She ran to the man who had led her so far astray*
> *And from under a velvet gown*
> *She drew a gun and shot her lover down*
> *Madam*
> *Miss Otis regrets she's unable to lunch today*

"Miss Otis Regrets" embodies a bewildering nexus of cultural contradictions. Written by a gay white man, sung (here and in many versions) by a straight Black woman, and concerning a patrician white socialite offed by a plebeian mob for the revenge killing of a cheating beau, the song turns presumptions about race, class, and gender inside out and upside down. Most lynching victims were Black, most were poor, most were men, and most were dispatched by unwashed rabble with at least tacit approval from blue-blood elites. That the song achieves humor and pathos under the weight of such paradox testifies to the genius of its creator, the acerbic songwriter Cole Porter. Written in 1934 and an instant success in the composer's upscale Manhattan milieu of well-did-you-evah? parties and nightspots, it was included in an English musical revue no one remembers called *Hi Diddle Diddle* the same year. (In that staging, the number is sung by a stoic butler.) Unattached to a larger work, it became a favorite of the smart set it

---

but slightly syrupy accompaniment diminishes the latter, making the former the essential cut.

105   Armstrong, Holiday, and Fitzgerald were typically treated like royalty overseas but faced segregation, threats, and harassment in Jim Crow America. Fitzgerald was arrested in Texas in 1955 for singing to a racially integrated audience (she signed an autograph while in custody for a cop who was a fan). That same year, Marilyn Monroe successfully lobbied the Hollywood hotspot the Mocambo–reluctant to feature Black performers–to book Fitzgerald, promising to attract crowds by sitting in the front row for each performance (which she did).

satirized. An early recording by the Broadway stalwart Ethel Waters (also 1934) is mannered and self-conscious—stage-bound even on record.

Interestingly, Waters—a pioneering Black entertainer who gradually crossed the color barrier from segregated to integrated audiences—addressed lynching more directly in a little-remembered Irving Berlin song. "Supper Time" is sung from the perspective of a widow telling her children that their father will never return at mealtime ("I should set the table / 'Cause it's supper time / Somehow I'm not able / 'Cause that man of mine / Ain't coming home no more"). Berlin wrote the song with the lyricist Moss Hart for a 1933 musical called *As Thousands Cheer,* wherein newspaper headlines introduced musical numbers based on current events. Most were light-hearted, but Berlin insisted—to considerable pushback—on including the downcast song, accompanied onstage by the headline "Unknown Negro Lynched by Frenzied Mob." Waters, who'd encountered lynching in Georgia, gave the song her all. That the flag-waving composer of "I Like Ike" and "God Bless America" took such a stand might seem incongruous. But Berlin was a fervent civil-rights supporter, targeted (like Holiday) by Hoover's FBI. A sad footnote to Waters' performance is that three of her (white) costars—Helen Broderick, Marilyn Miller, and Clifton Webb—refused to bow with her at the show's tryout (theatrical stages were then strictly segregated). Berlin informed the trio that unless they did so in the future, there would be no bows at all.

It would take mid-century jazz singers (and, later, rock-era artists) to transform "Miss Otis Regrets" from a campy showpiece for the likes of Marlene Dietrich and Ornella Vanoni into something unaffectedly tragic. Even an amiable shuffle version by the bluesman Josh White, recorded a year after Fitzgerald's in 1957, sounds stiff and old-fashioned, never shaking its urbane East Coast roots.[106] Accounts of its composition vary, but Porter seems to have workshopped the song from the piano at parties, and based it on a droll phrase he either coined or overheard.[107]

Porter wrote "Miss Otis" at the height of public awareness about lynching—a turning point in its savage history when activism, political pressure, and print editorials coalesced to reduce the shameful practice after an epidemic of lawless violence that began with Reconstruction and finally slowed during the Great Depression.[108] Porter often inserted headline issues into timely, tongue-in-

106 Among latter-day versions, a non-jazz interpretation that mines the song's heart but preserves its wit is Kirsty MacColl's folk-punk rendition with the Pogues. Cut for the AIDS fundraiser *Red, Hot + Blue* (1990), a collection of pop covers of Porter songs that range from the sublime (Annie Lennox's torchy but restrained "Ev'ry Time We Say Goodbye") to the ridiculous (U2's overwrought "Night and Day"), it movingly sets MacColl's mournful voice to funereal martial accompaniment. In a video for the song, band and singer perform onstage in music-hall finery before dancing couples in formal wear who enact Miss Otis's tragedy in stylized movement.

107 Ada "Bricktop" Smith, a cigar-smoking ex-pat performer, saloonkeeper, and doyenne of Parisian café society—mixed-race and born in West Virginia—claimed "Miss Otis Regrets" was written for her. She said the title phrase derived from a conversation with Porter (a friend), wherein she described a Southern lynching and pithily observed of the victim, "Well, that man won't lunch tomorrow" (Patrick Monahan, "To Bricktop, on Her Belated Birthday," *Paris Review,* 15 August 2011).

108 According to statistics compiled by the Archives of Tuskegee University, fifteen Americans died by lynching in 1934, the year Porter wrote the song. By contrast, in the peak year of 1892, 230 people were lynched (archive.tuskegee.edu/repository/

cheek spoofs (e.g., "Anything Goes," with its topical references to millionaires, movie moguls, and Eleanor Roosevelt). But lynching was an especially bleak topic for a satirical song, and Porter's ironic reordering of race, gender, and class renders the subject sufficiently absurd to contain that gravity. Plus, it's not really *about* lynching—rather, it uses lynching as a device to contrast extremes of refinement and brutality to comic but touching effect. Thus, the song condemns lynching while expressing empathy for social outcasts whose lives are made miserable by dullards, moralists, and miscreants.[109] Porter was neither Black nor poor. But he knew the pain of being gay in a hostile culture and had to tolerate a pompous retinue of the rich and famous whose patronage he needed to practice his craft. He spent years in the European demimonde of libertines and bohemians before resettling in America, ensconced in a lavender marriage. He had Black friends and lovers and seemed to have had no racial hang-ups.[110] Yet, for all his personal radicalism, like Fitzgerald, he wasn't the sort of artist to grandstand politically. Fitzgerald cut her version of "Miss Otis Regrets" two decades after Porter composed it, with the civil-rights movement underway, in the year *Browder v. Gayle* banned bus segregation. Beneath the song's surface levity lies a core of deep sadness—for composer and interpreter—clearly derived from its lynching theme.

Miss Otis's tale draws to a close with her summary execution. Taking her unflappable demeanor in the face of death to its natural conclusion, her last words are a terminal apology for her missed appointment. Fitzgerald's final vocal flourishes are heart-rending.

> *When the mob came and got her and dragged her from the jail*
> *Madam*
> *They strung her upon the old willow across the way*
> *And the moment before she died*
> *She lifted up her lovely head and cried*
> *Madam*
> *Miss Otis regrets she's unable to lunch today*

If Porter and Fitzgerald use misdirection and humor to address the despair and oppression of the marginalized, the most famous of all lynching ballads and its prime interpreter pull no punches. "Strange Fruit" is an unflinchingly direct evocation of lynching and an unabashed protest song targeting the practice—a polemic so uncompromising it would have been unimaginable

---

digital-collection/lynching-information). It is, of course, impossible to verify the accuracy of these figures, derived from public records, media accounts, and modern historical research, as the nature of the crime meant lynchings often went unreported. There is also considerable debate among researchers about what constitutes lynching (for a summary of relevant issues, see: plaintalkhistory.com/monroeandflorencework/explore).

109   "To a man like Porter," writes musical theater scholar Ethan Mordden, "art was stylized autobiography" ("A Critic at Large: Rock and Cole," *New Yorker*, 28 October 1991).

110   The scholar and musician Wilfried Van den Brande notes Porter's "strong empathy with the outcasts of society" and "[for the era] shockingly open attitude toward African-Americans" ("Cole Porter, European," in Don M. Randel et al., eds., *A Cole Porter Companion*, Champaign, Ill.: University of Illinois Press, 2016, p. 50).

Carl Van Vechten/Library of Congress

BILLIE HOLIDAY, 1949

just ten years earlier. The song was written in 1937—three years after Porter composed "Miss Otis Regrets"—by a Bronx-born Jewish schoolteacher named Abel Meeropol (under the snappier pseudonym Lewis Allan). Billie Holiday heard "Strange Fruit" in 1939 and swiftly incorporated it into her stage act. Its performance became a solemn, theatrical ritual for the rest of her career: she would insist on silence in the room, introduce the song's provenance and theme, then sing it under a single spotlight that framed her haunted face and went dark when she finished.

Southern trees bear a strange fruit
Blood on the leaves and blood at the root
Black bodies swinging in the Southern breeze
Strange fruit hanging from the poplar trees

The tune is balletic but slight—less memorable than the chilling, poetic words and thus strengthened by sensitive singing and thoughtful accompaniment. For all its intrinsic horror, the song is unnervingly slow and steady—neither screed nor rant, it lulls the listener into a waking nightmare. Its reserved tone creates a stillness wherein wretched details like the gentle sway of dangling corpses and the intermingling odors of flowers and scorched flesh become unbearably real and immediate.[111] Noteworthy is the original ghostly 78 side with minimal backing from 1939 (for Commodore Records; her label, Columbia, wouldn't touch the song) and a fuller, more dramatic version from the 1956 *Lady Sings the Blues* LP. Throughout her career, she invested every line with nuance, deep feeling, and elegant restraint, whether in her youthful prime (she was just twenty-four when she first recorded the song) or her reduced-voice "Lady in Satin" period.[112] Despite industry misgivings, her 1939 recording became an unlikely hit. It tapped into a shifting zeitgeist

---

111 Such directness, shocking in 1939, was, in fact, highly selective. Then and now, lynching was too often imagined as mere extrajudicial hanging–uncivilized but essentially a crime of racially motivated denial of due process. In truth, lynching victims were frequently beaten, tortured, disfigured, castrated, and burned to death to the whoops and hollers of crowds, their bones, teeth, and hair kept (or sold) by onlookers and participants. A horrific example was the lynching of Sam Hose, a twenty-four-year-old Black man accused of killing his white employer (Hose claimed self-defense) in Georgia in 1899. Apprehended by a mob, Hose was beaten, carved up with knives, and castrated. His face was skinned and soaked with kerosene, and he was chained to a tree and roasted alive before a cheering crowd of hundreds (some reports say thousands). His bones, heart, and liver were cut out and sold as souvenirs. *Libera nos a malo.*

112 A live performance for television from 1959, the year of her death, collected as a music video for the *Reelin' in the Years* archive, captures a powerful late-career version. Her once glorious voice is diminished, ravaged by years of hard living, but what it lacks in refinement, it gains in raw emotion. (www.youtube.com/watch?v=-DGY9HvChXk).

and was heard on jukeboxes across the country and on the airwaves of braver radio stations. Over time, "Strange Fruit" became part of the soundtrack of the emerging civil-rights movement; anti-lynching legislation activists even urged supporters to mail copies of the 78 (backed with "Fine and Mellow") to recalcitrant U.S. senators. The song's unvarnished imagery and Holiday's intense reading could still a room.

Pastoral scene of the gallant South
The bulging eyes and the twisted mouth
Scent of magnolias, sweet and fresh
Then the sudden smell of burning flesh

"Strange Fruit" is now an iconic song—a kind of aural *Guernica* for the American racial holocaust. Like Picasso's anti-war painting, countless articles and entire books have been written about it.[113] And, like *Guernica,* it has had its detractors—racists and reactionaries, obviously, but also musicians and critics sympathetic to its theme but skeptical of it as art. Some of this pushback came from jazz lovers who felt that the stiff, art-song-like style of "Strange Fruit" stifled the improvisatory freedom at the heart of America's only entirely original music. Others felt its self-conscious seriousness—the grandstanding that Porter and Fitzgerald avoided in "Miss Otis Regrets"—reduced its quality (and impact). "Moving propaganda, perhaps," wrote the jazz critic Martin Williams, "but not poetry and not art."[114] Similarly, John Hammond, Holiday's producer at Columbia (and a civil-rights activist), opined that, after "Strange Fruit," Lady Day became more "mannered" as a singer.[115] Today, such criticisms seem parochial and out of touch. Holiday was a seminal figure in jazz, but, like Fitzgerald (not to mention Ray Charles, Dinah Washington, and Frank Sinatra), she transcended genre and drew equally from blues, show tunes, and Tin Pan Alley.

But the charge of self-consciousness holds water. "Strange Fruit" applies a leveling gaze at an atrocity, gives no quarter, and offers no escape. It also privileges content over form, for righteous reasons that nevertheless repel some listeners. In this, it embodies a classic conflict between medium and message, art and agitprop, that provokes legitimate questions. If the words are paramount, why set them to music? If the content is so unyielding it thwarts interpretation, is it still art? Jerry Wexler, the legendary producer who coined the term "rhythm and blues," put it this way: "A lot of people who had tin ears and who wouldn't know a melody if it hit them in the head embraced ["Strange Fruit"] only because

---

113   One such book, thoughtful and thorough, is *Strange Fruit: Billie Holiday and the Biography of a Song* by David Margolick (HarperCollins, 2001). It tells the song's story, clears up some myths (e.g., Holiday's claim to have co-written its music: Meeropol was, in fact, its sole composer, but Holiday–an improviser of genius–certainly adapted his tune), and is rich with media accounts and recollections by cultural figures of first encounters with the song. Of the former, Holiday's first notice in *Time* magazine–in 1939, prompted by "Strange Fruit"–is jarring for its mix of praise and condescension. It exalts the song's message and "grim and gripping" lyrics but refers to Holiday as a "roly-poly young colored woman with a hump in her voice . . . [who] does not care enough about her figure to watch her diet [but] loves to sing" (p. 56).

114   Margolick, p. 60.

115   Ibid., p. 59.

of its politics . . . I absolutely approve of the sentiment. I think it's a great lyric. But it doesn't interest me as a song."[116]

In the end, it's apples and oranges. Some people exalt words over music; some extol fiery confrontation over subtler forms of subversion. "Strange Fruit" is now larger than life, less a song than a cultural touchstone. That the veiled "Miss Otis" and the stark "Strange Fruit" can coexist in the same conversation about a still-gaping wound seems a healthy stasis.

> *Here is a fruit for the crows to pluck*
> *For the rain to gather*
> *For the wind to suck*
> *For the sun to rot*
> *For the tree to drop*
> *Here is a strange and bitter crop*

In 1965, Bob Dylan opened his apocalyptic dreamscape, "Desolation Row"—the epic final track on his careening folk-rock masterpiece *Highway 61 Revisited*—with these curious words:

> *They're selling postcards of the hanging*
> *They're painting the passports brown*
> *The beauty parlor is filled with sailors*
> *The circus is in town*

For ten verses, he then serves as tour guide on an excursion through the alleys and byways of a hallucinatory America whose denizens personify national anxieties and contradictions. Unlike earlier, more whimsical travelogues (e.g., the *Moby-Dick*-inspired "Bob Dylan's 115th Dream"), the humor on "Desolation Row" is caustic. While the eleven-minute track mesmerizes with its grotesque imagery and withering wit, the cumulative effect is less cathartic than disquieting.

The song opens with an image of preposterous callousness ("postcards of the hanging") that mocks sensationalism and consumerism while evoking hawkers peddling wares at an Inferno-like entry gate ("Abandon all hope, ye who enter here"). But it also alludes to a ghastly historical reality. Souvenir images of lynchings, professionally photographed, were once mass-printed, sold in stores, and circulated cross-country as postcards by the U.S. Mail. Often these vile mementos featured bystanders posing beside victims. In postcard form, they were sometimes inscribed with sociopathic "wish you were here"–style messages.[117] More than a century after their heyday, these artifacts still shock. Dylan and Meeropol must also have found them hard to fathom or forget, as they inspired both Dylan's lyric in "Desolation Row" and the song "Strange Fruit."

---

116 Ibid., p. 60.

117 The circulation of these postcards peaked in the late nineteenth century. In 1908, the U.S. postmaster general banned their distribution by mail, but their production continued.

Dylan (birth name: Robert Zimmerman) grew up in Hibbing, Minnesota, but his father, Abram Zimmerman, had been raised in the busy port town of Duluth. In 1920, when Dylan's dad was nine, the circus came to town for a one-night performance. After the show, a pair of white teenagers claimed they were robbed and assaulted at gunpoint by Black workers dismantling the big top. One of them, nineteen-year-old Irene Tusken, was supposedly raped (though a medical exam showed no evidence of this). In answer to their accusations, police lined up 150 Black roustabouts and took six of them—identified by the teens—into custody. Within twenty-four hours, a mob of thousands had gathered at the jail. They broke into the building and dragged out the men. A farcical "hearing" followed, after which three of them—Elias Clayton, Elmer Jackson, and Isaac McGhie—were beaten and hanged from a lamppost.[118] A photograph of the aftermath, carefully composed with a smiling all-white crowd surrounding the murdered men, was printed as a postcard. The lynching occurred just blocks from Abram Zimmerman's childhood home.

Dylan learned about the lynching and the postcard from his father. That "Desolation Row" opens with a reference to this event, however indirect, is striking. At the time Dylan made *Highway 61 Revisited*, he had abandoned what he called "finger-pointing songs"—topical protest anthems like "Masters of War" and "The Lonesome Death of Hattie Carroll" that had made him a hero to idealistic youth and a darling of the New Left. Impatient with literalism and the pressure of being a movement spokesman, he pushed his art in more discursive directions with Symbolist and Beat-inspired works like "Mr. Tambourine Man" and "Desolation Row." But his rejection of explicit "issue" songs hardly meant he'd foregone his conscience; he'd merely grown weary of confining his muse. Racism is a recurring theme in Dylan's early work, and an unreleased song, "The Death of Emmett Till," is about lynching. So it's fitting he should launch this sprawling phantasmagoria in his new style with an allusion to an appalling manifestation of racial pathology. That Dylan, a grandson of Jewish immigrants, draws on a generational memory from childhood in a cutting satire of his inherited culture—complete with historically accurate and metaphorically rich circus references—seems canny and apt.

Abel Meeropol, too, was a second-generation immigrant and, though gentle and soft-spoken, he was, like Dylan, an intellectual gadfly. He earned his living as a high-school English teacher (James Baldwin was one of his students) but aspired to change the world through art. His creative output straddled popular and elite camps: he wrote a song covered by Frank Sinatra ("The House I Live in") but also the libretto for an operatic war satire (Robert Kurka's *The Good Soldier*). It's a fitting range for a committed leftist who, with his wife, Anne, adopted the orphaned children of Julius and Ethel Rosenberg after their execution. "Strange Fruit" began life as a poem called "Bitter Fruit" that Meeropol published in a teachers'-union journal. He soon set it to music, and the song was performed— initially by Anne, an amateur musician—at social gatherings. Both poem and song were inspired by a photograph Meeropol stumbled on in a magazine and couldn't shake from his mind.

---

118 A subsequent civil investigation exonerated all six.

On a summer night in 1930, a photographer in Marion, Indiana, snapped a dreadful picture that grows more nightmarish the longer one looks. It shows an arching tree branch that bears the hanged corpses of two Black teenagers, their bodies swollen with wounds, their clothing bloody and shredded. Below them, a crowd of white spectators poses for the camera. The onlookers include a teenage couple dressed like they're on a date. The boy grins leeringly, and the girl's mouth hangs open in scorn. She and another girl clutch scraps of the dead teens' clothing in their hands like trophies won at the fair. Nearby, an elderly woman turns primly away from the bodies while a smug-looking man stares into the camera and points to the dangling corpses. "We did this," he seems to say.

The photo is from a lynching postcard—a late entry in the repugnant practice and perhaps the most famous such image. It documents the murders of J. Thomas Shipp and Abraham S. Smith—suspects in the killing of a white laborer and the sexual assault of his white girlfriend—who were busted from jail by a mob of thousands, then tortured and killed while police looked on. The picture haunts both for its relative modernity—bygone images, turn-of-the-century or older, afford the viewer some distance and are more easily assimilated—and for the low-key savagery of its small-town citizens, who resemble stock characters from a homespun Norman Rockwell painting or '60s rural sitcom.[119] Meeropol found the photo in a magazine article about lynching; it so disturbed him he wrote "Strange Fruit" in response. But lynching photography went down the collective memory hole for most Americans, quietly buried and forgotten for generations. It resurfaced in an exhibit that reintroduced the phenomenon to the general public a century after its heyday.

"Without Sanctuary: Lynching Photography in America" was a traveling display of actual lynching postcards (including the Marion and Duluth photos), collected by an antique dealer, James Allen, that debuted at the New York Historical Society in 2000. The exhibit proved popular but controversial; it traversed the country for years, and a book of the photographs was published under the same title.[120] "Without Sanctuary" polarized critical opinion. While no one denied the power of the exhibit or the need to confront its horrific history, perspectives split over whether immersion in such imagery inured viewers to their brutality or awakened their humanity. Susan Sontag argued the former: "What is the point of exhibiting these pictures?" she wrote in a book-length essay called *Regarding the Pain of Others*. "Are we the better for seeing these images? Do they actually teach us anything?"[121] The critic Roberta Smith countered that the exhibit disproved claims that inundation numbs our reactions to morally shocking images, causing a kind of defibrillation of the soul instead. "These images," she wrote in a *New York Times* review, "refute the notion that photographs of charged historical subjects lose their power . . . Instead they

---

119 The Marion photo documents the last known lynching in the state of Indiana and the northern U.S.

120 James Allen, *Without Sanctuary: Lynching Photography in America* (Santa Fe, N.M.: Twin Palms Publishers, 1999). A sampling of the images can be viewed at the website: withoutsanctuary.org.

121 Susan Sontag, *Regarding the Pain of Others* (New York: Farrar, Straus and Giroux, 2003), pp. 91–92.

Lawrence Beitler, Loewentheil Collection of African-American Photographs, Cornell University Library/Creative Commons

LYNCHING OF THOMAS SHIPP AND ABRAM SMITH, MARION, INDIANA, 1930

send shock waves through the brain ..." While the photos "will burn a hole in your heart," she wrote, they offer "the gift of knowledge, the chance for greater consciousness and caring."[122]

Confronting a tragedy as immense as lynching—one that can't truly be absorbed, only faced and refaced with the hope of greater insight—calls for a range of approaches, direct and indirect. For some, immersion in horror catalyzes conscience and the drive for change; others will only feel brutalized and helpless. Just as "Miss Otis Regrets" and "Strange Fruit" offer contrary but equally valid entryways for such engagement, there's no right or wrong. So long as responses circulate, there's an antidote for the sinister postcards themselves.

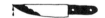

THE DAY JOHN KENNEDY DIED

O! why did you leave us, Eoghan? Why did you die?
Your troubles are all over, you're at rest with God on high,
But we're slaves, and we're orphans, Eoghan!—why did you die?
—Thomas Davis, "Lament for the Death of Eoghan Ruadh O'Neill," 1842

In 1975, Lou Reed made a shocking confession. To tender instrumental backing and doo-wop-style vocal accompaniment, the ornery poet of the New York netherworld revealed his ultimate high-school dream: "I wanted to play football for the coach." He prefaced the admission with "believe it or not," but the soulful six-minute track—with Reed singing passionately about regret, loneliness, and giving it all up for the "glory of love"—removed all doubt. Lou had been gentle and romantic before—his pioneering art-punk

---

122   Roberta Smith, "An Ugly Legacy Lives On, Its Glare Unsoftened by Age," *New York Times*, 13 January 2000.

band, the Velvet Underground, alternated love songs and ballads with scabrous noise and debauched reportage—but always from an outsider's perspective. On "Coney Island Baby," the title track from his then most earnest set of personal songs, the cantankerous iconoclast copped to his most deviant desire: wanting to belong.

This was a new Lou—wistful, unironic, and seeking connection—in a chameleon-like career. Always dead serious about making rock a literate art form, Reed's output post-Velvets had been wobbly and hard to gauge.[123] He'd hit it big with the David Bowie–produced *Transformer* (1972), an entertaining pastiche of glam-era decadence and gender-bending that the critic Lester Bangs called a "comic strip" version of his former band.[124] He then confounded new fans with intense no-fun art statements like the somber song-cycle *Berlin* (1973) and the feedback-without-guitars *Metal Machine Music* (1975). The rest of the '70s saw him treading water critically and commercially. By decade's end, he seemed weary of his contrarian stances. He quit drugs and drink, got married, and—starting with the aptly named *Growing Up in Public* (1980)—began writing introspective songs about family, relationships, and his personal demons. The first fully realized work in this new phase was *The Blue Mask* (1982)—a portrait of the artist, newly sober and nearly forty, that alternated anthemic and low-key songs about inner turmoil and fleeting peace. Amidst the thunder and light, he made another confession: he had been devastated by the assassination of John F. Kennedy.

> *I dreamed I was the president of these United States*
> *I dreamed I replaced ignorance, stupidity, and hate*
> *I dreamed the perfect union and a perfect law, undenied*
> *And most of all I dreamed I forgot the day John Kennedy died*

On the surface, this was hardly shocking. Born in 1942, Reed was a boomer and, like most of his generation, November 22, 1963, was an epochal event in his young life—his cohort's defining "Where were you when it happened?" moment. Yet it still jarred coming from Reed, whose nihilistic attitudes and poses in the '70s—personified by the sneer, the deadpan, the shades—had so petrified his persona in the public eye that his early-'80s "mature" move made some doubt his sincerity.[125] In retrospect, the song and album are clearly on the level. But it's still surprising to hear Reed—who at that point was uninterested in politics—ruminate so unaffectedly on the iconic tragedy.

---

123 The Velvets' ahead-of-their-time narrative is now well known: minimal impact during their short career, followed by Beatles/Dylan/Hendrix-scale influence years later. The band released four studio albums to critical acclaim but limited sales from 1967 to 1970, then broke up.

124 Lester Bangs, "Let Us Now Praise Famous Death Dwarves" in Greil Marcus, ed., *Psychotic Reactions and Carburetor Dung* (New York: Alfred A. Knopf, 1987), p. 175.

125 In a brusque statement it's impossible to imagine him making a few years later, he told the *New Musical Express* in 1976 that "[a]ll the albums I put out after this are going to be things I want to put out. No more bullshit, no more dyed hair, faggot junkie trip" (Nick Johnstone, *Lou Reed: Talking*, London: Omnibus Press, 1992, p. 59).

"The Day John Kennedy Died" is easily the oddest song on *The Blue Mask*—a plaintive reverie about lost innocence that sets homely words to fragile bass and guitar interplay with minimal drums. It stretches two of Reed's trademark tics nearly to the breaking point: his use of quotidian language and his tendency to recite, not sing. But the song is poignant in its midlife-rethink context. *The Blue Mask* opens with "My House," a touching ode to another man of Kennedy's age—Reed's college mentor, the poet Delmore

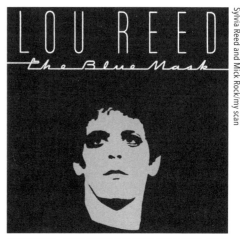

LOU REED, *THE BLUE MASK* COVER ART, 1983

Schwartz, who haunts the singer's artistic integrity as well as, Reed tells us, his rural hideaway home. It ends with "Heavenly Arms," a panegyric to his wife Sylvia and her revitalizing role in his life and art. In between, he muses on personal struggles in tones ranging from harrowing ("Waves of Fear") to humble ("Underneath the Bottle") to humorous ("Average Guy"). Reed's renewed commitment is buttressed by his best band since the Velvets: Robert Quine on guitar, Fernando Saunders on bass and background vocals, and Doane Perry on drums. "The Day John Kennedy Died" combines a series of idealistic "I dreamed" statements with Reed's own "Where were you?" JFK memory to bumpy but heartfelt effect.

> *I dreamed that I could do the job that others hadn't done*
> *I dreamed that I was uncorrupt and fair to everyone*
> *I dreamed I wasn't gross or base, a criminal on the take*
> *And most of all I dreamed I forgot the day John Kennedy died*

The chorus repeats the title, and Saunders' falsetto adds fragile eloquence to Reed's unadorned monotone.

> *Oh, the day John Kennedy died*
> *Oh, the day John Kennedy died*

The Kennedy in Reed's song is more symbol than man. He's the handsome young humanist, defeater of the odious Richard Nixon, on whom postwar liberals and the young projected near-messianic hopes at the dawn of the '60s—before the decade's tumultuous latter half and before neoliberalism and rightward shift devolved the Democratic Party into Republican Lite.[126] Just as

---

126 This shift is the subject of a scathing book by the old-school progressive Thomas Frank. *Listen Liberal; or, What Ever Happened to the Party of the People?* (New York: Henry Holt & Co., 2016) documents the Democrats' abandonment–starting

there's both a historical and a mythic Jesus, the convergence of which is likely irreconcilable, separating JFK the man from JFK the icon is a formidable task. Kennedy, the man, was personally flawed and politically erratic—equal parts social liberal and (moderate) Cold Warrior. But compared to today's tepid "liberals"—called "centrists" in mainstream discourse but more accurately described by the dissident intellectual Noam Chomsky as "pretty much what used to be called 'moderate Republicans'"[127]—JFK was a standard-bearer for the progressive politics of New Deal Democrats.[128] And Kennedy's worldview evolved: after the nightmare brinkmanship of the Cuban missile crisis, he launched earnest efforts to roll back the U.S. war and spy machines that, had he lived, might have transformed the nation's future.[129] None of this affects Reed's song, which evokes the mythic JFK from the reduced-expectations vantage point of the Reagan '80s—at the time, the seeming nadir of postwar progressivism. Reed's adult perspective merges with his younger self, who'd recently wanted to play football for the coach.

The song's "I dreamed" statements are interrupted by Reed's "Where were you?" memory. In artless language but urgent tone, he recalls the transformative moment:

> *I remember where I was that day, I was upstate in a bar*
> *The team from the university was playing football on TV*
> *Then the screen went dead and the announcer said,*
> *"There's been a tragedy*
> *There are unconfirmed reports the president's been shot*
> *And he may be dead or dying"*

Reed the writer often alters details to make a better story, and his biographer Anthony DeCurtis, notes that Syracuse University, Reed's alma mater, had no football game that day. But DeCurtis suggests something more intriguing than artistic license, noting that millions of Americans learned about John Lennon's murder on December 8, 1980, during *Monday Night Football*, when the sportscaster Howard Cosell broke the news mid-broadcast.[130] Perhaps Reed conflated the events. If so, the fusion was likely intentional: Lennon died less than a year before the song's recording, making faulty memory less likely. And Lennon's death must have haunted Reed; both were respected but diminished

---

with the Democratic Leadership Council (DLC) that helped elect Bill Clinton in the '90s—of its traditional pro-labor, pro-working-class, pro-minority values for a pro-corporate, anti-worker, tough-on-crime agenda virtually indistinguishable from that of the GOP.

127 Noam Chomsky and C.J. Polychroniou, *Optimism over Despair: On Capitalism, Empire, and Social Change* (Chicago: Haymarket Books, 2017), p. 125.

128 Barack Obama in 2012: "[M]y policies are so mainstream that if I had set the same policies that I had back in the 1980s, I would be considered a moderate Republican" (interview, *Univision Noticias*, 14 December 2012, youtube.com/watch?v=677elaGlsKU).

129 Among his goals before he was assassinated were de-escalation of the Vietnam War, improved diplomatic relations with Cuba and the USSR, and the dissolution of the CIA. Each of these initiatives made him powerful enemies.

130 Anthony DeCurtis, *Lou Reed: A Life* (New York: Little, Brown & Co., 2017), p. 286.

figures in rock, contemporaries trying to reestablish themselves as mature artists after years absent or adrift.[131] Lennon's comeback album (with his wife Yoko Ono), *Double Fantasy* (1980), hit number one the year before *The Blue Mask* was released. That an assassin felled Lennon on the cusp of artistic rebirth just as Reed was attempting the same, just as JFK was murdered on the verge of a sea change in his presidency, creates a compelling subtext.

Reed's recollection finishes, still guileless and dire:

> *Talking stopped, someone shouted, "What?"*
> *I ran out to the street*
> *People were gathered everywhere, saying*
> *"Did you hear what they said on TV?"*
> *And then a guy in a Porsche with his radio hit his horn*
> *And told us the news*
> *He said, "The president's dead, he was shot twice in the head*
> *In Dallas, and they don't know by whom"*

A final "I dreamed" sequence returns us to the present and provides a closing threnody. It's stark and mournful—the older Reed remembering his younger self's shock and discovering it still matters. Even as the language intensifies, the mood is consistent—less angry than vulnerable, an appropriate tone for a former outsider now seeking community:

> *I dreamed I was the president of these United States*
> *I dreamed I was young and smart and it was not a waste*
> *I dreamed that there was a point to life and to the human race*
> *I dreamed that I could somehow comprehend that someone*
> *Shot him in the face*

Guitar and bass interweave delicately. The chorus recurs before the fadeout, and once more, Saunders' falsetto adds tenderness to Reed's doleful voice.

> *Oh, the day John Kennedy died*
> *Oh, the day John Kennedy died*

"In Dallas, and they don't know by whom." It's striking that Reed ends his assassination narrative here, with the shooting and an unknown assailant. While doing so focuses the listener on the song's main theme—the trauma of the murder and the loss of a national symbol of hope and renewal—it also injects a note of ambiguity. So does the song's final verse, which evokes the crime's brutality but again names no names ("*someone* shot him in the face" [my italics]). These lyrical choices needn't imply anything beyond staying on point; they

---

131 Reed, who disliked the Beatles, admired Lennon's solo work (interview with Joe Smith, Library of Congress, 20 March 1987, www.loc.gov/item/jsmith000151).

seem to be Reed's way of saying, "I'm not going there," or, "That's not what this song is about." But such a line in the sand does acknowledge perceived pressure to go further.

Doing so, of course, would mean naming or not naming Lee Harvey Oswald as Kennedy's killer. And that would mean taking sides in an inexhaustible controversy: endorsing a conventional scenario stridently maintained by the powers that be or throwing one's lot in with subversives who challenge that narrative. And the choice is far-reaching: the status quo view—that Oswald was the killer, a deranged and pathetic attention-seeker who acted alone—preserves America's self-image as a noble democracy, though one beset by aberrant outsiders. Whereas the alternative view—that Oswald may not have been the planner and may not have pulled the trigger in the assassination, but that Kennedy was killed for political reasons by a powerful conspiracy—levels fantasies of American exceptionalism and locates the threat within.

Sixty years on, the JFK assassination seems to encompass three related tragedies. Each involves shattered innocence and a shift in consciousness. Some people accept all three, others accept one or two, and a minority rejects them all. The first tragedy is mythic, elegiac: the shocking loss of a great leader, cut down in his prime, and resulting numbing grief over the senseless crime. It's a childlike response, appropriate to (then) young boomers. The second tragedy is prosaic and political: the sense that Kennedy's murder and the slayings of other transformative figures like his brother Robert F. Kennedy, Martin Luther King Jr., and Malcolm X diminished the chance for a more peaceful, just society by clearing the national stage of charismatic agents of change, allowing authoritarian power to gradually fill the vacuum. It's a coming-of-age perspective, more pragmatic than the first. The third tragedy is most sweeping and controversial: the likelihood that Kennedy's death resulted from angering the wrong U.S. elites who collaborated in his demise; that deep-state actors, sponsored by powerful interests in government, intelligence, the military, big business—all of the above, or take your pick—murdered him just as they murdered foreign leaders perceived as hegemonic threats, and for the same reason.[132] Substantial evidence backs this conclusion, but for many, the implications are too disturbing to consider. Consequently, the lockstep rejection and scorn heaped on challengers of the official narrative by mass media and the powerful offers an attractive buffer of denial.[133]

---

132   The list of such leaders is long and ignoble, and includes Patrice Lumumba (Congo, 1961), Rafael Trujillo (Dominican Republic, 1961), Ngo Dinh Diem (Vietnam, 1963), and Salvador Allende (Chile, 1973). Failed attempts to kill Cuba's Fidel Castro are well documented, and in the '60s, under the auspices of the CIA's Operation Mongoose, involved direct collaboration with the Mafia.

133   There isn't room here to present and debate this evidence. But I will recommend three recent books that assemble facts diligently and theorize intelligently: *22 November 1963: A Brief Guide to the JFK Assassination* by Jeremy Bojczuk (Boxgrove Publishing, 2014) is a fine just-the-facts primer, its unsensational approach captured in its first chapter title ("Who Killed President Kennedy?") and opening sentence ("This short book is not going to give you the answer, but it will try to illustrate the best way to think about the question"); *JFK and the Unspeakable: Why He Died and Why It Matters* by James W. Douglass (New York: Simon & Shuster, 2008) focuses on the shifts of policy and character that made Kennedy powerful, possibly homicidal enemies; and *The Devil's Chessboard: Allen Dulles, the CIA, and the Rise of America's Secret Government* by David Talbot (New York: HarperCollins, 2015) is a kind of anti-biography of the former CIA director, who loathed (and was fired by) Kennedy.

Reed's song never strays past tragedy one. In this, it resembles most musical elegies for the dead president, which rarely venture beyond shock, grief, and loss. While it's an understandable focus, rooted in personal experience to maximize poignancy (and frankly, wordy analyses of complicated events don't make for sellable singalongs), the dearth of alternatives is noteworthy.

Songs that push the JFK-assassination envelope do exist, but most were penned by later generations. The Fall's post-punk "Oswald Defense Lawyer" (1988) is an abstruse meditation on the accused assassin inspired by a 1986 mock trial of Oswald by two American attorneys (Oswald, of course, was assassinated two days after Kennedy and was thus never tried). Pearl Jam's grunge-rock "Brain of J" (1998) is an elusive rant about the disappearance of the president's brain from the National Archives, built around the recurring refrain, "The whole world will be different soon / The whole world will be relieving." And the Death Cab for Cutie offshoot the Postal Service's electro-pop "Sleeping In" (2003) pines ironically for a world without troublesome complexities like the Kennedy assassination and climate change—where, instead, "everything was exactly how it seemed." Points of view vary, but each attempts to get beyond subjective experience or '60s pieties. Of boomer responses, Bob Dylan's late-career "Murder Most Foul"—an epic, "Desolation Row"–style tour of JFK-related facts and ephemera from *Rough and Rowdy Ways* (2020)—is one of the most interesting and alludes elliptically to all three tragedies. But media commentary predictably focused mainly on the song's myriad cultural references, treating the incantatory 17-minute track like a highbrow "American Pie" or "We Didn't Start the Fire."

Dylan's song is an outlier among his peers. Reed's "The Day John Kennedy Died" effectively evokes a youthful sense of trauma and estrangement. Yet it never leaves the shelter of post-adolescent perspective to ask hard questions or seek broader context. Consequently, though written by a sophisticated man, it mirrors a childlike quality of the American character, an insular naïveté about power and politics and an attendant desire for parental surrogates, whether politicians, media figures, academics, or celebrities, to keep us informed and keep us safe.

The most famous of these elegies began life as a traditional folk song but was transformed by a contemporary of Reed's into a lament forever associated with JFK and November 22nd.

He was a friend of mine
He was a friend of mine
His killing had no purpose
No reason or rhyme
Oh, he was a friend of mine

Talbot argues that Dulles was a major player in the assassination. Dulles also played a critical role, behind the scenes, in the 1964 Warren Commission Report, which tried (and failed) to squelch public conjecture about the crime and place the blame solely on Oswald.

Roger (Jim) McGuinn, co-founder of the folk-rock pioneers the Byrds, recast the traditional "He Was a Friend of Mine" as a tribute to JFK on the night of his murder, reworking the song's generalized lyrics about a lost friend to reflect the tragedy. At the time, the Byrds didn't exist. In 1963, McGuinn was a California session musician and songwriter-for-hire, an aspiring folkie who also loved the Beatles. He merged those passions into a workable group the following year with two kindred spirits, David Crosby (guitar, vocals) and Gene Clark (vocals), plus the bluegrass enthusiast Chris Hillman (bass) and the beach bum Michael Clarke (drums). The band launched its career and the folk-rock idiom with *Mr. Tambourine Man* (1965). With the assassination hardly a distant memory, the band recorded McGuinn's variant of "He Was a Friend of Mine" for their follow-up LP, *Turn! Turn! Turn!* (also 1965), alongside the pacifist title track and various Dylan covers.

The earliest known version of "He Was a Friend of Mine" is a field recording of a song called "Shorty George"—one of eleven sides by Smith Casey, an obscure Texas prison inmate singer, cut by the archivist John Lomax in 1939. The folk revivalists Rolf Cahn and Eric Von Schmidt adapted Casey's song—a mournful remembrance of a companion who "died on the road" with "no money to pay his boa'd [board]"—as "He Was a Friend of Mine" in 1961. Dylan reworked their version for his eponymous 1962 debut album. Lyrics vary, but the McGuinn–Byrds version transforms what Lomax's son Alan called an anonymous "dirge for a dead comrade" into an elegant memorial for the fallen president.[134]

JFK also died "on the road," but in drastically different circumstances. McGuinn's encomium includes assassination narrative in its second verse only, bare-bones, and derived from contemporary media accounts.

> *He was in Dallas town*
> *He was in Dallas town*
> *From a sixth-floor window*
> *A gunman shot him down*
> *Oh, he died in Dallas town*

What's most striking about McGuinn's revision is the earnestness with which the folk-rocker, just twenty-one when Kennedy died, declares JFK his friend. As with Reed, the loss feels deeply personal. Indeed, the two songs are of a piece: both capture generational anguish, but Reed's adds a still-dazed middle-aged perspective. The result is a curious leveling of differences—the hippie and the proto-punk, both born the same year, eclipsing sunny and cynical perspectives to feel the same grief.

> *He never knew my name*
> *He never knew my name*

---

134 "Archive of American Folk Song: Afro-American Blues and Game Songs," Library of Congress/American Folklife Center, www.loc.gov/folklife/LP/AFS_L4_sm.pdf.

Though I never met him
I knew him just the same
Oh, he was a friend of mine

McGuinn transcends subjectivity in the final couplet, obliquely touching on tragedy two: the sense of lost opportunity for political transformation—a dream deferred.

Leader of a nation for such a precious time
Oh, he was a friend of mine

IMPROMPTU REMARKS: DAVID CROSBY AT THE MONTEREY POP FESTIVAL, 1967

"He Was a Friend of Mine" remained a staple of the Byrds' live repertoire for years, as the halcyon mid '60s became the incendiary late '60s. They performed the song at the 1967 Monterey Pop Festival—the first major multi-artist outdoor rock concert, famous for its "Summer of Love" vibe and for the documentary film by D. A. Pennebaker (*Monterey Pop,* 1968). The Byrds' set was cut from the final print but is restored in the DVD/Blu-ray reissue, and their performance of the song—in a reworked country-rock version better suited for hipper, hairier times—is ragged but heartfelt. Crosby notoriously introduced McGuinn's tribute with some unscripted remarks, and they make for a moment of awkward drama. Noting that the performance is being "shot for television" (ABC planned to screen *Monterey Pop* as a "Movie of the Week" but got cold feet after they saw the footage), and assuming he'll be censored, the vociferous musician, resplendent in fringe jacket, muttonchops, and raccoon-fur hat, vents some spleen: "When President Kennedy was killed, he was not killed by one man. He was shot from a number of different directions by different guns. The story has been suppressed, witnesses have been killed, and this is your country, ladies and gentlemen."

The delivery's a tad pompous, and Crosby is visibly nervous. But the audience responds first with pin-drop silence, then with ardent applause. Crosby's bandmates, by contrast, were less enthused. He and McGuinn were temperamental opposites—fire and ice, respectively, their collaboration marred by constant clashes. McGuinn resented Crosby's soapboxing, and the incident contributed to the latter's firing from the band soon after.[135] Still, the

---

135 All parties agree that Crosby had grown difficult to work with (Crosby in 2018: "I was an asshole"). But McGuinn and Hillman, who orchestrated his dismissal, deny that his JFK comments were the last straw. Interestingly, both McGuinn and Hillman now identify as conservative Christians–McGuinn (who campaigned for RFK in 1968) is a moderate, anti-Trump Republican; Hillman describes himself as "very conservative." Crosby remained left/liberal and in 2020 supported Bernie Sanders for president (Crosby quote from A. J. Eaton's film *David Crosby: Remember My Name,* 2019; Hillman quote from Mike Greenblatt, "Chris Hillman Reminisces about Joining the Byrds–and Why a Reunion is Unlikely," *Goldmine,* 5 August 2014).

incident was a rare example of a rock demigod putting his neck out on the matter, however haphazardly. For the most part, JFK tributes—even good ones like McGuinn's and Reed's—have played it safe.

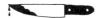

CHARLES MANSON MURDERS THE '60S

I sung of Chaos and Eternal Night ... —Milton, "Paradise Lost"

Two songs released a decade apart, by iconic rock artists of consecutive generations. The first is an anarchic anthem by underground anti-heroes, the second, a nervy rocker by a chameleon-like troubadour. Each addresses the same notorious slayings—horrific crimes linked so inextricably to their turbulent era they remain difficult to assimilate today. A much-quoted statement by the '60s chronicler Joan Didion contextualizes both: "Many people I know in Los Angeles believe that the Sixties ended abruptly on August 9, 1969."[136]

In 1985, a creepy-looking LP with a burning jack-o'-lantern-headed scarecrow on its cover haunted browser bins at hipper U.S. record stores. *Bad Moon Rising* was the first recording of note by Sonic Youth—a quartet of New York art-school types whose brand of noisy, experimental rock seemed doomed to the cultural margins in the heyday of Michael Jackson, Madonna, and "We Are the World." ("We're just dying to be mass-marketed," the band's bassist, Kim Gordon, sarcastically told *Creem* magazine at the time.) And doom was *Bad Moon Rising*'s métier. A somber soundscape of detuned guitars and stream-of-consciousness lyrics that starts faint and finishes *triple forte*, the album was a bad-vibes extravaganza—an impressionistic document of Reagan-era unease filtered through layers of feedback and postmodern detachment. Its one moment of true catharsis, "Death Valley '69," was about the Charles Manson murders.

Coming down
Sadie, I love it
Now, now, now
Death Valley '69

From 1969 to 1972, Manson and his followers (including Susan Atkins—the "Sadie" in Sonic Youth's song) brutally murdered at least eleven people. These horrific crimes, replete with ritualistic overtones and bloody writing on walls, and the bizarre beliefs that motivated them—Manson's messiahship, an impending apocalyptic race war, an Elysian hideout in the California desert for him and his nomadic Family—have been documented and debated in mind-numbing detail elsewhere.

But the Manson murders—especially the slayings of the movie actress

---

136   Joan Didion, "The White Album" in *The White Album* (New York: Farrar, Straus and Giroux, 1979), p. 47.

James Welling

SONIC YOUTH, *BAD MOON RISING* BACK COVER ART (DETAIL), 1984

Sharon Tate (then eight months pregnant), four others, and the businessman Leno LaBianca and his wife ("pigs"—or affluent "establishment" types in Family parlance) on August 8-9, 1969—were also instant, macabre folklore, in part due to their myriad connections to potent cultural signifiers of the 1960s: Hollywood, rock and roll, the ruling class, and the counterculture. And Manson—a semi-literate, chronically incarcerated hood, seething with anti-authoritarian hostility, who used a domineering charisma to exploit hippie-era youth's hunger for gurus, with deadly results—remains a cultural icon of enduring, if profoundly negative, resonance. These factors provide critical context for understanding Manson's impact on music and on Sonic Youth's song.

I was on the wrong track
We're deep in the valley
Now deep in the gulley
And now in the canyon

Twenty-four albums and forty years after *Bad Moon Rising*'s release, it's common wisdom that Sonic Youth helped midwife a musical movement. They did so for a generation born too late for '60s rock or '70s punk yet eager to find or forge rebellious sounds of their own in a decade of glitzy materialism and reactionary politics. First called post-punk, then indie, and finally—blandest of the bland—alternative, the burgeoning genre came to encompass everything from the aggressive hardcore of Black Flag to the moody jangle-pop of R.E.M. and reached critical mass when Nirvana's *Nevermind* (1991) finally toppled the old-school rock of hair metal and Guns n' Roses. The new music was smarter, darker, more forward-looking, and Sonic Youth's LP—though no masterpiece, and several times bested by the band—was an especially grim manifestation of the new ethos (sample titles: "Ghost Bitch" and "I'm Insane").

It also symbolically straddled those critical decades when rock was first taken seriously, the '60s and '70s, serving as a bridge between the values—roughly hippie and punk—each represented. It was beautiful and ugly, transcendent and nihilistic, California and New York. Older than many of their contemporaries, the band members had actual memories of the '60s. There was even a possible Manson connection: Gordon, who grew up in Los Angeles, had an older brother who dated a young woman suspected by some of being murdered by the Family. And, through the New York underground, Sonic Youth had hands-on experience with punk at its most extreme.

She started to holler
She started to holler
I didn't wanna
But she started to holler

Punk had made merciless fun of hippies—out of an Oedipal need to destroy the old to create the new and in disgust over the perceived failure, with Reagan and Thatcher ascendant, of the '60s social revolution. Despite mutual antagonism and contrary dark and light sensibilities, both subcultures were overwhelmingly left-ish in spirit. As the '60s dream faded, bands spawned by '70s punk gave sympathetic nods to hippie-era values, often via fiery reinterpretations of iconic songs. Hüsker Dü's electrifying 1984 remake of the Byrds' "Eight Miles High" (1966), for instance, amps up the psychedelic anthem with volume, feedback, and a shredding vocal from the guitarist Bob Mould that's equal parts rage and pain. The result is mournful and cathartic simultaneously, a post-punk reckoning with countercultural collapse. But the band and their peers remained skeptical of the era's escapist tendencies—its preoccupation with what the Sonic Youth guitarist Lee Ranaldo (born in 1951) once called "flowers and unicorns and rainbows."[137]

In this context, revisiting Manson—once described (by his own defense attorney) as a "right-wing hippie"—made sense.[138] Loathed by conservatives, both as a killer and as a sex-drugs-and-rock-and-roll degenerate, his philosophy—autocratic, patriarchal, sexist, racist—was still far right of center. Equally despised by leftists, some radicals nevertheless portrayed him (mainly before his murder conviction) as a righteous revolutionary. Most infamously, the Weather Underground provocateur Bernardine Dohrn, in a 1969 speech, described the Family's use of its victims' own cutlery to desecrate their corpses with an approving, right-on-from-hell "far out!"[139]

Deep in the valley
In the trunk of an old car

---

137 Quoted in Timothy Greenfield-Sanders' film *Lou Reed: Rock and Roll Heart*, 1998.
138 Vincent Bugliosi and Curt Gentry, *Helter Skelter: The True Story of the Manson Murders* (New York: Bantam Books, 1995), p. 545.
139 Ibid., p. 296.

I've got sand in my mouth
You've got sun in your eyes

Like many cultural icons (and all good boogeymen), Manson seemed to personify irreconcilable opposites—love and hate, peace and violence, freedom and tyranny—at a time when each was being redefined. This sociocultural dissonance still resonates because it remains unresolved. By the '80s, the Summer of Love was a distant memory and Reagan's "Morning in America" breezily obscured the nation's post-Vietnam malaise—even as his administration slashed social programs at home and armed right-wing militias abroad. For some, Manson became a canny symbol of the country at a schizoid impasse: an unseen (because locked safely out of sight) but ever-present reminder of unfinished business between right and left, old and young, hippie and punk, who terrified all because he blurred the differences between each.

If Hüsker Dü looked back to the '60s with bitter resolve, like post-punk folkies, the Sonic Youth of *Bad Moon Rising* (its title lifted from Creedence Clearwater Revival's spooky 1969 Vietnam War song) did so with an irreverent glee worthy of the album's grinning-pumpkin-head-on-fire cover. "Death Valley '69," *Bad Moon Rising*'s explosive final track, wallows in the seediness of all things Manson with unclear motive and manic, musical overkill. Its perverse mix of taste (highbrow conceptual seriousness) and tastelessness (lowbrow scare-flick sensationalism) creates a tense art-vs.-trash dynamic that ultimately gives way under the sheer force of the music.

Despite the song's atonal attack and subversive spirit, its structure is fairly traditional: a long, taut, near-monotonal midsection bookended by a thrashy power-chord chorus, similar in design to Pink Floyd's 1967 psychedelic warhorse "Interstellar Overdrive." Musically, it delivers the cathartic goods the rest of the album's slow crescendo promises. Lyrically, it strings together artless quotes and phrases related to the Manson murders, evoking their frenzied horror through allusion and indirection.

And you wanted to get there
But I couldn't go faster
So I started to hit it
I had to hit it

Sung by the guitarist Thurston Moore and the guest vocalist Lydia Lunch, then a fixture of the New York underground and a pioneer of the city's no-wave style of noise-as-rock, the song's shrill, affected singing splits listeners, love-it-or-hate-it style. While Moore sings "straight," Lunch sings in a self-consciously flat tone that threatens the song's precarious art–trash balance. Gordon took over Lunch's part live, and her husky sensuality provided a less abrasive counterpoint to Moore. YouTube makes multiple live versions from the last four decades—of varying sound quality but sung by Gordon and Moore (and Ranaldo)—available for contrast. Though lacking *Bad Moon Rising*'s conceptual framing, the best of these topple the art–trash scales altogether. "Death Valley '69" emerges as art rock in the best sense: a dark tone-poem of layered guitars, pulsing drums, and passionate vocals performed by a quintet of now middle-aged New York art-school types.

    Ask an ex-hippie the perpetual question, "What killed the '60s?" and you're likely to get an answer that mirrors Didion's perennial observation: "The Manson murders." The uniformity of reaction is striking, as is the tone of reply, which typically ranges from elegiac head-shaking to sneering disgust.

    As a cultural force, the anti-hippie hobgoblin has had a truly profound impact on our era. While the cumulative accomplishments of '60s social movements (civil rights, antiwar, environmental, etc.) undeniably altered the country, they also drove a rancorous wedge between those who applauded and those who condemned the changes. Consequently, a broad sense of loss and betrayal was felt by those deeply invested in the dream of a fully transformed society—a freer, gentler, peaceful ideal that never came to be, much mocked in subsequent decades by conservatives, realists, and cynics. Many blamed this loss, literally or symbolically, on Manson and his execrable behavior. Superficially, this meant that the Family gave hippies, free love, communal living, etc. a bad name. But, at a deeper level, it meant that their vilest acts, committed less than a week before Woodstock, caused a tear in the social fabric that may never be repaired. A legacy of reflexive doubt that routinely scorns idealism as hopelessly naïve—the stuff of "flowers and unicorns and rainbows."

    Before true crime was a bookstore section and Amazon category, only a few such tomes existed. One of them, common in middle-class homes in the '70s, was *Helter Skelter: The True Story of the Manson Murders* (1974) by Vincent Bugliosi (with Curt Gentry). Written by the Los Angeles County deputy district attorney who tried and convicted Manson and eight of his followers for the Tate–LaBianca murders, *Helter Skelter* was a riveting piece of crime reporting and remains a classic of the genre. Reading it became a rite of passage for young people who, forbidden access by adults, did so piecemeal in surreptitious glances in stores, neighbors' houses, or in their homes when no one was looking. The book's black-and-white crime-scene photos were discreetly "whited out"—a respectful gesture unimaginable on the Internet, where ghastly images, including those of the Manson victims, can be found in seconds. An epigraph at the book's front said simply: "The story you are about to read will scare the hell out of you."[140]

    The other ur-text every Manson buff reads is *The Family* (1971) by Ed Sanders, a poet and member of the satiric '60s rock band the Fugs. Sanders not only offered a (highly critical) countercultural take on Manson but also uneasily befriended Family members still living at Spahn's Movie Ranch—the remote Hollywood film set and locale of a hundred B-movie westerns where the Family squatted

---

140 Ibid., front page.

for much of 1969-1970. Some of them were later convicted of murder. *Helter Skelter* is the more trustworthy account, but *The Family* better evokes the witchy tenor of the times.[141]

Both books offer vivid examples of the serpentine links between the case and other '60s signifiers. Hollywood is one such link but falls outside the range of this chapter. Suffice to say the Manson saga is riddled with filmic connections, from its Benedict Canyon and Los Feliz crime scenes to Tate's husband Roman Polanski's homicide- and occult-themed films (e.g. *Repulsion, Rosemary's Baby*). Manson's great scheme, after his 1967 release from prison, was to become some kind of star—preferably in music, but movies would also do. So he and the Family haunted film studios and stars' homes throughout 1968 and 1969 to catalyze what Sanders calls Operation Superstar.[142]

Rock and roll is where Manson's malignant influence was most keenly felt and lingers still. Inspired in prison by the Beatles' success, Manson, a competent guitarist and singer, became convinced that his meager musical skills and unorthodox philosophical insights ("No sense makes sense,"[143] "Total paranoia is just total awareness,"[144] "You can't kill kill"[145]) would rocket him to stardom once he was released into the hedonistic wonderland of '60s California. His consequent failure after his 1967 release—despite some surprisingly high-profile support in the music industry—played a critical role in his shift from sex-and-drugs messiah to vengeful maniac.

Brought to the attention of Terry Melcher (son of the actress Doris Day), who had produced seminal folk-rock records for the Byrds, Manson ultimately failed to impress the young executive, and the rejection inflamed his insecure ego. Melcher lived in Benedict Canyon with his girlfriend, the actress Candice Bergen, and when the couple moved out in mid-1969, their former home was leased to Polanski and Tate. On the night of August 8th, when Manson armed four followers and told them to kill the occupants of whatever house he sent them to, it was Melcher's old place—now occupied by Tate and her houseguests (Polanski was in Europe on business)—he selected.

Manson met Melcher through the Beach Boys' Dennis Wilson in 1968, after the handsome drummer picked up a pair of hitchhikers and drove them back to his Sunset Boulevard home. Unknown to the musician, both were Family

141   The trustworthiness of both accounts has been debated to the extent that contrary camps endorse one or the other, both, or neither (Manson-philes are an obsessive bunch, prone to exhaustive quarreling over minutiae and big-picture themes). Bugliosi's more conventional read focuses on the investigation and trial. But critics accuse him of, among other things, making himself the hero of the case, bending evidence to suit his theories, and misrepresenting Nietzsche as a proto-Nazi. Similarly, Sanders' reliance on anecdotes paints a vivid picture, but led to the deletion of a chapter due to its libelous claims about another '60s cult–the Process Church of the Final Judgment–in later editions. Some of his wilder claims (e.g., that sects practiced human sacrifice in late-'60s California or that the Family may have shot "snuff" films) strain credulity. Today, books, documentaries, and podcasts speculate about Manson from every conceivable angle. But the Bugliosi and Sanders books were the founding documents.
142   Ed Sanders, *The Family: The Manson Group and Its Aftermath* (New York: Signet Books, 1989), p. 19.
143   Bugliosi, *Helter Skelter*, p. 55.
144   David Felton and David Dalton, "Charles Manson: The Incredible Story of the Most Dangerous Man Alive," *Rolling Stone*, 25 June 1970.
145   R. C. Zaehner, *Our Savage God: The Perverse Use of Eastern Thought* (New York: Sheed and Ward, 1974), p. 66.

members, and when he returned late that night from a recording session he found his house swarming with nubile cultists and their guru-like leader. A dark period followed for Wilson, during which the Family moved in and helped themselves (over several months) to $100,000 worth of his money and belongings while pressuring him to boost Manson's music career. For a time, Wilson himself got swept up in the madness, promoting and recording the would-be superstar (he later erased the tapes, telling Bugliosi "the vibrations connected with them don't belong on this earth").[146] He called Manson "the Wizard" and admitted he was afraid of him. Eventually, he had the Family evicted and cut off contact, but extortion attempts followed. When Manson threatened his young son, an enraged Wilson—never one to shrink from a fight—pummeled him, according to the Beach Boys collaborator Van Dyke Parks. Still, the musician increasingly feared for his life.[147]

Manson's animus toward Wilson stemmed partly from his adaptation of one of Manson's songs for the B side of the 1968 Beach Boys single "Bluebirds over the Mountain." The move, ostensibly part of Operation Superstar, enraged Manson because Wilson substantially rewrote the song in an attempt to make it commercially viable. (He also took sole compositional credit—a mercenary but probably fair action considering the strain the Family put on his bank account.) Originally an acid-fried anthem to ego death with sadistic overtones called "Cease to Exist," Wilson changed "exist" to "resist" and reshaped it into an unlikely love song called "Never Learn Not to Love," replete with chant-like but appealing Beach Boys harmonies.

> *Cease to resist, come on, say you love me*
> *Give up your world, come on and be with me*

There are few creepier artifacts of the '60s than this admittedly slight but still haunting song. The Beach Boys cut the song during a rough patch in their career, when their resident songwriting genius, Dennis's troubled brother Brian, was withdrawn and inactive following the traumatic collapse of his psychedelic magnum opus, *Smile*.[148] "Never Learn Not to Love" marked the only time before Manson's final incarceration that one of his songs saw wide release. It was even performed on *The Mike Douglas Show*. Wilson croons the song with stoned sincerity, in the same slightly raspy voice he gave "Forever," a romantic ballad and minor hit in 1969.

---

146 Bugliosi, *Helter Skelter*, p. 340.

147 On a darkly humorous note, the teenage Box Tops singer Alex Chilton–a forebear of alternative rock through his '70s band Big Star–crashed briefly at Wilson's place during the Family's residence there and was once sent by a Manson follower to buy groceries (out of pocket) for the household. "When I got back," he later recalled, "[t]hey looked at the grocery bag and they said, 'Well, you forgot the milk!' I said, 'Aw, gee, I'm really sorry I forgot the milk' . . . By the time I got to the front door, they were standing in the doorway, blocking the door. And they said, '*Charlie says, "Go get the milk."*' The vibes were kind of weird." Chilton left soon afterward (Holly George-Warren, *A Man Called Destruction: The Life and Music of Alex Chilton, from Box Tops to Big Star to Backdoor Man*, New York: Penguin Books, 2014, p. 77).

148   Co-written with Parks and finally completed and released to ecstatic reviews in 2004.

Submission is a gift given to another
Love and understanding is for one another

Manson needn't have fretted over his potential big break, as the single flopped. But the demands for money continued and the threats of violence escalated when Wilson received .45 caliber bullets at his home delivered by a Manson associate. The cumulative intimidation took a toll. The drummer found himself in a state of constant paranoia (or "total awareness" in Family lingo)—an anxiousness that would not abate until Manson's arrest on suspicion of murder in late 1969. "I'm the luckiest guy in the world," Wilson told Bugliosi in 1970, "because I got off only losing my money."[149]

Another musician who spent time with Manson was Neil Young, the mercurial folkie and purveyor of feedback-drenched rock who served as a musical link between '60s and '70s iterations of the counterculture. In 1974, the year President Gerald Ford informed the country that "our long national nightmare is over" (referring to Watergate, though the sentiment also resonates with Manson), he released a caustic track—inspired by Manson and the Family—on a disquieting album about the transitional times.

Young had consecutive hits in the early '70s with *After the Gold Rush* (1970) and *Harvest* (1972)—mostly mellow folk-rock LPs that solidified his public persona as a thoughtful hippie balladeer. But, as the '60s waned, Young was in no mood to be anyone's flower child, so the irascible rocker made a trio of edgy, introspective albums designed to please no one but himself. *Time Fades Away* (1973), *On the Beach* (1974), and *Tonight's the Night* (1975) were records of tough, ambivalent rock unleashed on a public expecting earnest folk-pop (like 1972's "Heart of Gold") or at least obvious message songs (such as 1970's "Southern Man"). Instead, listeners got dark ruminations on a cluster of themes—drugs, dissolution, the downside of fame—that nagged Young as the new decade hit high gear. *On the Beach* was the least musically raw and despairing of the three. But its biting lyrics remained bitter, at times savagely so. A key track on the album was "Revolution Blues."

Well, we live in a trailer at the edge of town
You never see us 'cause we don't come around
We got twenty-five rifles just to keep the population down
But we need you now, and that's why
I'm hanging around

By 1974, the heyday of the Manson Family had passed. The Tate–LaBianca killers were behind bars, their death sentences commuted to life imprisonment when California abolished capital punishment in 1972. A ten-month trial had kept Americans entranced as the gruesome and bizarre details of the crimes

---

149 Bugliosi, *Helter Skelter*, p. 341.

were made public, and Manson made headlines by disrupting the proceedings and issuing threats while a circle of his followers kept vigil on the street outside the courthouse. Manson carved an "X" into his forehead ("I have X'd myself from your world," the evil messiah explained; later he modified it into a swastika), and Family members—after insisting for months that they acted independently from their guru—all followed suit.[150] For verdict day, they shaved their heads.

Mysterious deaths occurred during and after the trial. A Manson follower was found dead with a bullet in his head at a Family crash pad—from playing Russian roulette, those present told police (who had no idea they were talking to Family members). But the gun had been fully loaded and wiped clean of prints. A Family associate was found dead in a London hotel, his wrists and throat slit. It was ruled a suicide, though, once more, police were unaware of his Family connection. Mid-trial, one of Manson's defense attorneys (all forced on the accused mass murderer, who wanted to defend himself) disappeared. Weeks later, his decomposed corpse was found trapped under a boulder at Sespe Hot Springs. Some of these deaths may have been accidental or self-inflicted, but, at the time, each tweaked the paranoia of a nation still adjusting to the homicidal hippie paradigm. Meanwhile, police studied possible links between the Family and various unsolved murders.

So you be good to me and I'll be good to you
And in this land of conditions
I'm not above suspicion
I won't attack you, but I won't back you

In the early '70s, Young's career was at a crossroads. A veteran of the '60s band Buffalo Springfield but best known as one-fourth of the folk-rock supergroup Crosby, Stills, Nash, and Young, he had launched a successful solo career in 1968, with and without his band Crazy Horse. By the turn of the decade, he was, in his own words, a "rich hippie,"[151] but, despite wealth and critical accolades, he seemed squirrelly and discontented—especially within the confines of the country-tinged singer-songwriter genre he'd helped pioneer. "One of you fuckin' guys comes near me," he snapped at a cameraman before his debut with Crosby, Stills, Nash, and Young at Woodstock, "and I'm gonna fuckin' hit you with my guitar."[152] His best songs with that band (the keening "Helpless," the fiery "Ohio") outclassed those of his smoother-voiced collaborators. Always an odd mix of hippie and punk (before the latter term existed), his agrarian folkie sensibility meshed uneasily with his shrewder, mocking side.

He was also dogged by tragedy. In 1972, he was badly shaken by the overdose death of the Crazy Horse guitarist Danny Whitten. A subsequent tour became a rickety, if riveting, affair, with Young debuting new material—at times drunkenly—in looser, more hard-rock arrangements than his fans were used to or sometimes wanted (heard on *Time Fades Away*). Young hit bottom the

---

150 Ibid., p. 421.

151 Quoted in Jonathan Demme's film *Neil Young: Heart of Gold* (2006).

152 Quoted in Jimmy McDonough, *Shakey: Neil Young's Biography* (New York: Anchor Books, 2003), p. 320.

following year when his friend and roadie Bruce Berry also died of an overdose. Live shows became near-funerary rites: spooky, bluesy, musical wakes where Young confronted, night after night, the demons unleashed by his friends' deaths (*Tonight's the Night* documents the trauma). Amidst the turmoil in his band, his first two children were born with developmental disabilities.

These records and *On the Beach* took their place beside other albums of stripped-down, end-of-the-'60s rock like John Lennon's primal-scream break with the Beatles, *Plastic Ono Band* (1971) and Sly and the Family Stone's chilly negation of Woodstock-era optimism, *There's a Riot Goin' On* (1972). "The dream is over," sang Lennon and, while he wrote the line about the Beatles, it clearly applied to the peace-and-love decade as well. Three years later, Young's "Revolution Blues" heightened the disillusionment:

> *Well, it's so good to be here asleep on your lawn*
> *Remember your guard dog?*
> *Well, I'm afraid that he's gone*
> *It was such a drag to hear him whining all night long*

The Family's final flameout began on August 21, 1971, when five members and a white supremacist from the Aryan Brotherhood prison gang stole 143 rifles from an L.A. gun shop. They intended to free Manson by either busting him out of jail or hijacking a 747 jet and killing one passenger every hour until his release. A silent alarm alerted police, and an argument over whether to kill the store's captive clerks and customers (lying terrified on the floor) delayed the thieves long enough to thwart their escape in a gun-filled van. The police arrived, and a brief shoot-out occurred.

Remarkably, no one was killed. But the subsequent arrests and convictions removed some of Manson's most hardcore disciples from the streets, as did the 1972 slayings of a young ex-Marine and his wife in Stockton, California—both found shot to death, the former decapitated and buried near a hiking trail, the latter in a freshly dug grave in the dirt cellar of a rental home. Charged with murder or accessory were two Aryan Brotherhood members and two female followers of Manson, all later convicted. Eerily, police found the dead couple's infant daughter in the care of the Manson women.

The Stockton crimes are the last known murders with clear links to the Manson Family. With the bulk of his most steadfast supporters behind bars, Manson's media sheen dulled: he became, over time, less a demonic archetype of the age than a morbid curiosity of a bygone era. Separated from their abusive surrogate father figure, most of his followers—bourgeois teenage runaways who came under his influence at their most vulnerable and easily manipulated—regained their sense of self and gradually woke from their collective nightmare.

> *Well, I'm a barrel of laughs with my carbine on*
> *I keep 'em hopping until my ammunition's gone*

But I'm still not happy
I feel like there's something wrong

"Revolution Blues" is the first of three *On the Beach* songs with "blues" in the title (the others are "Vampire Blues," about the oil industry, and the wearily hopeful set-closer "Ambulance Blues"). Built around a simple, barbed-wire guitar riff played by David Crosby atop the fierce rhythm section of the Band's Levon Helm and Rick Danko, Young sings it with a snarl and plays lead guitar between verses (there is no chorus). Syncopated with irregular stanzas, the lyrics have a dashed-off but devout feel and are sung from the point of view of a Manson-like hood—a trailer-trash would-be revolutionary, disgusted by the gaudy rich and hungry for apocalypse. Young's artless tenor, redolent of the Appalachian "high lonesome" in gentler fare, sounds snide and ruthless, brimming with resentment and in love with chaos. The effect is all the more chilling because he sounds like he means every word. You begin to wonder if Young is revealing a facet of himself—basically, his inner Manson—we might not want to see.

I got the revolution blues
I see bloody fountains
And ten million dune buggies coming down the mountains
Well, I hear that Laurel Canyon is full of famous stars
But I hate them worse than lepers, and I'll kill them in their cars

Crosby, at first, wanted nothing to do with the song. "I played it for [him]," Young recalled years later, "and he said, 'Don't sing about that. That's not funny.'"[153] The former Byrd—a friend of Terry Melcher and too many *dramatis personae* of the Manson saga—was deeply spooked by the murders and feared overzealous drugged-out fans. Plus, he knew that Young knew Manson—had met him at Dennis Wilson's house in 1969 and been sufficiently impressed by his music to recommend him to a record executive. "[Manson's] songs were off-the-cuff things he made up as he went along," Young remembered. "And they were never the same twice in a row. Kind of like Dylan, but different because it was hard to glimpse a true message in them. But the songs were fascinating."[154]

Manson's music is critically divisive. Much scrutinized due to his infamy, assessing its quality is difficult for the same reason. Among his cadre of boosters, too many have obvious and often arrested-adolescent agendas of their own. Certainly, the songs he pitched in the late '60s—collected on the semi-legal LP *Lie: The Love and Terror Cult* (1970)—are largely undistinguished and forgettable. Melodically indistinct and stylistically derivative—less of folk or blues sources than radio crooners from Manson's youth, like Perry Como and Nat "King" Cole—what's inevitably most compelling is their sometimes morbid or psychotic-sounding lyrics. Consequently, it's music mostly for voyeurs. "Charlie never had a musical bone in his body," Wilson said two years after adapting one

---

153   Quoted in Ben Whalley's documentary film, *Neil Young: Don't Be Denied* (2000).

154   Neil Young, *Waging Heavy Peace* (New York: Plume, 2012), p. 104.

of his better compositions ("Cease to Exist") for the Beach Boys.[155]

Still, Young was on to something. Manson does impress—or at least "fascinate" (in Young's nomenclature)—when he's at his most free-form, as Young heard him in 1969. Unhindered by studios, Family backup singers, or the constraints of commercial songwriting, Manson finds his sinister, shamanic groove in largely improvised compositions driven purely by arcane motivations of his own. This side of Manson's music—not for everyone, but compelling in its way—is heard on another dubiously legal recording, *Charles Manson Live at San Quentin* (1983). It's an hour of uninterrupted performance, recorded in his cell and semi-arbitrarily divided into tracks with titles like "Marilyn Monroe Was My Childhood Shame." For added ambiance, men curse, cough, and occasionally flush toilets in the background.

By the mid-'70s, most of Manson's followers had denounced him, and those not imprisoned were in hiding. The bombastic exceptions were Lynette "Squeaky" Fromme and Sandra Good—Satan's most strident cheerleaders, nicknamed "Red" and "Blue" by their leader according to a new color-coded faith he devised called the Order of the Rainbow. Manson was now primarily preoccupied with man's abuse of Planet Earth (the Order would eventually evolve into ATWA—for Air, Trees, Water, and Animals), and Red and Blue proselytized passionately for him, writing press releases and admonishing corporate polluters for their sins. Like Manson, they became clichés out of time—bobble-headed revolutionaries wandering Sacramento in long, hooded robes, unaware that the '60s had ended. They also became pioneering eco-terrorists, sending threatening letters to the CEOs of ecologically unsound multinationals—a federal offense that landed Good in prison.[156]

The final incident of this footnote to the Manson affair occurred on September 4, 1975, when the flame-haired Squeaky, resplendent in scarlet gown and matching pixie cap, pointed a .45 automatic at Gerald Ford in a Sacramento crowd. The gun failed to fire and, in fact, had no bullet in the chamber (though the magazine was loaded). This led some to conclude that her assassination attempt was a bluff, a desperate attempt to refocus dwindling media attention on the Manson cause or simply get her beloved leader, lover, and father figure's attention and, perhaps, win his approval. "Every girl," Fromme had said in a 1973 documentary, "should have a daddy just like Charlie."[157]

From here, the road between Young's "Revolution Blues" and Sonic Youth's "Death Valley '69" is navigated with relative ease. If the Manson murders were

155 Bugliosi, *Helter Skelter*, p. 339.

156 "[Y]our homes will be bloodier than the Tate-LaBianca houses and Mi Lai [sic] put together," read a press release the pair delivered to Sacramento news media, warning the establishment to shape up (Sanders, *The Family*, p. 448).

157 Good was paroled in 1985. For years she co-ran a website dedicated to Manson (Access Manson, now defunct). In 1987, Fromme escaped prison to try and reach Manson, who was under treatment for cancer. Apprehended two days later, she was eventually paroled in 2008. Unlike nearly every other player in the Family drama, Good and Fromme remain unrepentant devotees of Manson. Charlie himself died from cancer in 2017 (Fromme quote from Robert Hendrickson and Laurence Merrick's film, *Manson*, 1973).

Bob Seidemann and Gary Burden

NEIL YOUNG, *ON THE BEACH* **COVER ART, 1974**

the symbolic death knell of '60s idealism, they cast a long shadow on the cynical decade that followed. For prime players in both eras, like Young, the '70s must have seemed especially purgatorial—a druggy, after-party hangover of torpor and decay, with flower children sleazily reborn as junkies, pimps, and coked-up A&R men. And when your faith is gone, nihilism beckons: "Though your confidence may be shattered," Young sang on another *On the Beach* track, "it doesn't matter."

The cover for *On the Beach* shows Young standing on the Pacific shore in gaudy yellow polyester—a rich hippie surrounded by quixotic comfort items (a potted palm, some beach furniture, a mostly buried '59 Cadillac). He stares out at the sea, his back to the camera as if waiting for the end of the world. (The image alludes to the album's namesake: Nevil Shute's 1957 novel, made into a film in 1959, about a group of people awaiting the arrival of deadly, wind-borne radiation after a nuclear war.) But no such reckoning came: the counterculture fell and was debased and the '80s brought spectacle, escapism, and bland reassurances as state power reasserted itself to tepid opposition. In between came punk, which, more than any other musician of his generation, Young welcomed and understood.

STEVEN L. JONES, *OPEN HYMNAL #2*, 2019

CHAPTER FOUR:
HARD WORK AND HARD TIMES:
SONGS OF LABOR AND STRIFE

AND WHO KILLED THE MINER?

To the tintinnabulation that so musically wells
From the bells, bells, bells, bells
Bells, bells, bells—
From the jingling and tinkling of the bells
—Edgar Allan Poe, "The Bells," 1849

"The Bells of Rhymney" opens with a cascade of arpeggiated guitar as instantly recognizable as the cannon-like snare shot that launches Bob Dylan's "Like a Rolling Stone." A shimmering sequence of D, G, and E chords peal on an electric twelve-string Rickenbacker, each tone ringing discretely yet resounding with the others in rich harmonic clusters. Jangly rhythm guitar joins alongside droning bass and minimal, pulse-setting drums. It's a stunning intro—bracing yet trancelike—that sets the stage in seconds for a vocal that's both earthy and ethereal, enhanced at the end of lines by layered harmonies. The words are similarly bejeweled and hypnotic—an enigmatic crisscross of colors and mysterious place names.

Oh, what will you give me?
Say the sad bells of Rhymney
Is there hope for the future?
Say the brown bells of Merthyr
Who made the mine owner?
Say the black bells of Rhondda
And who killed the miner?
Say the grim bells of Blaina

"The Bells of Rhymney" is a mining song—a haunting recitative in which anthropomorphized church bells converse cryptically about labor strife in South Wales. Adapted from a 1938 poem, the song is a soaring highlight of the Byrds' *Mr. Tambourine Man* (1965)—the seminal folk-rock album wherein the band and its producer, Terry Melcher,[158] first merged the ebullient sounds of British beat music with the reflective, moody lyrics of the '60s folk revival. The song blends these aspects masterfully, imbuing a mournful narrative that's simultaneously fantastic and social-realist with sonic power and sensory pleasure in a

---

158 His role in the Charles Manson saga is outlined in the previous section.

CONSTANTIN MEUNIER, *RETURN OF THE MINERS*, 19TH CENTURY

best-of-both-worlds hybrid. Both camps—beat enthusiasts and folkies—personified boomer youth culture but, before the Byrds' integrative experiment, they were largely treated as warring tribes: the former frivolous, the latter serious, and never the twain shall meet. The resulting mash-up was a smashing success. Dylan marveled that the band made the title track—one of four of his songs on the LP—danceable, and soon went full-tilt electric himself. Folk rock became a genre with far-reaching impact: garage bands covered Dylan, beat groups recast old ballads, and twee troubadours beefed up their sound with chiming guitars and rock drums. George Harrison even adapted the guitar part for "The Bells of Rhymney" in his then-best song, "If I Needed Someone," for his own band's folk-rock classic, *Rubber Soul* (1965). Folk music became fun—not just head but body music, still "serious" (i.e., contemplative and transformative) but you could frug to it.

Of course, folk purists suspicious of fun looked askance at this development. When Dylan went full-band that summer at the Newport Folk Festival, audience response was a hard-to-read mix of cheers and boos. But the organizer Pete Seeger—an old-school folkie and early champion of Dylan—saw red, condemning (by various accounts) the loud volume, poor sound (that obscured the lyrics), or simply Dylan going "pop." Seeger, in fact, composed "The Bells of Rhymney," setting words by the Welsh poet Idris Davies to music and making the song a stirring set-piece in his own stage act.[159] Davies was an ex-miner from Rhymney, a small village in Welsh coal country, who worked the pits as a young man, lost a finger in an accident, and participated in the failed 1926 General Strike for better wages and work conditions.[160] One of the largest labor disputes in British history, the strike involved millions of workers from multiple industries walking

159 The Byrds would cut another Seeger adaptation–"Turn! Turn! Turn!," his setting of a chapter from *Ecclesiastes*–on their follow-up album of that title.

160 Despite massive wealth generated (upward) by the coal industry, Wales was one of the hardest hit places in Europe before and during the post-World War I economic depression, with high unemployment and infant mortality rates in addition to hazardous working conditions.

off their jobs in solidarity with locked-out miners. When the mine bosses prevailed—their case boosted by anti-union politicians and media—it left a vast swath of the population jobless. In 1927, mass picketing and sympathetic strikes were outlawed in the U.K., further crippling the labor movement. The historian Gareth Elwyn Jones describes the strike's demoralizing aftermath:

> *The General Strike lasted for nine days; the miners stayed out for months until starved into submission . . . It was a traumatic period of near-starvation, educational opportunities blighted, victimization, blacklegging and abject poverty. Community support was outstanding and soup kitchens and concerts were organized to provide some money. In the end, there was disillusionment as the men were forced to surrender.*[161]

This was the background of "The Bells of Rhymney." Inspired by P. B. Shelley, Davies quit mining, educated himself, and became a poet. While on the dole, he wrote the poem Seeger adapted for a collection entitled *Gwalia Deserta* (Wasteland of Wales). Dylan Thomas and T. S. Eliot were fans, yet Davies died in relative obscurity at forty-eight. Seeger, a pro-labor leftist, blacklisted in McCarthyite America, admired Davies' poem and refashioned it as an elegiac anthem. Seeger adjusted a few words, but the Byrds version omits a whole verse:

They will plunder willy-nilly
Cry the bells of Caerphilly
They have fangs, they have teeth
Shout the loud bells of Neath
Even God is uneasy
Say the moist bells of Swansea
And what will you give me?
Say the sad bells of Rhymney

The singular structure of Davies' adapted poem, with its back-and-forth dialogue between bell towers, is derived from a morbid nursery rhyme with a pointed subtext—a children's "game song" (à la "London Bridge Is Falling Down"), sometimes sung as a folk song. If Davies' poem and Seeger's song are ominous, its model, "Oranges and Lemons" (Roud 13190), is suffused with dread—its fatalistic tone and themes of debt and stagnation made darker by its singsong style.[162]

Oranges and lemons
Say the bells of St. Clement's

---

161 Gareth Elwyn Jones, *Modern Wales: A Concise History* (London: Cambridge University Press, 1994), p. 262.

162 A weirdly cheerful rendition by Tim Hart and Maddy Prior is found on *My Very Favourite Nursery Rhyme Record* (1981)—a kiddie album, so understandably low on doom and gloom. A more sinister take is from the Mekons' excellent odds-and-sods set of outtakes and rarities, *I Have Been to Heaven and Back: Hen's Teeth and Other Lost Fragments of Un-Popular Culture, Vol. 1* (1999). The song is referred to several times in George Orwell's dystopian *Nineteen Eighty-Four*.

You owe me five farthings
Say the bells of St. Martin's

When will you pay me?
Say the bells at Old Bailey
When I grow rich
Say the bells of Shoreditch

When will that be?
Say the bells of Stepney
I do not know
Says the great bell at Bow

"Oranges and Lemons" closes with a grim encounter with a decapitating Reaper, implying that after economic immobility comes only death:

Here comes a candle to light you to bed
Here comes a chopper to chop off your head

The provenance and meaning of the song are much debated. The earliest known printed version dates from 1774, but scholars list older variants, which have not survived. Like many nursery rhymes, "Oranges and Lemons" mixes child's play with adult despair to unsettling effect. This blend of fantasy and didacticism survives in Davies' poem, confounding stereotypes of political firebrands as hardheaded realists. *Gwalia Deserta* is a committed socialist's portrait of the proud Welsh mining tradition in decline—devastated by accidents, closings, and corrupt, greedy owners, but, for all his political zeal, Davies was also a visionary Romantic—a familiar melding of seemingly contrary traits in Wales, where poets are lauded as national heroes. Davies was critical of the bland agitprop of well-meaning but drearily materialist writers: "Too many 'poets of the Left,'" he wrote, "are badly in need of instruction as to the difference between poetry and propaganda."[163] He urged literary activists to read William Blake and engage with his notion of Imagination as an immaterial but actual realm.

This quixotic blend of working-class realism and transcendent yearning informs both Seeger's and the Byrds' versions of "The Bells of Rhymney." But contrasting the two also highlights the gaps between rock and folk camps that the band (and Dylan) sought to bridge. "The Bells of Rhymney" debuted as a duet on *Pete Seeger and Sonny Terry*—a 1958 live album Seeger cut with the Piedmont bluesman. It's a dramatic, mannered performance and the template for later renditions by Seeger—less folk song than art song, with shifting tempo and dynamics, and a breakneck mid-song instrumental interlude. Its irregular beat and idiosyncratic delivery are commanding but preclude rhythmic engagement;

---

163 Dafydd Johnston, ed., "The Development of Idris Davies's Poetry," in *The Complete Poems of Idris Davies* (Cardiff: University of Wales Press, 1994), p. lvi.

Fred Palumbo/Library of Congress

PETE SEEGER, 1955

it's moving, but you can't move to it. A recording of a 1964 solo performance from Australia is available on YouTube and captures Seeger's stentorian style.[164] Solemn and erect, he delivers a deeply respectful reading of the song, alternately thunderous and calm.

Throw the vandals in court!
Say the bells of Newport
All will be well if, if, if, if, if—
Say the green bells of Cardiff
Why so worried, sisters, why?
Say the silver bells of Wye
And what will you give me?
Say the sad bells of Rhymney[165]

The Byrds, by contrast, perform the song with no jarring shifts—just a steady beat beneath a rich, unvaried sound. But the band's achievement isn't to enliven a brooding recitation with a sexy sway. Unlike Dylan, whose version of folk-rock was gritty, hip-shaking roots music, the Byrds' rendering was tuneful and expansive—proto-psychedelic with its chiming guitars, meditative tempo, and ascendant church-like harmonies. Indeed, "chiming guitars" is now pop shorthand for the Byrds' early sound, and "The Bells of Rhymney" rings like its namesake—less a monochrome tolling than a colorful carillon.[166] The Byrds' version is lyrically earnest but ultimately favors sonics over messaging. The song sparkles elusively like a garlanded painting converted to sound.

Oh, what will you give me?
Say the sad bells of Rhymney
Is there hope for the future?
Say the brown bells of Merthyr

---

164 See www.youtube.com/watch?v=vK_eVaLeiQ0

165 It's hard to knock Seeger. As a musician and activist, he was unfailingly generous, principled, and committed to elevating folk music for the masses. He resisted red-baiting and refused to answer questions or name names before the House Un-American Activities Committee. But, for the rock generation, he seemed stiff and stuffy–a cool old man, perhaps, but not groovy. His fellow folksinger Woody Guthrie–whose performing style was looser–famously emblazoned his guitar with the snappy legend "This machine kills fascists." Seeger, in homage, inscribed his banjo with "This machine surrounds hate and forces it to surrender." It's a thoughtful rejoinder, but the extra verbiage is telling–Seeger was too pensive, too concerned with being perfectly understood, to simplify sentiment for rhythm and feel.

166 It also resonates with another Dylan cover on the album–"Chimes of Freedom," which conflates a lightning storm with chiming bells and chiming bells with freedom from tyranny ("And we gazed upon the chimes of freedom flashing"). Dylan anticipated its fusion of natural and manufactured sounds in an earlier song, "Lay Down Your Weary Tune" (1963) ("The crying rain like a trumpet sang . . . The branches bare like a banjo moaned"), but without the topical allusions (to war, civil rights, and unjust imprisonment) of "Chimes of Freedom." Bells, of course, were once primary conduits for community communication, announcing time of day, religious services, births, marriages, deaths, and raising the alarm during local disasters (including mining accidents).

Who made the mine owner?
Say the black bells of Rhondda
And who killed the miner?
Say the grim bells of Blaina

"And who killed the miner ...?" The most striking lyrical change the Byrds made to Davies' poem and Seeger's adaptation is this line—"Who *robbed* the miner?" in both the song's sources. The substitution lends the track existential depth. "Robbed" evokes wage cuts and layoffs—economic insecurity among workers exploited by coal barons primarily concerned with profit. But "killed" ups the ante, reminding us that mining is deadly work and that mining companies routinely take the lives of workers—and by extension, their families and dependents—into their own hands. A corollary follows: in a just society, such workers would be protected at every level of employment, from health and safety to fair wages and meaningful participation in decision-making. Hence unions, hence union-busting, hence class war. The drama engendered by these basic labor issues animates countless songs, including mining ballads. And the lethal regularity of mining tragedies means many of the most memorable are disaster songs.

One widely performed ballad concerns a colliery accident that killed seventy-four men and boys in northeast England in 1882. "The Trimdon Grange Explosion" (Roud 3189) is a dramatic broadside that recounts the devastation caused by a massive detonation of coal dust and firedamp—a highly flammable methane-based gas found in mines. The explosion killed sixty-nine workers at Trimdon, a County Durham coal pit, plus five who died when the blast forced toxic fumes into an adjacent mine at Kelloe. The song's composer was a miner-bard named Tommy Armstrong—a pitman since 1857 (he started at age nine) who supplemented his income by writing, performing, and selling broadsheets of ballads he wrote about life and events in his native Durham. Such topical songs typically provide blow-by-blow accounts of tragedies, appropriate for times of limited literacy and scant news media. To make a profit, such balladeers had to work fast, and breathless sensationalized accounts were common.

"The Trimdon Grange Explosion" confounds these expectations. While it's true that Armstrong debuted the song just days after the disaster, funds raised went to the miners' families, and the song is entirely respectful and restrained, focused not on gruesome details of the calamity but the precarity of the miner's life and the loved ones left behind.

O let's not think about tomorrow
Lest we disappointed be
For all our joys, they may quickly turn to sorrow
As we all may daily see
Today we're strong and healthy
Tomorrow there comes the change

As we may see from the explosion
That has been at Trimdon Grange

Armstrong tells the tale in four verses of eight lines each, focused solely on the workers' routine, its deadly disruption, and the plight of shattered families. Other Armstrong songs protest mining conditions and support worker strikes. But "The Trimdon Grange Explosion" never sways from a compassionate account of human suffering in plain-spoken language. Armstrong sometimes toned down his politics to make his songs more palatable; he had fourteen children to feed and no illusions that militant sentiment expanded his audience. But "The Trimdon Grange Explosion" is no pulled punch. If anything, its resolute focus on human cost, sans sloganeering, sharpens its implicit critique of power and hierarchy. Like an Italian realist film, the song uses empathy, not ideology, to provoke pointed questions about the fate of the struggling many beside the prosperous few—e.g., Why are boys working in a mine? Why are workers so unsafe? Why is there no institutional relief for bereaved families? Why do those who take no risks profit from the perilous labor of those who do? The song's non-dogmatic tone and unspecific narrative give the song semi-universal appeal. "As a rule," the folklorist A. L. Lloyd wrote of Armstrong, "[his] songs were too local in spirit or language to spread far outside the north-eastern coalfield."[167] "The Trimdon Grange Explosion" defies this provincialism; aside from "Wor Nanny's a mazer"—a comical tune that lampoons the Geordie accent of his fellow countrymen—it's probably Armstrong's best-known song.

God protect the lonely widow
And raise each drooping head
Be a father unto the orphans
Do not let them cry for bread
Death will pay us all a visit
They have only gone before
And we will meet the Trimdon victims
Where explosions are no more

Like many ballads circulated both by singers and printed lyrics, "The Trimdon Grange Explosion" has been set to various tunes, but a stirring martial melody, described by Lloyd as a "'come-all-ye' type tune," is the best-known setting.[168] Armstrong died in 1920 and left no recordings. But the postwar folk boom produced many fine covers of the song—from the Tyneside balladeer Lou Killen's concertina-based lament (1962) to the folk-rocker Martin Carthy's more strident guitar-based version (1971). Full-band versions are rare but include a subdued rendering by the Scottish folkies the Battlefield Band (1997) and a genuinely peculiar orchestral pop version by the former Animals keyboardist

---

167 Quoted at the Tommy Armstrong Society website, www.pitmanpoet.org.uk.
168 A. L. Lloyd, *Come All Ye Bold Miners: Ballads and Songs of the Coalfields* (London: Lawrence & Wishart, 1952), p. 21.

Alan Price (1969). The latter is
ardently sung but ultimately sunk
by its schlocky, Muzak-meets-big-
band accompaniment.

An epic folk-punk version by
the Mekons provides *The Mekons
Honky Tonkin'* (1987) with a
fiery finale. For seven rousing
minutes at lumbering tempo,
booming drums propel a bagpipe-
like drone of wailing guitar,
accordion, and fiddle as Tom
Greenhalgh's mournful everyman
vocal recounts the disaster from
almost precisely a century before.
A hushed two-part coda follows

HONKY-TONKIN': THE MEKONS, 1987

the song's anthemic thunder: a ghostly cover of Hank Williams' forlorn
"Please Don't Let Me Love You" and a resigned paean to the local pub called
"Gin Palace." It's a powerful close to the final LP from their mid-'80s "country-
punk" period, when the Leeds-based band compellingly melded country and
folk influences into their brainy brand of left-wing punk. That conflation partly
arose from the band's drive to support the U.K. miners' strike of 1984-85—the
largest such action since the 1926 General Strike. It began as a flexing of union
muscle meant to prevent massive colliery closings and save countless jobs. But
Prime Minister Margaret Thatcher used the unrest to launch an unabashed
class war, demonizing strikers as the "enemy within." She and her Tory allies
gave no quarter until they had crushed the strike, vastly diminished union
power, and privatized the few remaining mines. This neoliberal onslaught
mirrored the concurrent Reagan revolution in the U.S., which similarly
decimated blue-collar industry, and in "Vengeance"—a Cajun-style hoedown
that closed *So Good It Hurts* (1988), the follow-up to *Honky Tonkin'*—the band
condemned both:

> *Don't be depressed, don't be downhearted*
> *There's a mighty crisis coming*
> *Peals of thunder, pearls of wisdom*
> *Reagan, Thatcher, dead and gone*

At the strike's start, the Mekons were a defiantly amateurish aggregate
of former art students whose mix of tuneless rant and experimental noise
attracted few fans. Reifying their commitment to the miners' plight thus
required a rethink and reconfiguration. "We weren't miners; we weren't on
strike," recalled the bassist and guitarist Kevin Lycett years later. "What can
we do? Well, the only thing we can do is the Mekons, and get out and play

benefits and raise money."[169] So stronger players were enlisted to shore up the band's sound, and a flirtation with American country and British folk crystallized from a dalliance to a full-blown mission statement. Punk, the band sensed, was spiritual kin to the stripped-down aesthetic and working-class expressionism of both genres.[170] On the critically acclaimed *Fear and Whiskey* (1985), the band hit artistic (if not commercial) pay dirt. A classic distillation of their roots-punk vision, it opens with "Chivalry"—a cry-in-your-beer song about alienation ("I was out late the other night / Fear and whiskey kept me going")—and closes with a spirited romp through Williams' end-of-his-rope classic, "Lost Highway." In between, a dour set of songs describes life in Thatcher's Britain with dark humor and a bipolar blend of rage and resignation. Pro-miner sentiment resonates throughout, most explicitly in "Abernant 1984/5"—a lament for lost jobs and shattered communities that alludes to a once prosperous Welsh mine, shut down forever after the strike. When the Mekon and South Wales native Jon Langford performs the song today, he typically introduces it with the throwaway line, "This is a song about coal-mining." His understatement obscures the song's urgency. The shortest track on *Fear and Whiskey*, its fiddle-drenched fury and despairing vocals place it at the album's heart and the spiritual center of the band's strike-inspired honky-tonk experiment.

The wind and the rain beat on his fair head
As he stood in the darkness, wishing he was dead
Only seventeen when he went down the mine
And it's a year that he's been out on the line

It's the most resolute blend of punk and folk on the album, a stripped-down protest song that shakes the rafters but, like "The Trimdon Grange Explosion," never sacrifices empathic connection with flesh-and-blood humans for dogmatic sloganeering. Nearly forty years on, the song remains gripping, and, while the events that inspired it have receded into memory, the themes it dramatizes—power and hierarchy, the struggling many and the prosperous few—are unresolved as ever, keeping its fire alive.

The weeds choke and the rust corrodes
You'd think it'd have been fifty years
Since the place was closed

---

169 Quoted in Joe Angio's film *Revenge of the Mekons* (2013).

170 Fans of the Mekons' early work savor the band's zealous commitment to punk's DIY/anyone-can-do-it ethos, but Steve Goulding–the "proper" drummer recruited for their new phase–was initially unimpressed. Asked to join, the young pro (who'd already played with, among others, Nick Lowe, Elvis Costello, and Graham Parker) at first said, "[N]o way, because I thought they were horrible. I went to see them a few times and they were drunk, they were onstage yelling and screaming with a drum machine. I didn't get it" (quoted in Angio, Revenge of the Mekons). Luckily, the band's earnest desire to "dig deep for the miners" assuaged his doubts. It's a cliché that a band's only as good as its drummer; still, it's often true. With Goulding's solid playing anchoring their new incarnation, alongside Susie Honeyman's fiddle, Lu Edmonds' bass, and the ex-Pretty Thing Dick Taylor's blazing guitar leads, the Mekons never sounded better.

Vengeance is not ours, it belongs to those
Who seek to destroy us
How much more is there left to lose?

Idris Davies would approve.

HONEY, TAKE A WHIFF ON ME

When I die, bury me low
Bury me deep in a nice bunch of snow
—"Hop Song," Anonymous[171]

In 1928, a hillbilly quartet cut a boisterous, if cautionary, song about an unexpected subject: getting high. And not on moonshine or marijuana. "Tell It to Me," by the awkwardly named Grant Brothers and Their Music, startles the modern ear in two ways. First, for its evocation of a drug, associated not with country folk in the prewar South but upper-class urbanites in the '70s and '80s. Second, for its enduring appeal as an infectious, catchy tune. It's one of those rare rural sides that plays well as a pop song, with no eccentric meter or impenetrable lyrics—just a good-time melody with singalong verses and a punchy chorus. Only the words seem out of place.

Goin' up Fifth Street, comin' down Main
Tryin' to make a nickel for to buy cocaine
Cocaine's gonna kill my honey dead

Tell it to me, tell it to me
Drink corn liquor, let your cocaine be
Cocaine's gonna kill my honey dead

It's not what you expect from an affable hoedown. Yet its subject—cocaine use, addiction, and procurement—occurs regularly in old-time music, both hillbilly and blues, testament to a time when the drug was neither illegal nor chiefly associated with the glamor and decadence of the upper crust.

"Tell It to Me" is a string-band gem—a genial jamboree propelled by banjo, guitar, a catchy fiddle hook, and the simple close-harmony singing of Jack and Claude Grant (plus the fiddler and vocalist Jack Pierce). The Grants formed a quartet called the Tenneva Ramblers in 1924 with Pierce and the banjo player Claude Slagle and the personnel on the track is, in fact, the Ramblers under a different name. It's also one of seven sides they cut for seminal "open call"

171 Collected in Frank Shay, *More Pious Friends and Drunken Companions: Songs and Ballads of Conviviality* (New York: Macaulay Company, 1928), p. 79.

sessions of early country music in Bristol and Johnson City, Tennessee. The Bristol sessions (1927) saw the talent scout Ralph Peer record, among others, the country pioneers the Carter Family and Jimmie Rodgers, to launch the Victor label's "hillbilly" line. Rodgers even played briefly with the Tenneva Ramblers, convincing them to change their name to the Jimmie Rodgers Entertainers. But "Tell It to Me" came from the lesser-known Johnson City sessions (1928-29), where the A&R man Frank Buckley Walker recorded regional talent for Columbia.[172]

Sniff cocaine on the point of a knife
Sniff cocaine if it takes my life
Cocaine's gonna kill my honey dead

Tell it to me, tell it to me
Drink corn liquor, let your cocaine be
Cocaine's gonna kill my honey dead

The song debuted in tandem with the less memorable "When a Man Is Married"—a lament for premarital freedom—and the 78 disc sold 7,600 copies. The late '20s proved to be the Grant Brothers' peak. They performed live and on the radio for two more decades but by the '40s had blue-collar day jobs. "Tell It to Me" is now their most famous song. Periodically revived over the years (e.g., by the New Lost City Ramblers in the '60s and by Doc and Merle Watson in the '70s—as "Let the Cocaine Be"), it became a staple of old-time revival tunes after Old Crow Medicine Show opened their

THE TENNEVA RAMBLERS WITH JIMMIE RODGERS, SECOND FROM LEFT, C. 1927

eponymous debut album (2003) with a rave-up rendition. But the original's jubilant blend of mountain music and urban squalor is hard to beat.

Sniff cocaine, sniff it in the wind
Doctor said it'd kill me, but he didn't say when
Cocaine's gonna kill my honey dead

---

172 Among tracks cut by Walker were three classics that turned up on Harry Smith's *Anthology of American Folk Music*: Clarence Ashley's "The Coo-Coo Bird," Bill and Belle Reed's "Old Lady and the Devil," and the Bentley Boys' "Down on Penny's Farm." The name switch from Tenneva Ramblers to Grant Brothers and Their Music was meant to disguise the fact that the Grants were recording for both Peer/Victor and Walker/Columbia.

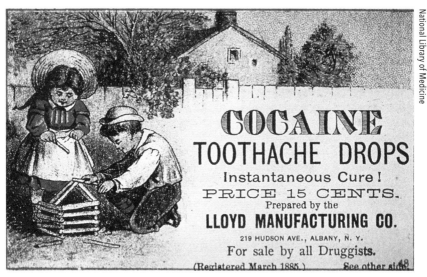

ADVERTISEMENT FOR COCAINE TOOTHACHE DROPS, C. 1885

Tell it to me, tell it to me
Drink corn liquor, let your cocaine be
Cocaine's gonna kill my honey dead

Cocaine has a wildly contradictory history in this country—a culture not known for levelheaded wisdom when it comes to mind-altering substances. Andean and other indigenous people used the coca leaves that produce the drug for medicinal and ritual purposes long before colonization. But it wasn't until the post–Civil War narcotic explosion—when cocaine, a stimulant, and opiates like opium and morphine were used for analgesic purposes and as all-purpose feel-good balms—that the drug became a fixture of North American life.[173] Largely unregulated until the 1920s, these drugs were sold over the counter at pharmacies and saloons and found in health tonics and restoratives (including Coca-Cola, which was originally a "medicinal" brew that contained small amounts of cocaine; the Coca-Cola company has been doing damage control ever since). By the turn of the century, narcotic addiction was at pandemic levels, and in 1910 President Taft declared cocaine Public Enemy No. 1. Regulation ensued, as did *Reefer Madness*–style demonization. By the Roaring Twenties, coke had become, like booze, valuable contraband.

The drug's widespread availability and affordability before its prohibition meant that users and addicts came from all classes and walks of life; its reputation as a costly "status" drug came later. It was used heavily by poor and working-class people, rural and urban, Black and white, who valued its dual nature as a stimulant and euphoric. It could keep workers alert and awake during tedious

---

173 Opiates were the miracle pain-killers of the War Between the States. After Appomattox, doctors prescribed them for everything from headache to menstrual cramps, soothing suffering but creating a massive wave of addiction in America.

or dangerous labor but also provide instant pleasure and release from dreary, oppressive lives. "Tell It to Me" is a souvenir of this era—when the drug was familiar to a wide swath of middle- and lower-income Americans who knew its pros and cons well.

Not surprisingly, the song has a tangled lineage. Already credited to "Traditional" in 1928, it's often confused with "Cocaine Blues"—a variation of the American murder ballad "Little Sadie," written and sung by the Western-swing musician T. J. "Red" Arnall in 1947 (with W. A. Nichols' Western Aces) and famously covered by Johnny Cash at his 1968 Folsom Prison concert. Despite similar lines in various versions (e.g., "Lay off the whiskey / And let that cocaine be"), the song's basic tune, words, and story are entirely different from "Tell It to Me" (which is, confusingly, sometimes called "Cocaine Blues"). After that, one faces a plethora of related songs with sometimes interchangeable titles—"Cocaine," "Cocaine Blues," "Coco Blues"—clear kin that share lines, verses, choruses, and melodies like progeny from some lost ur-text. One could write a book sorting out the strains and strands.[174]

If "Tell It to Me" surprises with its frank depiction of drug dependence, its exuberant style can be equally perplexing. Modern listeners who expect "serious" subjects to have "serious" musical settings can find its upbeat tone troubling or bizarre. Yet such incongruity typifies blues and hillbilly music. Both are rooted in a light–dark duality—a tug of war between perceived opposites like body and soul, abasement and redemption, hard times and high spirits. They also derive from the resourceful way that poor Blacks and whites escaped crushing limits by singing their woes. The resulting music can be heartbreaking, but, more often, it's desperate and uplifting simultaneously, and humor and infectious beats and tunes facilitate the merger. It's hard to fathom the instinct to *resolve* such contradictions—to smooth edges and neutralize clashes of tone. Novices are often shocked to discover that blues can be lighthearted and hilarious, that country can be both fatalistic and celebratory. But these qualities aren't errors needing correction—they're part of the lifeblood that makes the music glorious.

All you rounders[175] *think you're tough*
Feed your women on beer and snuff
Cocaine's gonna kill my honey dead

Tell it to me, tell it to me
Drink corn liquor, let your cocaine be
Cocaine's gonna kill my honey dead

The psychoanalyst Robert A. Johnson believed that incongruity deeply troubles Westerners because of our entrenchment in rational thought. "Truths always come

---

174 I tried to organize these songs into a coherent lineage while writing this and finally gave up. It's frustrating and fascinating to find songs so enmeshed that they require near-surgical precision to separate. It also speaks to the ubiquity of cocaine use in late nineteenth and early twentieth-century America.
175 A rounder is a rowdy drunk.

in pairs," he wrote, "and one has to endure this to accord with reality."[176] Logic rejects the idea that we can be opposite things at once, as does our deeply dualistic religious tradition. But real life knows better: liberals can be conservative, atheists can be spiritual, the unmusical can love music. Johnson differentiated between contradiction, which he characterized as conflicting traits that cause inner turmoil, and paradox, which he exalted as acceptance of coexisting but contrary truths. He extolled the "divine progression" from "conflict to paradox to revelation."[177] In this schema, if an inner conflict troubles us, we must determine whether it's a superficial clash or an intrinsic set of opposites. If the latter, we should embrace the discordance as *paradox*—a respectful stasis between conflicting archetypes.

This reconciliation can facilitate insight (revelation). But logic and ideology play little role in the transformation, which is mostly achieved through symbolic expression—i.e., through ritual, ceremony, and art. In Johnson's words, "Great poetry makes these leaps and unites the beauty and the terror of existence."[178]

That sounds like music—especially in its glorious, non-conflict-resolution mode.

Missing from Johnson's disquisition on paradox is humor—whether witty and droll or brash and vulgar. It, too, can unite beauty and terror in poetry. "Tell It to Me" uses lively music to address a tragic truth: drug dependence in a partner and the fear that interminable use will prove fatal. But it also uses dark humor—in its tongue-in-cheek tone and perverse "drink-don't-snort" admonition. "Better to drink heavily" is hardly approved advice, but at least booze is a slower death. There are, in fact, a slew of similar songs about drinking, many of them sung by a man about a woman (e.g., Cootie Williams' 1946 "Juice Head Baby"—"I've got a juice-head baby / She's drunk all the time"), and another old hillbilly side, Charlie Poole's "Take a Drink on Me" (1927), shares structure and feel with "Tell It to Me."[179] Its titular chorus also appears in another comic blow ballad, with booze exchanged for powder.

"Take a Whiff on Me" (Roud 10062) is both a song and a recurring line found in songs about recurrently doing lines. The best-known version is also the best: the bouncy Memphis Jug Band side (1930), which—surprise—goes by a different title: "Cocaine Habit Blues":

> *Cocaine habit mighty bad*
> *It's the worst old habit that I ever had*
> *Hey, hey, honey, take a whiff on me*
> *I went to Mr. Lehman's in a lope*
> *Saw a sign on the window says "no more dope"*
> *Hey, hey, honey, take a whiff on me*

---

176 Robert A. Johnson, *Owning Your Own Shadow: Understanding the Dark Side of the Psyche* (San Francisco: HarperCollins, 1991), p. 82.

177 Ibid., p. 91.

178 Ibid., p. 103.

179 It also contains the immortal couplet, "If you keep on stallin', you'll make me think / Your daddy was a monkey and your mama was an ape."

If "Tell It to Me" is exuberant hillbilly, "Cocaine Habit Blues" is saucy jug-band. The song lollops good-naturedly for three minutes, a congenial jam of guitar, harmonica, and kazoo over simple blasts of tuba-like jug. The (female) singer laments her habit, not with despair but comic resignation—a kind of "so it goes" head-shaking. She's equally bugged by her addiction and by her supplier's lack of product. Such unapologetic hedonism is wildly out of step with both old-school temperance and modern-day recovery models—ultra-earnest approaches that save lives but discourage fond memories of past indulgence.[180] Yet the whimsical backing and tongue-in-cheek delivery root the sentiment in an exaggerated persona that mediates the paradox. In other words, it's not a tract, it's a hoot.

Jug bands were also a hoot. They sprang up in the early twentieth century, centered in Louisville, and by the late '20s were a full-fledged craze.[181] There's no more jovial style in old-time music due to their loose, low-key presentation and eclectic mix of musical sources: ragtime, early jazz, string band, and country blues, but also minstrel show, vaudeville, and double entendre-laden hokum. They extolled a DIY ethos and were anarchic by design, with shifting lineups, non-effete instruments (banjo, guitar, and fiddle, but also spoons, washboard, washtub bass, and the ubiquitous jugs), and were as likely to busk street corners as play saloons, joints, or riverboats. In similar proto-punk fashion, jug-band musicianship ranged from rudimentary to virtuoso, often in the same group. The eclectic kitchen-sink sound and bawdy lyrics imbued the style with a surreal, carnival-like atmosphere that defiantly celebrated life's ups *and* downs.

Jug bands first recorded in the early '20s, and a flurry of groups cut sides before the craze petered out in the '30s. Harry Smith included a handful of tracks on his *Anthology* (1952), including two by the Memphis Jug Band. Will Shade was the leader and only constant member of this august troupe—possibly the first jug band in Memphis. Scores of musicians came and went during the band's four-decade career, but their heyday and artistic peak coincided with their recorded output—nearly 100 sides cut from 1927 to 1934.[182] "Cocaine Habit Blues" features Hattie Hart, a frequent guest vocalist and local Beale Street character who sang jocular songs about lust and intemperance in an earthy alto voice.

> *If you don't believe cocaine is good*
> *Ask Alma Rose at Minglewood*
> *Hey, hey, honey, take a whiff on me*

---

180 Plenty of old blues songs treat the subject more gravely–e.g., Tommy Johnson's death-by-Sterno "Canned Heat Blues" (1928), about an alcoholic straining the jellied fuel for a Prohibition-era drink ("Crying, 'Mama, Mama, Mama / You know, canned heat killin' me'"). These include more conventionally rueful (if still dark-humored) sides by women–e.g., Victoria Spivey's "Dope Head Blues" (1926), which contrasts the addict's plea ("Just give me one more sniff, another sniff of that dope") with the addict's denial ("Got double pneumonia, and still think I got the best health").

181 A priceless 1930 film clip of Louisville's Whistler and His Jug Band features a line of jug blowers in top hats performing "Folding Bed" in what looks like a vacant lot in Derby City (www.youtube.com/watch?v=rwo6HVTacYs&t=32s).

182 A superb compilation of twenty-three of these, issued as a double LP on the Yazoo label in 1981 (with iconic R. Crumb art) and reissued on CD in 1990, remains one of the essential roots music recordings.

I love my whiskey, and I love my gin
But the way I love my coke is a doggone sin
Hey, hey, honey, take a whiff on me

The father and son folklorists John and Alan Lomax collected "Cocaine Habit Blues" (as "Honey, Take a Whiff on Me") in *American Folk Ballads and Songs* (1934)—their compendium of tunes and lyrics gathered from cross-country travels and field recordings in the early twentieth century. They describe the tune as a "cheerful ditty of the dope-heads" but make no Child-like attempts to trace its source.[183] They list the "Mr. Lehman" verse and others that wound up in the Jug Band version, as well as this familiar-sounding stanza:

Goin' up State Street, comin' down Main
Lookin' for a woman that use cocaine
Ho, ho, honey, take a whiff on me

This hybrid of "Tell It to Me" and "Cocaine Habit Blues" suggests a common origin for both songs and shows how a pool of floating lines contributed to each. The verse comes from Lead Belly (Huddie Ledbetter), the folksinger incarcerated for attempted murder in 1930 and recorded by the Lomaxes, whose 1933 recording includes this cognate:

Walked up Ellum [Elm], and I come down Main
Tryin' to bum a nickel just to buy cocaine
Ho, ho, honey, take a whiff on me

Other lines—from Lead Belly, James "Iron Head" Baker, and sources unnamed—are pretty risqué. "Most of the stanzas," the Lomaxes note, "as we heard them in the prisons, are unprintable."[184]—which sure makes you wish they'd printed them. A verse that made the cut comes from Lead Belly's rendition:

The blacker the berry, the sweeter the juice
Takes a brown-skin woman for my particular use
Ho, ho, honey, take a whiff on me

Here, "whiff" takes on olfactory overtones and playfully extends the motif from cocaine use to carnal pleasure.

If the cocaine blues, as experienced by poor and ordinary folks, found broad expression in '20s and '30s roots music, it also affected popular and upscale entertainment. Pre-Code Hollywood can still startle with its frank takes on sex, race, crime, and drugs—alternately sensationalistic and

---

183   John A. Lomax and Alan Lomax, *American Ballads and Folk Songs*, (Mineola, N.Y.: Dover, 1994), p. 186.
184   Ibid.

CAB CALLOWAY, 1947

thoughtful, often simultaneously—as well as its outlandish musicals (e.g., the outrageously sexualized song-and-dance spectacles of Busby Berkeley). Traumatic periods often inspire edgy popular art but also escapist fantasy, and the Great Depression found Americans weary of moralistic condescension and hungry for adult fare. A vivid example is the number one chart-topping song of 1931—an "adult" take on drugs, lowlifes, and the high life that matches the jug bands for bawdy wit and carnival atmosphere:

Folks, here's a story 'bout Minnie the Moocher
She was a red-hot hoochie-coocher
She was the roughest, toughest frail[185]
But Minnie had a heart as big as a whale

"Minnie the Moocher" was the signature tune of Cab Calloway—the flamboyant, zoot-suited singer and bandleader whose Jazz Orchestra was the house band at Harlem's Cotton Club from 1931 to 1934. Mob-run and racially segregated, the venue featured many of the era's great Black entertainers but catered to an affluent, all-white, smart-set clientele. "Minnie the Moocher" lampoons that world. It's a cartoony portrait of a Jazz Age hoofer, hooker, and bonne vivante who lives for good times and fine things, including drugs. Minnie is an unapologetic hedonist and gold-digger—a flapper version of the Memphis Jug Band's Hattie Hart and with better connections. She's also a fantasy figure of no limits in a time of deprivation and uncertainty. Part of a cast of recurring characters in Calloway songs (she got a full-fledged sequel the following year in the nutty nuptial tribute "Minnie the Moocher's Wedding Day"), she shares the stage with oddballs that resemble campy, dope-enhanced rejects from a Disney Silly Symphony. Calloway establishes her badass credentials in four lines, and, by verse two, she's already indulging:

She messed around with a bloke named Smoky
She loved him, though he was cokey
He took her down to Chinatown
And he showed her how to kick the gong around

"The gong" is opium, and Chinatown—whether the literal enclave or a euphemism—is a wonderland of its refined derivatives. Smoky sounds like a

185 Thirties slang for a woman, à la dame or doll.

pimp (in "Minnie the Moocher's Wedding Day" he's rechristened Smoky Joe and marries Minnie). In verse three, we meet a drug kingpin who plies her with luxuries, presumably in exchange for intimate favors.

> *She had a dream about the King of Sweden*
> *He gave her things that she was needin'*
> *He gave her a home built of gold and steel*
> *A diamond car with platinum wheels*

What the radio-listening and record-buying public that sent "Minnie the Moocher" to number one made of all this is anyone's guess. The song is sufficiently whimsical that its obscure lyrics may have sailed over most people's heads while giving those in the know a chuckle.[186] "Minnie the Moocher" is an infectious, multi-part romp, its colorful lyrics punctuated with growling horns and Calloway's wacky scat singing. The song's catchy "Hi-dee hi-dee hi-dee ho" call-and-response refrain follows each verse. These novel qualities probably ingratiated "Minnie the Moocher" with the public more than its evocation of a jazzy, dreamlike demimonde. Calloway based the song's structure, dope theme, and parade of pimps and panderers on "Willie the Weeper" (1927), a piano-and-vocal novelty tune popularized by the vaudevillian Frankie "Half-Pint" Jaxon:

> *Have you ever heard about Willie the Weeper?*
> *Had a job as a chimney sweeper*
> *He had the dope habit, and he had it bad*
> *Listen, while I tell you about a dream he had*[187]

But Calloway drastically improved his source and made it his own. The cartoon vividness of his adaptation made "Minnie the Moocher" ripe for animation and, in 1932, Fleischer Studios used the song in a classic pre-Code Betty Boop short. The cartoon opens with a haunting, live-action tableau of Calloway doing a jazzy, slo-mo dance in front of his band. It then switches to an animated scenario in which Betty—a red-hot hoochie-coocher to rival Minnie—runs away from home and is serenaded in a cave by Calloway in the form of a ghostly walrus.[188] Calloway rerecorded the song for the spooky short, slowing it to a bluesy dirge.

The resulting cartoon is another kind of hoot: a hallucinatory distillation of the upscale debauchery of "Minnie the Moocher" to match the Memphis

---

186 The situation recalls Lou Reed's "Walk on the Wild Side" (1973), with its cavalcade of marginal characters (scenesters from Andy Warhol's Factory and with similarly cartoony names–e.g., Little Joe and Sugarplum Fairy). "Walk on the Wild Side" topped the charts despite its kinky (if obscured) themes and the line, "But she never lost her head / Even when she was giving head." Radio programmers apparently didn't know the term (giving head), as the record made the hit parade unmolested.

187 The song, of unknown authorship, is at least as old as 1904, when the vaudevillian Kitty Bingham performed it onstage in Boston. The Lomaxes include the tune in *American Ballads and Folk Songs* in their "Cocaine and Whisky" chapter and note that the lyrics "floated around in Texas a quarter century ago" (p. 184).

188 The Fleischer Brothers (Dave and Max) made some of the weirdest cartoons of the Depression era–loopy, menacing, but always sexy and surreal. Some feature early jazz greats. Louis Armstrong appears in "I'll Be Glad When You're Dead You Rascal You" (1931), and Calloway returns in "The Old Man of the Mountain" and "Snow White" (both 1933). He sings "St. James Infirmary" in the latter, which features the clown character Koko in a dance sequence based on a rotoscoped Calloway.

Jug Band's carnival recast of "Cocaine Habit Blues"—souvenirs of a hedonistic past that forged folk poetry from addiction's beauty and terror.

Hey, hey, honey, take a whiff on me.

HARD TIME KILLING FLOOR

Now and then a visitor wept, to be sure; but this slaughtering machine ran on,
visitors or no visitors. It was like some horrible crime committed in a dungeon,
all unseen and unheeded, buried out of sight and of memory.
—Upton Sinclair, The Jungle, *1906*

Scratchy electric guitar plays a three-chord intro and launches a funky, up-tempo groove. A walking bass line is doubled on acoustic guitar, its rhythm also tapped on drum rims. Tinkling piano fills the empty spaces, and saxophones accent an infectious guitar riff. It's one of the catchiest backings in all of blues, in frisky 4/4 time with no lugubrious triplets. By the time the big voice booms in, thirty seconds into the song, you're hooked and bobbing to the sly, sexy beat.

I shoulda quit you long time ago
I shoulda quit you, babe, long time ago
I shoulda quit you and went on to Mexico

The voice growls, swaying like a restless beast. It bellows regret, but the music is too boisterous for self-pity. Rueful words recall Delta blues, but the band is pure Chicago—sweaty electric boogie played by hot, skillful players.

If I had-a followed my first mind
If I had-a followed my first mind
I'd-a been gone since my second time

The singer takes a break, and the guitar takes a solo—rollicking, choppy chords with no picked notes. The big voice comes back, bemoaning the woman he should have quit and wishing he was south of the border.

I shoulda went on when my friend come from Mexico at me
I shoulda went on when my friend come from Mexico at me
But no, I was foolin' with ya, baby, I let ya put me on the killin' floor

"Killing Floor" by Howlin' Wolf is one of the most bracing moments in recorded blues—a seamless blend of gruff vocal and searing accompaniment that utterly captivates from first note to fade-out. Just two and a half minutes long, it fills one side of a 45 single with intricate musical interplay but never sounds busy. Lyrically, it couldn't be simpler: a fling has run its course, and the singer wishes he'd ended it sooner. He wants to be far away but instead finds himself "on thc killin' floor."

Lord knows, I shoulda been gone
Lord knows, I shoulda been gone
And I wouldn't've been here down on the killin' floor

It's a dour metaphor for an upbeat song. The killing floor is the site in slaughterhouses where animals are killed and their carcasses initially processed. In Wolf's Chicago—"Hog Butcher for the World," where the vast Union Stock Yards saw more animals killed for meat in a century than anywhere else in the world—it was a notorious workplace for African Americans who, like Wolf, left the Deep South for the Windy City during the Great Migration. Wolf never worked the stockyards, but he did general labor on family farms in Mississippi and Arkansas, where he killed his share of livestock.

"Killing floor" in the song's context refers to a state of depression, of feeling defeated by circumstance, burdened by the weight of the world. That the filthy environs of old-school abattoirs inspired the trope is fitting. These were hellish places, awash in blood and gore, where low-wage workers with few rights performed hazardous labor in a claustrophobic environment of chaos and cruelty. The labyrinthine Chicago yards, with their boundless sprawl of livestock pens and multi-level processing plants, were especially dismal; one needn't be an activist to describe them as death camps for animals. But they were also debilitating and deadly for workers: injuries and fatalities were common, and the impact of daylong assembly-line slaughter on mental health was profound.[189]

Wolf recorded "Killing Floor" in 1964, three decades into his career and twelve years after settling in Chicago. But the phrase had been in blues vernacular for much longer. It appears in Son House's "Dry Spell Blues" (1930) ("The dry spell blues have put everybody on the killing floor") but before Wolf's song was best known from "Hard Time Killing Floor Blues," a 1931 side by the idiosyncratic bluesman Skip James. Both songs use the term as a metaphor for mental depression,[190] inspired by the then-current Great Depression. Perhaps its metaphoric use was as old as the Chicago stockyards (founded in 1865). Workers who traveled back and forth from rural South to urban North, often struggling to save enough money to relocate their families, no doubt brought

---

189 Recent studies document the harmful effects on workers of killing animals at great speed in loud, enclosed spaces. Slaughterhouse employees are far more likely to be injured on the job than other laborers, but the mental toll is equally calamitous: in 2002, the psychologist Rachel McNair coined the term Perpetration-Induced Traumatic Stress (PITS) to describe a PTSD-like condition where workers are traumatized by causing trauma. Note that these data pertain to more modern and better regulated slaughterhouses than were imaginable in the heyday of the Chicago yards.

190 As does every variation I'm aware of. Even the comic bluesman Peter Joe "Doctor" Clayton's song "On the Killing Floor" (1942) is a lighthearted look at despair, wherein "high-priced whiskey and women done put me on the killin' floor."

the term with them. But the South had slaughterhouses too, and "killing floor" was also a farm term. Notably, the phrase only exists in blues *as* a metaphor— i.e., there are no blues songs about ubiquitous and brutal meatpacking work. This is hardly surprising, as blues was meant to provide *release* from despair, plus income for performers.

Still, it was better than sharecropping in the Jim Crow South. Wolf (born Chester Arthur Burnett in 1910) did hard labor there, but a chance meeting with Charley Patton—Father of the Delta Blues, whose showboating style influenced the fledgling musician—set him on the path to Chicago and fame. It was a circuitous route but, by the time he recorded "Killing Floor," he was a towering figure of the form who, like his rival genius Muddy Waters, lived long enough to be lauded by a mass audience before his death in 1976. Wolf's larger-than-life persona and deep, raspy voice left an indelible imprint on blues, rock, and R&B. The stellar backing on "Killing Floor" includes his labelmate Buddy Guy on acoustic guitar. But the linchpin of the arrangement is the lead guitarist Hubert Sumlin—a Wolf sideman for a decade, whose twangy electric riffing creates an earworm as addictive as the song's springy rhythm section. Credited to Wolf, "Killing Floor" is a mid-'60s highlight from his last period of good health (heart and kidney ailments would curtail his touring and recording in the early '70s), a time when blues-obsessed rock-and-rollers (the Rolling Stones, the Yardbirds, the Doors) were discovering his music and covering his songs.

But if rockers were immersing themselves in the blues, blues players were also learning from rock. "Killing Floor" integrates influences from '50s rockabilly and nascent funk (a still embryonic style in 1964) yet remains blues in form and content. Its funky feel belies its standard twelve-bar structure. The song's crossover appeal registers in diverse covers by non-blues artists in various styles, from Jimi Hendrix (heavy rock, late '60s) to the Electric Flag (soul-gospel, 1968), while blues covers tend toward funk, whether slow-burn (Albert King, 1969) or fiery (Smokey Wilson, 1993).[191]

Wolf's "Killing Floor" exemplifies blues as good-time catharsis—a down-and-dirty nighttime antidote to daytime trials and tribulations, redolent of smoky rooms, bawdy dancing, and ample corn liquor. Even the morose lyrics sound triumphant. Put in a funk by a past-its-shelf-date affair, the singer shakes his way off the killing floor by singing about it. Before his death in 2011, Sumlin claimed a comical subtext for the song. He told the author and musician Debra Devi that "Helen," a girlfriend of Wolf, suspected him of infidelity on the road. So she searched his tour bus for evidence and uncovered some ladies' underwear. Sumlin insisted the drawers implicated not Wolf but one of his band. But Helen would not be appeased. "She shot him with a double-barrel shotgun with buckshot," said Sumlin. "Out the second-floor window. This woman, oh man,

---

191 The best-known rock version, really a variant, is Led Zeppelin's "The Lemon Song," from *Led Zeppelin II* (1969). It adapts Sumlin's riff and some of Wolf's words but also arbitrarily throws in Robert Johnson's "squeeze my lemon 'til the juice runs down my leg" line from "Traveling Roadside Blues" (1937). It's one of Zeppelin's least inventive blues appropriations— comparatively plodding beside "Dazed and Confused" or "When the Levee Breaks," which reimagine blues as expansive, Wagnerian psychedelia.

he wrote that song about her!"[192] It's possible the incident inspired the song, though the bare-bones lyric contains no verifying details. The anecdote does add weight (and comedy) to its forlorn lines ("I shoulda quit you, long time ago," indeed). Sumlin: "They picked shots out of him for a whole week." Wolf married the love of his life, Lillie Handley, in 1964 (they had lived together since the '50s). She never shot him, and they remained happily married until his death.

HOWLIN' WOLF, 1972

While Wolf enjoyed a late-career peak, Skip James—whose Depression-era lament "Hard Time Killing Floor Blues" likely inspired his song—was being belatedly rediscovered. James had released one of the most challenging sets of blues ever recorded in 1931: twenty-six songs featuring his eerie falsetto and intricate guitar work that he cut in Grafton, Wisconsin, for the Paramount label. Despite their high quality and innovative sound, sales were poor and James felt financially shafted. The experience was sufficiently devastating that he quit music. In the aftermath, James was twice ordained as a minister (Baptist and Methodist), though it's unclear whether he worked as a preacher. Mostly, he farmed. Forty years later, he was still bitter, telling the music writer Peter Guralnick, "Why'd I quit? I was so disappointed ... I cut twenty-six sides ... I didn't get paid but forty dollars. That's not doing very good. Wouldn't you be disappointed?"[193] A moody man convinced (with reason) of his greatness, he felt sidelined and forgotten by history. In June 1964, two months before Wolf cut "Killing Floor," a trio of white blues fans (Bill Barth, John Fahey, and Henry Vestine) located James in a Tunica, Mississippi, hospital. They brought him a guitar (he didn't own one), paid his bills, and coaxed him out of retirement. That July, he mesmerized a crowd of mostly white, college-educated blues enthusiasts at the Newport Folk Festival. He was grateful for the renewed interest, performing live and releasing several albums of old and new material before his death in 1969. But he remained cautious with businesspeople and aloof with fans.

Nehemiah "Skip" James was nine years older than Wolf. Born in 1901 in Bentonia, Mississippi, he built levees and worked on road crews in the '20s. His father was a bootlegger turned preacher, and, as a teenager, James played church organ (after quitting the blues in the early '30s, he worked for a time as choir director for his father's congregation). He learned guitar and piano,

192 Debra Devi, *The Language of the Blues* (Jersey City, N.J.: Nature Books, 2012), pp. 156-157.
193 Peter Guralnick, *Feel Like Going Home: Portraits in Blues and Rock 'n' Roll* (New York: Harper & Row, 1989), p. 111.

developing unique styles on both. His guitar had a resonant, otherworldly sound that resulted partly from using open D minor tuning (D–A–D–F–A–D). Combined with his keening vocals, the effect was spine-tingling. He strongly influenced Robert Johnson, whose chilling "Hellhound on My Trail" (1937) was inspired by James's "Devil Got My Woman" (1931). James shunned standard song structures as he shunned standard tuning, and his deeply personal take on the blues sounded like no one else.

"Hard Time Killing Floor Blues" was a highlight of his Paramount sessions—a rare topical tune inspired by the desperate mood that enveloped the country after Black Tuesday, 1929. Its mournful opening lines set the scene like a jittery newsreel of breadlines and Hoovervilles, the scratches on the source record mimicking abrasions on old film stock.

Hard times here and everywhere you go
Times is harder than ever been before

And the people are driftin' from door to door
Can't find no heaven, I don't care where they go

The words are slow and steady, the voice a hypnotic moan. After the second couplet, James hums a doleful countermelody and, for the rest of the song, alternates singing with humming—the latter, a wordless lament.

Let me tell you people, just before I go
These hard times'll kill you, just dry long so[194]
When you hear me singin' my true lonesome song
These hard times can last us so very long

James rerecorded "Hard Time Killing Floor Blues" more than once before his death, with improved sound and slight lyrical variations. But he never bested the original. It remains an affecting artifact of the pre-FDR Depression—when recovery for all but the wealthy seemed like a pipe dream and proud people taught that charity was wrong had to choose between begging and starving.

If I ever get off-a this killin' floor
I'll never get down this low no more

It's a far cry from Wolf's slinky hootenanny—a dark night of the (collective) soul laid bare rather than purged. Both approaches characterize blues but rarely so divergently. Partly it's temperament—the two men were opposites in many ways. James was introspective, a loner who never left the South. He spoke in a

---

194 "To be 'dry long so' is to be worn out by poverty to the point where it feels like you're not going to make it" (Devi, *The Language of the Blues*, p. 100).

stiff, at times portentous manner, and in performance his high voice and refined playing elicited concentrated silence from listeners. Wolf, on the other hand, was plainspoken, widely traveled, and an over-the-top entertainer—Dionysus to James's Apollo. He roared from his gut onstage, shaking his 6' 3", 300-pound frame, tossing his guitar in the air, and lewdly straddling his mic stand. These contrary natures extended to their careers: while both men could be self-pitying, it's impossible to imagine as driven a performer as Wolf giving up after an early setback as James had done.

If you say you had money, you better be sure
Lord, these hard times'll drive you from door to door

James repeatedly returns to this image of panhandling "door to door." It must have symbolized the worst losses of the economic catastrophe: independence and self-sufficiency, but also pride and hard-won dignity—especially gut-wrenching privations for a Southern African American. The phrase also appears in Son House's "Dry Spell Blues," released a year before James's song and in the same hard-times context:

The dry spell blues have fallen, drive me from door to door
Dry spell blues have fallen, drive me from door to door
The dry spell blues have put everybody on the killing floor

It turns up in Doctor Clayton's comical "On the Killing Floor" as well:

Lord, it's zero weather, and I ain't got a lousy dime
Lord, it's zero weather, and I ain't got a lousy dime
I'm walkin' from door to door, and I can't find a friend of mine

It's a common phrase but likely found its way into the Clayton song from James.

Two little-known but commanding films further explore the killing-floor theme. *The Killing Floor* (1984) is a dramatic episode of the PBS anthology series *American Playhouse* about a Mississippi sharecropper migrating to Chicago. He finds work in the stockyards and transforms from an apolitical transplant grateful to have a job to a union organizer anxious to secure rights for his fellow workers. It's a well-made TV movie (by a first-time director, Bill Duke) featuring the athlete-turned-actor Damien Leake as the worker-turned-activist. The fact-based film begins during the First World War and ends with the race riots that shook Chicago in 1919. Decades after release, it's still striking to see a mostly Black cast in a historical drama that's neither *Masterpiece Theater* snooty nor Spielberg sentimental and that portrays labor struggles honestly in a country where the powerful have always been overwhelmingly anti-union.

The odyssey of Leake's character, from migrant to man-with-a-mission, is a psycho-geographic tour of killing-floor blues. He starts as a hayseed in a family shack, driven by Great Migration dreams to head north for a better life. Once in Chicago, his only goal beyond survival is to make enough money to relocate his family from Mississippi. "Mister," he tells a German-American union man who tries to recruit him early in the film, "I come up here to make a living. I ain't gettin' in no white man's war, no sir." But the realities of job insecurity and exploitation explode his simple worldview.

The slaughterhouse is the backdrop to his awakening—an oppressive maze of dingy stone-and-metal rooms where men, bound by economic need, kill to survive and argue bitterly over whether to fight for more or settle for less. A triumph of the low-budget film is its smooth integration of live action with (often non-contemporary) stock footage of the Union Yards. Images of workers killing and chopping livestock, factory-style, add somber ambience and imply links between workers and animals without hammering viewers over the head. The literal killing floor contrasts with the sunny union hall, where Leake is converted to collective action and helps helm a fragile coalition of racially and ethnically diverse workers. When the war ends, industrialists move to crush labor gains by replacing unionists with returning troops and fomenting racial distrust. Racial and ethnic tensions exacerbate economic turmoil as segregated communities fight over jobs, housing, and turf. The 1919 riots erupt, further crippling the coalition. (The real-life trigger of the tumult goes unmentioned in the film: white–Black rancor exploded when an African American teenager drifted into a "whites only" swimming area and died from a hurled stone. Violence swept the city for days, and authorities exploited the conflagration to weaken the labor movement.) The film ends in tragedy, with no uplifting finale.[195]

The Killing Floor's balance of optimism and despair mirrored its times. Filming began just two years after Ronald Reagan fired 11,345 striking air traffic controllers—the opening volley in an aggressive (and ongoing) effort to reverse a century's worth of labor advancement. But it also coincided with the election of the pro-union candidate Harold Washington as Chicago's first Black mayor. Washington was a non-machine politician elected by a coalition of minority and left-leaning voters. He served one fruitful term and won a second but died in office. Mayoral politics quickly reverted to establishment mode, but Washington had briefly given hope to the city's least powerful. His campaign volunteers played extras in the film, and multiple unions worked on the production.

If *The Killing Floor* is superior entertainment, the second film, *Killer of Sheep* (1977), is unabashedly arthouse—a nearly plotless assemblage of vignettes about life in '70s Watts, centered on a dispirited slaughterhouse worker. *Killer of Sheep* is the debut film by Charles Burnett (it was, in fact, his MFA thesis), a critically acclaimed African American director whose work has never found a mainstream audience, and, like many first films by serious directors, it's an

---

195 *The Killing Floor's* dour ending recalls another fact-based film about union-busting–John Sayles's despairing *Matewan* (1987), about West Virginia coal miners. Neither film is fatalistic, but both are unflinching about the uphill struggle of class war.

experimental and uncompromising work that rejects Hollywood conventions and aspires unapologetically to art.

Killer of Sheep is an immersive experience, its washed-out black-and-white photography as vital as the glimpses it gives into its protagonist's downcast life. He lays linoleum, scolds his kids, helps repair a friend's car, tries (and fails) to make love to his wife, tries (and fails) to take his family on a racetrack outing. Poverty and despair are omnipresent, and every morning he returns to his soul-crushing job at the slaughterhouse. The film's tone is simultaneously naturalistic, dreamlike, and hard to shake. *Killer of Sheep* germinated from a chance encounter on a bus between Burnett and a meatpacker. Burnett asked the man what he did, and he replied, "I kill sheep." In those days, Burnett recalled, "they would hit the animal in the head with [a] sledgehammer and crush the skull. And I couldn't imagine someone doing that every day, day in and day out, without creating some nightmare effect."[196] The film's protagonist, played by Henry Gayle Sanders (a non-actor, like much of the cast), lives out that disturbance. His depressed affect is equally rooted in the trauma of his work, the poverty that engulfs him, and his inability to escape. Unsurprisingly, we learn that he is a migrant who left the South for a better life (as were Burnett's parents, who left Mississippi for Los Angeles when the director was three).

Music is central to *Killer of Sheep*, and Burnett uses an eclectic mix, from Paul Robeson to Sergei Rachmaninoff, as reflective counterpoint to the film's austere visuals. Many scenes involve children who romp and squabble in their dust-and-debris ghetto playground. To emphasize their vulnerability, Burnett often cuts from their mischievous play to the sheep in the slaughterhouse. (The slaughterhouse footage, used sparingly in the film, is all real.) In one scene, young bike riders careen recklessly on a neighborhood street, laughing as cars slam brakes and loose dogs scamper in circles. We then see a grim montage of sheep carcasses on meat hooks, slid down an overhead line to the dirge-like blues of Little Walter's "Mean Old World" (1953).

This is a mean old world
Try to live it by yourself
This is a mean old world
Try to live it by yourself

Can't get the one you're lovin'
Have to use somebody else

The film's last sequence begins with a rare upbeat scene: a disabled young woman tells female friends she's pregnant, tracing a baby bump with her finger to laughter and smiles. Burnett follows this hopeful shot with haunting images of live sheep hoisted by workers onto hooks, stunned with bolts and bled out, to the mournful strains of Dinah Washington's "This Bitter Earth" (1961).

196   Robert E. Kapsis, ed., *Charles Burnett: Interviews* (Jackson: University Press of Mississippi, 2011), p. 166.

And if my life is like the dust
That hides the glow of a rose
What good am I?
Heaven only knows

Oh, this bitter earth
Yes, can it be so cold?
Today you're young
Too soon you're old

It's a poignant moment that pulls together strands of narrative, image, and sound. It also highlights how the film doesn't simply dramatize scenes with music. Instead, it integrates all elements—low-key episodic plot, everyday visuals, subdued, moody soundtrack—into a seamless whole. The result has few dynamic shifts and emphasizes getting by over hurling oneself at the world. In this, it resembles the music that first gave voice to the killing-floor theme, from Skip James to Howlin' Wolf.

Non-fans complain that blues is monotonous, repetitive, and passive—that it lacks variety and never breaks from despair. Yet these qualities reflect the life experience of the Black Americans who created the form—the drudgery, immobility, and sense of being trapped that results from poverty and racism. "You don't necessarily win battles," Burnett once said, "you survive."[197] His film captures this rueful sense of inertia—in its story but also the oppressive sameness of its design. In other words, *Killer of Sheep* isn't just a bluesy evocation of lives lived on the killing floor. Rather, it *feels* like the blues—like the blues reimagined as film.

WORSE THAN THE THING THAT POSSESSED ME

What is the knocking?
What is the knocking at the door in the night?
It is somebody wants to do us harm.

No, no, it is the three strange angels.
Admit them, admit them.

—D. H. Lawrence, "Song of a Man Who Has Come Through," *1914*

Three songs, all post-punk. Each concerns a young woman enduring inner turmoil, attended by (mostly) male caregivers. Two of them, drawn from life, suffer baffling physical symptoms. Both die. The third, a cipher based partly on a real person, fades with the song.

An electric guitar peals like thunder, evoking a late-night storm. The turbulence is mild, not overpowering—moody like the unfolding, mid-tempo

197   Michael Sragow, "Explorer of the Black Mind Looks Back, but Not in Anger," *New York Times*, 1 January 1995.

track. The ambience is Gothic, not goth: echo-drenched guitar, accordion, violin, and vocal over hypnotic bass and drums, with words that seem to place us in a decaying manor house on a windswept heath—like something from the Brontë sisters with a dash of Vincent Price. Lyrics are vivid but impressionistic, swaying like a pendulum between clarity and dreamlike vagueness.

He stood naked outside the door
Handsome with dark eyes flashing
The winds blew straight in off the moor
The sisters stopped their pacing

Through the flickering firelight
Shadows jumped across the room
Pounding hearts and rushing blood
Romantic thoughts and fears

It's a gem of associative scene-setting, grounding the listener in the menace and mystery of dark Romantic tropes ripe with tempestuous but sublimated passions. But no Heathcliff or Roderick Usher bursts in the door, naked or otherwise. Instead, the chorus introduces a tragically resigned protagonist, her storied name not from Victorian literature but seminal psychiatry.

Dora, Dora, looking in the mirror
Dora, Dora, acting out in Mother's clothes
Dreaming, dreaming
No one will ever know
Dora, Dora

The name derives from an early case of Sigmund Freud's—a pseudonym the founding psychoanalyst gave to a patient he treated but failed to cure, as outlined in an influential treatise on his theories and methods called *Dora: A Case of Hysteria* (1905).[198] The song "Dora" comes from *So Good It Hurts* (1988), the sixth studio album by the pioneering British post-punks the Mekons. It is less "about" Freud's Dora than a musing on her legacy and the notion that damaged women were often further damaged by men given authority over their well-being.

Dora (real name: Ida Bauer) was a depressed middle-class teenager in Vienna who, during a family crisis, inexplicably lost her voice.[199] Freud believed that profound trauma, left unconfronted, could manifest in physical disorders and dubbed the phenomenon "hysteria." That insight remains controversial with ongoing debate about psychosocial ramifications, proper treatment, and mind–body dynamics. In feminist circles, the term "hysteria"—redolent of pejorative nineteenth-century diagnoses of sexually uninhibited women (that predated Freud)—aroused resentment; it's since been replaced with the blander epithet

---

198   Original title: *Fragments of an Analysis of a Case of Hysteria*.
199   Medical term: aphonia, and typically caused by disease of or injury to the larynx or mouth. Dora had none of these conditions.

"conversion disorder."[200] Freud felt Dora's aphonia was a subconscious response to interfamily drama with repressed sexual overtones.[201] She made progress under his care but, after eleven weeks, abruptly ended treatment.

Dora's lost voice reverberates through time and culture. As a symbol for the whole or true self, its restoration is the goal of psychoanalysis, but, as a metaphor for women denied agency and expression, it has tragic echoes. An uneasy undercurrent suggests that men tinkering with women's psyches, especially in the past, was problematic at best, even by healers with good intentions. Masculine ego, ambition, aggression, condescension, and, at times, outright misogyny jeopardized female patients and asserted orthodoxies of normalcy that stifled authentic voice.[202]

"Dora" by the Mekons is a standout track on a transitional album—a foray into Caribbean and other non-rock styles after a trio of trailblazing records merged existential, left-wing punk with American country music. "Dora" stuck out from amid the experimentation—partly because it was atmospheric rock amidst reggae, Cajun, and calypso dabbling, rooted less in "world music" than in the band's West Yorkshire heritage, but also because it showcased the soaring vocals of the band's (relatively) new secret weapon, the soprano Sally Timms, whose clear singing and formidable presence gave the track added power.[203]

After the chorus name-check, "Dora" picks up not on the moors but in posh London on a fashionable psychoanalyst's couch.

The autumn leaves are falling
Through a dreary evening sky
In St. John's Wood, a woman waits
Sitting on a leather sofa

The psychiatrist smiled sadly
As she uncrossed her legs
The ticking of an antique clock
Penetrates the gloom

---

200 This pre-Freudian milieu was typically misogynistic and anti-sex. Sexually active women were condemned as immoral and masturbation was demonized as a practice that led to drooling imbecility. Women who "self-abused" could face institutionalization, and cures proposed by clinicians and clerics ranged from ascetic living to graver remedies (cold enemas, irritants applied to the genitals) to reduce recidivism—up to and including clitorectomy. Freud rejected such savagery and sought a healthier, more humane attitude toward sex.

201 A drama sufficiently complex to preclude summarization here, involving a syphilitic invalid father, parental affairs, lesbian urges, a mother with a house-cleaning mania, and improper advances by a paternal family friend. Steven Marcus described the scenario in his *Representations: Essays on Literature and Society* (New York: Random House, 1976, p. 253) as a "classical Victorian domestic drama, that is at the same time a sexual and emotional can of worms."

202 Here, Freud's record is mixed. He failed to question many chauvinistic assumptions of his era (e.g., that women needn't be educated and should confine themselves to domestic life). But his rejection of puritanical sexual attitudes was liberating, and throughout his career he dismissed notions of "normalcy" as relative and untenable. Thornier are his (often contradictory) notions of female desire: he acknowledged its existence but seemed incapable of seeing it as an active, not passive, trait.

203 Timms debuted on *The Edge of the World* (1986) and immediately expanded the Mekons' sound and sensibility—her graceful singing augmented the band's more rough-hewn male vocals, and her outspoken, at times outrageous, personality recalibrated their gender dynamic.

In a song of shifting locales, where plot never fully takes hold, Dora most resembles Freud's patient here. But it's all shorthand—a dreamy collage of cultural signifiers like the previous Gothic pastiche, wherein motifs trigger associations through juxtaposition. If the moors evoke a Dionysian squall of repressed emotion and London an analytical coolness, Dora remains passive in both—submissive and half-formed. Timms's ascendant but sad vocal seems to hover over her, urging her to take wing.

> *Dora, Dora, see the man is writing*
> *Writing down all the words you say*
> *We know, don't we*
> *The truth is locked away*
> *Dora, Dora*

Tom Greenhalgh, who co-wrote the song, confirms this lyrical approach. "I can't remember exactly why I picked on Dora," he told me. "I hadn't at that time read any primary-text Freud, but was reading Juliet Mitchell's *Psychoanalysis and Feminism,* which I had heard was a really good exposition of Freud with feminist correctives . . . The whole Brontë Romanticism/sublimated female sexuality allusions fit perfectly."[204]

Mitchell's book is, in fact, sympathetic to Freud—a non-knee-jerk attempt to square his innovation and compassion with his failings and overreach and, in the process, save what is valuable in his psychology. "The greater part of the feminist movement has identified Freud as the enemy," Mitchell wrote, "[but] a rejection of psychoanalysis and of Freud's works is fatal for feminism."[205] Freud himself felt he had failed Dora through poor handling of her transference—the tendency of patients to project thoughts and feelings about troubling people in their lives onto their analyst. But second-wave feminism also took him to task for badgering her. In the words of the scholar Peter Gay, "Freud . . . has been charged with still another failure: a striking inability to set aside his male prejudices, a lack of empathy with a suffering adolescent girl being victimized by egoistic adults—including her father." He then acknowledges, "There is a good deal to this charge."[206]

Reading *Dora* one is struck at times by how he harangues her, how he seems to forget she is a fragile teenager, how his eagerness to prove his theories makes him pushy and insensitive. No doubt this played a role in her cessation of treatment. Greenhalgh told me, "If I remember rightly, Dora [eventually] tells Freud to shove it."[207]

Appropriate for a cipher, "Dora" ends with a last shift of environment—this time to a scene of ritual debauchery, seemingly in an upscale bordello, where Dora has either disappeared or gone to work.

---

204 Interview by the author, 2022.
205 Juliet Mitchell, *Psychoanalysis and Feminism: Freud, Reich, Laing, and Women* (New York: Random House, Vintage, 1975), p. xiii.
206 Peter Gay, introductory remarks, *The Freud Reader* (New York: W. W. Norton & Co., 1989), p. 173.
207 Interview by the author, 2022.

In the pitch-black dungeon
Slaves touched up the black paint
Upstairs the maid took details on the phone
"She's twenty-seven with a lovely figure
Experienced in these careful arts"
The purr of an expensive car
In the alleyway outside

At the risk of spoiling a good mystery, Greenhalgh and his fellow Mekon Jon Langford both told me that this lyric was inspired by stories they heard from the musician Dick Taylor. The former Pretty Things guitarist and founding Rolling Stone played blistering lead guitar on the Mekons' country-punk records when such virtuosity was beyond their capabilities. At the time, he supplemented his musical income as an odd-jobber. As Greenhalgh said, "Dick Taylor was doing various delivery jobs to make ends meet and told us some amusing details about this upmarket S&M brothel [where] he'd been delivering furniture . . . As I remember, it was all very droll, business-like, and down to earth."[208]

Second song. Less descriptive, more abstract and abrasive. Also mid-tempo, but built on asymmetrical guitar hooks and jarring, syncopated drums. Where the vocal in "Dora" is plaintive but smooth, this singer sounds tightly wound—struggling to communicate without coming unglued.

That last one messed me up
Things look bad, things look tragic

It's a strange opening line. We have no idea what the singer's talking about, but it feels ominous. The carefully sketched, allusive scenes from "Dora" are gone, replaced with urgently sung staccato phrases. Quickly, a new woman is named—another elusive central figure whose presence haunts the song.

I keep looking in the mirror
Afraid that I won't be there
Courting Ellen West, dancing on her grave
Saving Ellen West

The singer fears she will vanish or is already gone. As her identity crumbles, or shatters, or simply fades away, she invokes this mystery woman, fully aware that she's inaccessible by mortal means. The day-lit, lucid world gives way to a realm of spirits where there is no rest.

My house is full of demons, I swear to God
I need to go to bed

---

208 Ibid.

I need to go to sleep
I'm awake with a vengeance

The "need"s of this refrain are drawn-out and desperate (*I neeeeeeeeed*)—
pleas for relief from exhaustion and attendant madness as waking and dream
states merge. The music builds and releases like labored breathing—all barbed-
wire guitar and thunderous drums. Verbs accumulate confusingly: *courting,
dancing, saving.*

Courting Ellen West, dancing on her grave
Saving Ellen West
'Cause she wanted it this way

Ellen West is another lost voice from the past—like Dora, a tormented soul
attended by a revered psychiatrist who failed to cure her. She was a bright,
creative young woman, an engaging writer and poet, who suffered from a severe
eating disorder and death obsession that ultimately took her life. In 1921, she
was treated by Ludwig Binswanger, a Swiss-born analyst who incorporated ideas
from existentialism into his psychology. Like Dora, her name is a pseudonym
(her real name remains unknown). Her case haunted Binswanger, who published
an account of it decades after her death.[209]

The song "Ellen West" is a harrowing highlight of *The Real Ramona* (1991)—the
fourth album by the college rockers Throwing Muses, a band that gave voice
to the tempestuous inner vision of the songwriter and vocalist Kristin Hersh.
Like the Mekons' "Dora," the Muses' "Ellen West" evokes both a flesh-and-blood
person and an archetype of a fractured psyche that still haunts history.

West grew up in a middle-class family with a history of depression and
suicide. Spirited and intelligent, she kept diaries and wrote poetry starting
in her teens. In her twenties, she became acutely weight-conscious and
developed symptoms of anorexia nervosa and bulimia. She craved food but
feared gaining weight, so she starved herself, took laxatives, and binged
and purged. She grew fixated on death—both as a release from debilitating
depression and the absurdity of her can't eat/must eat to survive predicament.
One of her poems opens: "Creator, Creator / Take me back! Create me a second
time / And create me better!"[210] Like a modern Gnostic, she split the world
into opposing realms—a "tomb world" of banal materialism and an "ethereal
world" of transcendent freedom. She associated her body, with its incessant
need for nourishment, with the former. Trapped in irresolvable conflict, she
used her poetic gifts to express her plight and suicidal urges as a Phoenix-like
rebirth by fire:

---

209 Initially in German. Widespread attention followed the publication of a translated account in a collection of essays edited
by the American psychologist Rollo May (with Ernest Angel and Henri F. Ellenberger) in 1958: *Existence: A New Dimension in
Psychiatry and Psychology* (New York: Basic Books).
210 C. George Boeree, "Ludwig Binswanger," *Personality Theories* website, 1997/2006, webspace.ship.edu/cgboer/
binswanger.html.

I'd like to die just as the birdling does
That splits his throat in highest jubilation;
And not to live as the worm on earth lives on,
Becoming old and ugly, dull and dumb!
No, feel for once how forces in me kindle,
And wildly be consumed in my own fire.[211]

Maternal instinct kicked in, like the life force asserting itself. She wanted a child and, at twenty-eight, married a cousin, but her emaciated body couldn't sustain a pregnancy and she miscarried. She sought psychiatric treatment and, after several suicide attempts, checked into Binswanger's private hospital. He prescribed a healthy diet, sedatives, and psychoanalysis. She improved slightly under his care, then discharged herself. Like many desperate people who take their lives, she became strangely calm at the end. She wrote letters to family and friends and, for the first time in years, ate her fill of favorite foods. She then took poison and died.

Hersh discovered West's story in college. She told me she was moved by the tragic finality of her story, wherein "the lead character is beyond help." West's powers of expression struck Hersh as "raw and rich and human, at a time when the animal in women was something to be ashamed of, or, at best, downplayed." West also resonated with her life and music.[212]

Throwing Muses were formed by the stepsisters Hersh and Tanya Donnelly while still in their teens.[213] Their sound was earthy yet abstract, reconfiguring folk, pop, and punk influences with shifting dynamics and off-kilter rhythms. In 1986, they signed to 4AD, the British indie label that took post-punk in a dark, dreamy direction with bands like Bauhaus, Cocteau Twins, and the Pixies. Hersh dominated vocals and songwriting, and her stream-of-consciousness lyrics dove headfirst into emotional chaos, but, if the operative template was coffeehouse confessional, the resulting music exploded stereotypes of bad poetry by thrift-store bohemians. Hersh's songs are intense and idiosyncratic—surreal, obtuse, at times impenetrable, but rarely precious.

For years, she had no memory of writing them. Words spilled uncensored from her unconscious, and she dutifully set them to music. "Automatic writing," she called her process, and the allusion to Spiritualist practice resonates with her lyrics, in which ghosts, hauntings, and possession are recurring themes.[214] Such metaphors allowed her to express the dislocation and despair caused by a lifelong struggle with mental illness—of feeling ghostlike, half-there or half invisible, coexisting with an alien personality. Over the years, she was diagnosed with schizophrenia, bipolar disorder,

211 Ludwig Binswanger, "The Case of Ellen West," in Rollo May, Ernest Angel, and Henri F. Ellenberger, eds., *Existence: A New Dimension in Psychiatry and Psychology* (Lanham, Md.: Rowman & Littlefield, 2004), p. 246.

212 Interview by the author, 2022.

213 Donnelly left the band after *The Real Ramona*, in 1991. She went on to co-form the Breeders and front her own band, Belly.

214 Multiple interviews, including Alex Swift, *Buzz* magazine, 19 March 2019, www.buzzmag.co.uk/kristin-hersh-interview.

and post-traumatic stress disorder (PTSD) and treated with talk therapy, medication, and hospitalization. Finally, after more than thirty years of uncertainty and spottily effective treatment, she was diagnosed with a dissociative disorder.[215] The description fit: she often felt "outside" of herself while writing and performing and credited her early music with Throwing Muses to another personality.[216] A subsequent regimen of EMDR (Eye Movement Desensitization and Reprocessing) helped her turn a corner toward wellness.[217]

KRISTIN HERSH, 2010

Part of EMDR's premise is that the mind, like the body, moves naturally toward self-repair when injured but traumatic events can cause blocks in smooth functioning that require confrontation and assimilation. Such self-repair has particular relevance for artists, who turn instinctively to creativity as a form of healing.[218] Hersh was hit by a car while bicycling at sixteen, and a double concussion triggered auditory hallucinations she felt compelled to turn into songs. West used poetry to express life-threatening internal contradictions in nonobjective ways. Both women's turmoil was multilayered, with physical, mental, and spiritual dimensions, and cried out for holistic healing. Unfortunately, integrative perspectives are rare in our culture of specialization: niches are the norm, with body, mind, and spirit treated separately.

Binswanger sensed this dissonance and sought to resolve it. His colleague Freud saw neurosis as symptomatic of social maladjustment—a flaw that needed fixing to achieve successful assimilation, but, for Binswanger, it was existential: it expressed a need to adapt oneself not to society but to all of existence. Thus, he rejected the privileged position given "objective" reality in psychology and elevated subjective truth. He strove to understand the personal reality of his

215 "Dissociative disorders involve problems with memory, identity, emotion, perception, behavior and sense of self. Dissociative symptoms can potentially disrupt every area of mental functioning … [S]ymptoms include the experience of detachment or feeling as if one is outside one's body, and loss of memory or amnesia. Dissociative disorders are frequently associated with previous experience of trauma" (American Psychiatric Association).

216 She dubbed this doppelgänger "Rat Girl" and, in 2010, published a memoir of the same name that documented a year in her life (1985-86) in which she coped with her band's ascendant popularity, her first pregnancy, and her mental health struggles.

217 EMDR is a psychotherapeutic treatment developed in the late twentieth century wherein controlled eye movement and talk therapy help people process and recover from traumatic memories.

218 The psychiatrist Kay Redfield Jamison's book *Touched with Fire: Manic-Depressive Illness and the Artistic Temperament* (New York: Free Press, 1993) documents how artists with mood disorders, from Lord Byron to Vincent van Gogh, instinctively used creative work for self-healing. Jamison, herself bipolar, argues that this is an innate mechanism–that the fragmented psyche seeks integration through art, music, and writing.

patients—their *Eigenwelt*, or "way of being" in the world—and treat the total person. Tragically, by the time he treated West, her way of being was a closed system—an unsustainable cycle of wanting to be fully alive, like the jubilant birdling, while slowly self-immolating. Binswanger felt helpless to help her. She had, in a sense, died long ago; it was only a matter of her body catching up with her "existential" death. Ultimately, she turned a passive suicide into an active one, and Binswanger refused to condemn her for it. He grieved her loss but felt she had at least taken control of her tortured life by ending it with an act of will.

"Ellen West" ends with a last litany of "needs"—urgent but unobtainable:

I need to go to bed
I need to go to sleep
I need that hope chest
I need it to breathe
I need you here
I need to disappear

Last song. This one is lumbering and loud, a shrill rant set to booming drums, speaker-shaking bass, and a slashing two-chord guitar riff. It runs for nearly seven minutes and seems to dare you to last as long. If "Dora" is a moody nocturne and "Ellen West" is a warped pop tune, this song is an aural assault. Lyrically, it trades the hazy half-narrative of "Dora" and the dreamlike soliloquy of "Ellen West" for a full-tilt screed.

Think I'm proud to be your enemy?
Take your hands off of me
You're worse than the thing that possessed me

Every line is shriek-sung in bold with an exclamation point. The singer doesn't so much tell a story as editorialize around fragments of narrative. Dub-style bass plays a thunderous pattern while drums pound four beats to the bar. Only the guitar varies, adding dissonant cadenzas to its basic riff. The barrage of words comes in verse-like blocks, each ending with a woman's name.

The way they were
The way they should have been
Annalisa

The name is drawn out, its syllables stretched and tremulous, like a deranged call to prayer ("Anna-liiiiiiiii-saaaaaa").

Annalisa was 15 years
Stole her soul
But I hear no tears
Ever been alone

And heard the voice?
Not your own
I've seen those fears
Annalisa

It's a rant worthy of one of the all-time ranters, and, on the surface, its scenario seems like the most cut-and-dried case of a victimized woman in this essay. But the monolithic song strips nuance from a complex tragedy.

Anneliese Michel (the song anglicizes her German name) is a last lost voice—a final haunted figure who sought institutional help, fruitlessly and (in her case) fatally. She was a devout Catholic girl from Bavaria who experienced worrisome mental and physical ailments in adolescence. When conventional treatments failed, she and her equally devout parents became convinced she was possessed by demons. She endured months-long rites of exorcism that left her profoundly weakened before she died of malnutrition at twenty-three. This didn't happen in the Middle Ages but in 1976. Her parents and two Catholic priests were subsequently found guilty of negligent homicide, fined, and given suspended sentences.

The song "Annalisa" is from *First Issue* (1978)—the debut album by Public Image Ltd (PiL), the former Sex Pistol Johnny Rotten's post-punk project, in which he tried to create a new non-rock style and revived his given name, John Lydon. On the original LP, the track closed side one—a suite of songs roughly about religion and Lydon's disdain for it.

Michel's story is difficult to summarize. Accounts are deeply biased according to conflicting worldviews. Everyone has an axe to grind, and prying facts from partisan context is no small task. She grew up in a pious middle-class home. She began having seizures in her teens and was diagnosed with temporal-lobe epilepsy. The diagnosis was tentative; most of her attacks were unseen by doctors, who described them as "epilepsy-like."[219] For her part, Michel reported symptoms resembling night paralysis—a frightening sense of pressure and inability to move or scream. Tests were inconclusive, and her autopsy showed no brain lesions. Her diagnosis meant she was given powerful anti-convulsive medications for years, which may have aggravated other symptoms. Her condition worsened when she went away to college, and medication provided little relief. Ordinarily shy but cheerful, she grew depressed.

She began having bizarre experiences. She saw frightening faces and heard voices. Hospitalization and anti-psychotic medications were similarly unhelpful. She grew intolerant of sacred places and religious objects and became convinced that she was under the spell of dark powers. Her parents agreed and consulted with Catholic clergy to request an exorcism. Church officials refused and advised her to continue medical and psychiatric treatment. She grew worse. She began to harm herself and lash out at others. She wet herself, drank her urine, ate insects, barked and growled like a dog, and spoke in a guttural, alien voice. Eventually,

---

219 Felicitas D. Goodman, *The Exorcism of Anneliese Michel* (Eugene, OR: Resource Publications, 1981), p. 205.

the church relented and approved an exorcism. Between 1975 and her death the following year, she underwent sixty-seven such rites. During these, she shook, went rigid, and vocally manifested various entities. She grew exhausted, stopped eating, and seemed to accept that she would not survive her ordeal. Yet she insisted the rites continue. During periods of lucidity, she repeatedly knelt in prayer. She also wrote down her increasingly disconsolate thoughts: "I have no choice anymore. I see that sometimes like clear lightning, hopelessness sits at the root of where life is."[220] Ten months after the exorcisms began, she died in her sleep, her body battered and worn. She weighed just 66 pounds.

It was an appalling tragedy, and, in its aftermath, finger-pointing filled the air. The need to blame became paramount, and battle lines were drawn— between believers, non-believers, and various "experts." In the process, Michel, the person, was sidelined: she became a fetish for feuding ideologues and a tabloid headline-grabber in the heyday of the film *The Exorcist* (1973). There was, in fact, plenty of blame to go around. Every authority engaged to help her, whether familial, medical, psychological, or religious, ultimately failed her, but a careful review of the record reveals no mustachioed villain; parents, doctors, psychiatrists, and priests all showed compassion and an earnest desire to help. But each was blinded by assumptions endemic to their vocation or role. The problem of niches recurs: of specialization, not synthesis, of a person in crisis not treated as a multifaceted whole.

None of this plays a part in the song. For Lydon, the unambiguous villain is religion, and he lays the blame squarely on the parents, the priests, and the church. "[It's] about these silly fucking parents of this girl who believed she was possessed by the devil, so they starved her to death," he said in a 1978 interview.[221] But Lydon's polemic disregards inconvenient truths—e.g., that Michel also believed she was possessed, that she approved her exorcism, that she was a legal adult, that she stopped eating on her own, and that neither she nor her parents ever claimed she was possessed by "the devil," but instead by multiple entities.

Annalisa had no escape
Starved to death in a waiting room
Cheap concern and rosary beads
Did not solve screaming needs
Annalisa

Lydon, of course, has a history of making contentious, un-nuanced statements in songs and interviews. His scabrous anti-charisma was always rooted in shrill iconoclasm, and his impact as an artist—with the Pistols and PiL—was more about tearing down than building up.[222] Childhood strife reveals much about

---

220　Ibid., p. 75.

221　Chris Brazier, "The Danceable Solution," *Melody Maker*, 28 October 1978.

222　The author and musician Gary Lachman, himself a punk pioneer and co-founder (as Gary Valentine) of Blondie, described this thrilling but ultimately self-defeating nihilism: "They [the Sex Pistols] know what they don't like, and want to shout about it, but suggest nothing in its place" (*Beyond the Robot: The Life and Work of Colin Wilson*, New York: TarcherPerigee, 2016, p. 358). Lachman eventually left music, earned degrees in philosophy, and wrote scores of erudite and readable books about

Lydon's adult temperament. He grew up in an impoverished Irish Catholic household and, at age seven, contracted spinal meningitis. Hospitalized for a year, he drifted in and out of a coma for six months. The illness left him with staring eyes and a slight hunchback. But it also ignited something inside him—a core of anger and fierce individualism that gave no quarter and ultimately set him on his unconventional creative path.[223] This stridency put him at loggerheads with his family's faith and all forms of authority.

Similarities between Lydon's illness and Michel's are telling. In his memoir, Lydon recalls disorienting headaches, frightening visions, inability to eat, and painful medical procedures—all of which Michel experienced—plus unwanted visits by nuns and priests. His rage at her fate is cogent but was likely triggered partly by his identification with her, hence his inability to see her as anything but a hapless victim. He seems to have delved no deeper than the lurid press accounts that sprang up after her death and latched on to her story as a springboard for an anti-religious rant.

Such tunnel vision diminishes her experience. Like Dora and West, Michel was a unique individual caught up in a complex, devastating crisis. Authorities in all three cases tried to fit the sufferer's subjective perceptions into objective categories that were simplistic and incomplete.

In the most comprehensive account of Michel's ordeal, *The Exorcism of Anneliese Michel* (1981), the anthropologist Felicitas D. Goodman applies her discipline's broad-minded, flexible approach. Like Binswanger with West, she tries to understand Michel's "way of being" in the world—the distinct traits that filtered her experience—without judgment or bias. Goodman argues that the most fruitful starting point would have been to take Michel's religious interpretation seriously, whatever one's views on the subject, and that the stalemate between secular and religious approaches likely doomed her. "Had the psychiatrists who saw Anneliese as a patient been trained to also look at the culture that had decisively shaped her, namely, a Catholicism deeply rooted in peasant tradition, their diagnosis might have been entirely different."[224] She posits that Michel was a "hypersensitive," burdened with an "overly sensitive nervous system," who responded to troubling ailments by withdrawing into a "religious altered state of consciousness" (RASC).[225] Such visionary states are familiar in preindustrial cultures but are typically glossed over, despite recurrence, in the "civilized" West. Goodman notes that trance states and convulsions, easily mistaken for epileptic seizures, are well-documented facets of RASC, such as speaking in tongues (glossolalia). Similarly, "possession" occurs in numerous cultures around the world, whether contextualized as a

Western esoterica. Lydon has struggled to remain musically relevant, and his audacity hasn't aged well: youthful attacks on the music business, the monarchy, and bourgeois mediocrity gave way in middle age to griping about homeless people in his Venice Beach neighborhood, supporting the anti-labor Donald Trump as a "workers'" candidate, and childish confrontations with fellow aging punks.

223   In his autobiography, he refers to the experience as "the first step that put me on the road to Rotten" (*Rotten: No Irish, No Blacks, No Dogs*, New York: Picador, 1994, p. 16).

224   Felicitas D. Goodman, *The Exorcism of Anneliese Michel* (Eugene, Ore.: Resource Publications, 1981), p. 202.

225   Ibid., p. 204.

medical condition, a psychiatric disorder, literal congress with demons (or the Holy Spirit),[226] or a poorly understood anomalous phenomenon. Despite her religious framework, Michel seems, at times, to have grasped the archetypal quality of her experience. While being treated medically for a mood disorder, she told a doctor, "This is not a depression, this is a condition."[227]

Michel was ill-served by clashing factions. How different things might have been had the transcultural approach invoked by Goodman held sway, because bullying the fragmented self—demanding it conform to an outside perspective of what is "real" and "normal"—is unlikely ever to generate its spontaneous reassembly. Such shortsightedness is central to all three tragedies. A sense of futility haunts each—a recognition that entrenched traditions and analytical methods can be useless at healing the torment of multifaceted human beings, and, while the songs that remember them can't possibly "explain" what happened to Dora, West, or Michel, they keep the fates of these "three strange angels" alive for others to ponder.

Admit them, admit them.

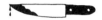

226　Horror movies and tabloids aside, most cases of "possession" involve positive, not negative, entities.

227　Goodman, *The Exorcism of Anneliese Michel*, p. 206.

STEVEN L. JONES, *PROMISCUOUS SISTERS/UNKNOWN BEAST* (DETAIL), 2019

CHAPTER FIVE: FANCIES OF LOVE, FANTASIES OF DEATH

WHISPERER IN DARKNESS

Real things in darkness seem no realer than dreams.
—Murasaki Shikibu, The Tale of the Genji, *11th century*

Songs of murder and tragic death are not always grounded in reality. A compelling subset exists outside the continuum of facts and recollections, rooted entirely in folklore or fantasy. This shift from actual to imaginary events privileges subjective interpretation since there's no objective truth to seek. Instead, such songs take on the quality of dreams and, like dreams, can yield rich but elusive meanings. A haunting example, culled from eighteenth-century literature and converted to nineteenth-century classical music, blends myth with modern introspection to unnerving effect.

The first sound is a rhythm, a staccato burst of piano triplets beneath a brief, rising-and-falling melody evoking hoofbeats. A horse races through a windswept wood at night, bearing a beleaguered boy and his worried father toward safety. The tone is tense, the tempo swift, the key E minor. The ominous intro repeats, its jackhammer speed straining the pianist's widespread fingers. A booming voice begins to sing, in the language the devil in Thomas Mann's musical novel *Doctor Faustus* (1948) calls "good old German."[228] It tells of a boy menaced by both nightmare and neglect, by a spectral predator only he can sense, and a disbelieving father who thinks his frightened, possibly feverish son is imagining things.

Rhythms recur, maintaining tension, but the song's tune is through-composed. Each musical line uniquely complements a corresponding sequence of text. Singer and composer masterfully interweave characters—narrator, father, son, supernatural villain (and horse, on the piano)—giving each a distinct sonic personality. Urgency grows as manifestations increase; the dark figure whispers temptations only the boy can hear. His terror compounds with each paternal reassurance until, finally, a cold claw of his phantom assailant seems to grip his pounding heart. The father's steed completes its trek; hoofbeats—and piano triplets—cease. But safety comes too late: the boy arrives dead.

It is one of the finest performances of one of the world's great songs. Written by Franz Schubert and most famously performed and recorded by the lyric baritone Dietrich Fischer-Dieskau and the pianist Gerald Moore, for three and a half

---

228 Thomas Mann, Doctor Faustus: *The Life of the German Composer Adrian Leverkühn as Told by a Friend*, (New York: Vintage International, 1992), p. 223.

ALBERT STERNER, *DER ERLKÖNIG*, C. 1910

riveting minutes—the length of a classic 45 single—it flawlessly balances words and music, content and form. Its text source is a poem by Johann Wolfgang von Goethe, its musical idiom *Lied,* or art song. Its title is "Der Erlkönig," which is German for "Erl-King." And while it's unclear what an Erl-King is supposed to be, the song implies that it, or a fantasy of it, takes the boy's life before the song's final chords.

> *Who rides there so late through the night dark and drear?*
> *The father it is, with his infant so dear*
> *He holdeth the boy tightly clasp'd in his arm*
> *He holdeth him safely, he keepeth him warm*

(Bowring translation)[229]

"Der Erlkönig" is the best known *Lied* by the greatest composer of the form, the Austrian genius Franz Schubert (1797–1828). First published and publicly performed in 1821, the song sets to music the 1782 poem of the same name by the German cultural titan Johann Wolfgang von Goethe (1749–1832). Neither the first nor last adaptation, critical and popular consensus rate it the best.

---

229 Multiple English translations of "Der Erlkönig" exist. I will be using those of Edgar Alfred Bowring (*The Poems of Goethe: Translated in the Original Metres*, New York: Hurst & Company, 1881) and Edwin H. Zeydel (*Goethe the Lyricist*, Chapel Hill: University of North Carolina Press, 1955).

Goethe's poem—a high-water mark for early Romanticism—derives its subject from folklore generally and from the pre-medieval Scandinavian ballad "Elveskud" specifically. *Elveskud* is Danish for "Elf-shot," and *Erl-König* is commonly translated as "Elf-King." In fact, the song title's etymology is thorny. While the Danish word *Ellerkonge* does indeed mean "Elf-King," the German cognate *Erlkönig* literally translates as "king of the alder trees," and a race of elf-like "alder tree people," the *Ellefolket,* figure in Danish folklore. This implies that the sinister entity portrayed in "Der Erlkönig" is closely allied with the forest. He also clearly has little in common with modern notions of elves—as either Santa's twinkle-eyed helpers or the mystic Aryans of Tolkien-style fantasy.

But the Erl-King has everything to do with Romanticism, that revolutionary style that straddled the eighteenth and nineteenth centuries, rattling Enlightenment-era rationalism by exalting the monsters unleashed by reason's sleep. Goethe and Schubert spanned the (Neo-)Classical and Romantic periods and served as cultural bridges between the two. Their renderings of "Der Erlkönig" compellingly blend the former's values of balance and restraint with the latter's themes of dramatic emotion, turbulent nature, and occult realms of fairy and folk tale.

"My son, why cover your face in such fear?"
"You see the elf-king, father? He's near!"

(Zeydel translation)

"Dost see not the Erl-King, with crown and with train?"
"My son, 'tis the mist rising over the plain"

(Bowring translation)

Lied worked well with such motifs. An intimate art better suited to drawing rooms than to opera houses, its focus on the expressive powers of a lone vocalist mirrored Romanticism's elevation of the individual. "All the knowledge I possess, everyone else can acquire," wrote Goethe, highlighting the movement's exaltation of subjective truth, "but my heart is all my own."[230] *Lied*'s mission to match poetry with music, word for word and line for line, squared with the Romantics' call to swap a century's dispassionate, didactic verse for, in the words of one reformer (William Wordsworth), "the spontaneous overflow of powerful feelings."[231]

Today, *Lied* has the stuffy reputation of an ultimate snob's art, but, in the Victorian era, art song was, in a sense, the folk music of the bourgeoisie. Long before Western living rooms were organized around televisions, houseguests were typically seated in relation to a piano. And if you had such an item (and

---

230   *The Sorrows of Young Werther* (New York: Signet Classics, 1962), p. 83.
231   Nicholas Halmi, ed., *Wordsworth's Poetry and Prose: A Norton Critical Edition* (New York: W. W. Norton & Company, 2013) p. 265.

many middle-class people did), someone in the household could probably play and knew at least a parlor song or two. Many of these were sentimental and unimaginative, the pop schlock of their era, but, in those pre-Victrola days, more refined, meaningful fare by Schubert or Gabriel Fauré or Johannes Brahms provided moments of respite—in one's own home and, possibly, one's own voice.[232]

The rhythmic piano triplets continue. The boy clings to his father but hears the Erl-King whisper in his ear.

"Oh, come, thou dear infant! Oh come thou with me!
For many a game I will play there with thee
On my strand, lovely flowers their blossoms unfold,
My mother shall grace thee with garments of gold"

(Bowring translation)

Perhaps there's solace to be found in the fact that the Erl-King, whatever he is, has a mother. Regardless, with his sepulchral voice now close by, the terrified child turns once more to his sole protector and ally. But his father focuses relentlessly on the task at hand: driving his horse to safety through the desolate wood. He assures his son that he hears only "the sad wind that sighs through the withering leaves." The boy's recurrent cries of *Mein Vater, mein Vater* grow panicked and pitiful.

"Wilt go, then, dear infant, wilt go with me there?
My daughters shall tend thee with sisterly care"

(Bowring translation)

"In the night my daughters their revelry keep,
They'll rock you and dance you and sing you to sleep"

(Zeydel translation)

That the Erl-King has daughters, presumably produced through conventional means, might further demystify him. Inexplicable phenomena, after all, frighten precisely because they're unexplained. Fight-or-flight terror might recede to cooler-headed caution if the vague shapes of supernatural night gain focus in preternatural day. But Enlightenment rationalism is of little use in a Romantic

---

232 Fischer-Dieskau performed "Der Erlkönig" countless times over a forty-six-year career. To watch his dynamic reading from a 1959 BBC broadcast accompanied by Moore is to be struck both by its musical excellence and the singer's compelling but subtle theatricality. Beefier in youth than middle or old age, his broad face emotes in nuanced tandem with his voice, shifting characters on a dime. It's a shame that such potentially accessible art has been consigned to the esoteric margins in today's world (see www.youtube.com/watch?v=PaBNUzVSnj8).

nightmare. Once the Alder Tree King offers sensual pleasures in exchange for the boy's—what exactly? fealty? body? life? soul?—his characterization takes on newly menacing overtones, both sexual and satanic.

Now less a baleful spirit than an alluring Mephistopheles, he tempts the boy with beautiful things, maternal nurturing, and his daughters' "sisterly care." The latter enticement seems distinctly libidinous ("They'll rock you" sounds lewd even for 1821). It's the kind of randy coaxing to which a diabolical figure might subject a preadolescent boy, with no concern for exploiting his confused desires or damaging his young psyche. The father is unfazed; his son's erotic glimpse of the Erl-King's daughters is merely "the aged willows deceiving [his] sight." But darker lusts emerge and the wraith's language, at least, turns toward rape.

"I love you, your comeliness charms me, my boy!
And if you're not willing, my force I'll employ"

(Zeydel translation)

"Der Erlkönig" resembles a dark fairy tale or scary story set to music. One can imagine children sharing such a yarn—whispering, like the mysterious Erl-King, around a campsite fire or at a basement sleepover by flashlight. While some themes would evade them, the dreadful conclusion would likely haunt and disturb: that, despite the father's efforts to save him, the boy dies and is presumably "taken" by the Erl-King.

The child psychologist Bruno Bettelheim's classic book *The Uses of Enchantment: The Meaning and Importance of Fairy Tales* (1976) argues that parents risk harming their children if they reduce the threat found in fairy tales to make them less frightening. Bettelheim believed such stories are valuable to healthy child development precisely because they *are* frightening—because, through them, a child learns that seemingly overwhelming adversaries like giants and witches and goblins (and all they symbolize in life) can, in fact, be defeated. "The child intuitively comprehends," wrote Bettelheim, "that although these stories are *unreal*, they are not *untrue*."[233] Thus, Jack outmaneuvers the giant, Hansel and Gretel outsmart the witch, and the miller's daughter wins her freedom by tricking Rumpelstiltskin. In Bettelheim's view, to defang such villains is to remove the threat necessary to rally a child's courage and will to survive.

To this thesis, Bettelheim tagged a single proviso: in order to learn such lessons, a child must feel safe, and what makes a child feel safe is knowing that all fairy tales start with "Once upon a time" and end with "They lived happily ever after." "Der Erlkönig" breaks this rule. While the presence of fairies, however malevolent, might imply a Fairyland setting, it lacks Bettelheim's reassuring denouement. In its place is an ending almost modern in its starkness: evil goes

---

233   Bruno Bettelheim, *The Uses of Enchantment: The Meaning and Importance of Fairy Tales* (New York: Vintage Books, 1989), p. 73.

unvanquished, the father's efforts fail, the child hero perishes. Compounding the horror are the two ambivalent father figures—the whisperers in darkness. One is a flesh-and-blood *Vater*, entrusted with his son's welfare yet strangely aloof to his fears, the other an immaterial monarch intent on snuffing out his life and stealing his soul.

None of this is the fault of "Der Erlkönig." It's a song, not a fairy tale, and while it draws from a common storehouse of themes and motifs, neither Goethe's poem nor Schubert's *Lied* was intended for the preschool set.

Great art is never simple. Like myth and dreams, it comprises puzzle boxes of resonance and interpretation. In "Der Erlkönig," the listener faces, from the start, a choice between what might be called literal and realist accounts of its narrative. Does the story occur as described, a supernatural mystery? Or is the boy hallucinating from an illness that ultimately takes his life? Neither alternative entirely satisfies, so the listener must concoct a hybrid view or veer unsurely between options. This conflict between irrational and rational outlooks, between subjective and objective interpretations, opens a gateway to deeper exploration.

"Oh, come, thou dear infant! Oh come thou with me!" The Erl-King's shift from inchoate nature spirit to infernal tempter can be read as two-thirds of a tripartite schema (triplets again). In this model, he transforms from a primitively perceived natural force to an anthropomorphized—and therefore more manageable—devil figure. Both are terrifying, but the former is a chaos while the latter has morality and a name. Part three of this configuration culminates with the demonic pied piper revealed as death itself, in all its irremediable anti-glory. Thus, the Erl-King passes through phases that mirror evolving human concepts of the awesome unknown—from prehistoric–animistic, to theistic–Abrahamic, to modern–existential.

A specifically Christian reading might find a dark inversion of the Trinity, wherein the Son suffers but is forsaken by the Father and the Spirit is Unholy (picture a winged demon in place of the dove of peace and hellfire instead of Pentecost's cleansing flames). In this grim theology, death is triumphant: the stone of the tomb stays unmoved.

The theme is despairingly circular. If "Der Erlkönig" begins, in a sense, in primordial darkness, it finishes there as well, its nemesis revealed as the Grim Reaper in elfin or sylvan disguise. We find ourselves huddled once more around a fire with our primitive ancestors, trying to make sense of nature's tumult and the end of consciousness.

The father now gallops, with terror half wild,
He grasps in his arms the poor shuddering child.

(Bowring translation)

Austrian Gallery Belvedere/Creative Commons

MORITZ VON SCHWIND, *DER ERLKÖNIG*, C. 1830

The father's role is perplexing. It makes sense at both literal and realist levels: whatever troubles his son, surely the wisest course of action is to get the boy to safety at all costs. But his stubborn single-mindedness, his refusal to take his son's fears seriously, might signify a destructive subtext. What is it the boy so fears that the father wishes to keep him from? Perhaps the Erl-King's offer of sensual pleasures provides a clue. Does the father wish to keep his son a child—to prevent his transition to adulthood by "protecting" him from his emerging sexuality (still half-conscious and therefore frightening to the boy) in a contrasexual riff on Rapunzel? In this light, the boy's death is recast as a triumph of sorts—his initiation into manhood despite his father's meddling—but the result is the same: he discovers that death is real and that no person or deity can save him from it. As in Genesis, there's no turning back: once the forbidden fruit is sampled, the mortal knowledge it imparts bars us forever from Edenic childhood.

No metaphoric framework fully satisfies, nor should it. Just as the Romantics intuitively grasped that classical rationalism left out approximately half of human experience, there's no "solution" to the song's mystery. Thus, the essence of "Der Erlkönig" will always be its final image, fixed and immutable:

He reaches his courtyard with toil and with dread—
The child in his arms finds he motionless, dead

(Bowring translation)

There is a curious mirroring of this final image, conceptually reversed, in another nineteenth-century work of dread and doubt: Henry James's Gothic Revival novella *The Turn of the Screw* (1898). In this late-Romantic work, an unreliable narrator—an aging, virginal governess—is sent to care for two wealthy children. She becomes convinced they are menaced by the ghosts of a servant couple, now deceased, who she believes corrupted the children's innocence in life and crave their souls in death. A subtext of possible sexual abuse was seized on by modern readers in the age of Freud. In various stage and film adaptations, this theme rises to the surface. The best include Benjamin Britten's 1954 chamber opera of the same name and Jack Clayton's 1961 film *The Innocents*.

In the book's terminal scene, the oppressive paranoia of the unstable governess achieves deadly apotheosis. Alone with the boy Miles and convinced a vile spirit is at the window waiting to "take" him, she shields the terrified child with her body until the manifestations cease, only to find him dead in her arms: "We were alone with the quiet day, and his little heart, dispossessed, had stopped."[234]

In both "Der Erlkönig" and *The Turn of the Screw*, a boy is menaced by an unseen fiend. These adversaries could be imaginary: in Schubert's song, he may be the boy's fever dream, in James's book, a neurosis of the sexually repressed governess. Parental figures try to "save" both boys—the father in "Der Erlkönig," a maternal surrogate in *The Turn of the Screw*. Each fails and may, in fact, cause the boy's demise—the father through neglect (by not taking his son's fears seriously), the "mother" through abuse (by projecting her own terror on the boy until she frightens him to death).

Versions and variants of "Der Erlkönig" abound in classical music, but the song has made few inroads into other styles. The folksinger Steve Gillette opened his eponymous 1967 debut LP with a comparatively soothing adaptation of Goethe's poem, set to his own tune. Gillette's crooning voice and jangly guitar (in Celtic-friendly D-A-D-G-A-D tuning) create a self-described "spirited rendition" that emphasizes fairy tale over dark psychology.[235] While Gillette doesn't alter the narrative, he fleshes out the father's response in the boy's final moments, smoothing over his ambivalent behavior.

> *Clutching the reins in his trembling hands*
> *With pain and despair that he can't understand*
> *Alone on the road with the stars overhead*
> *Fearful and hopeless, the boy in his arms is dead*

In Schubert's *Lied*, the father arrives home "with toil and with dread" and discovers the child has died, and the song ends with no reassuring denouement. Gillette's lyrical tweak—"with pain and despair he *can't understand*" (my italics)—rehumanizes the remote patriarch by imbuing him with a confused state of mind that's missing from the source. In a final verse Gillette wrote for the song, the grieving parent cries out to the impassive night.

---

234   Henry James, *The Turn of the Screw* (New York: Book-of-the-Month Club, 1996), p. 280.
235   Steve Gillette, "The Erl King," *About the Song* website, 2019-2022.

To the trees in the night wind he cries aloud
He seeks out the face of death in every passing cloud
Down in the meadow where the boy's grave is laid
Nothing but the willows that wave in the glade.

The former Carolina Chocolate Drop Dom Flemons raises the creepy quotient, channeling the high lonesome balladeers Clarence Ashley and Dock Boggs in a banjo-and-vocal variant on his 2007 solo debut, *Dance Tunes Ballads and Blues*. Flemons transforms Schubert's Erlkönig into a proper name for a folkloric boogeyman—"Earl King"—an Appalachian-style haint that pursues father and son through "mumblin' winds" and "gaunt and bony trees" across an Americanized tableau. In Flemons's song, the father is well-meaning but clueless as the disembodied bogey torments his son, and there's no end-of-song closure, only ambiguity and doom.

The child laid back, his eyes both closed
He gave the impression of sleep
Yet as he closed his lids, he saw Earl King's smile
And his eyes so deep, so deep

On the modal flip side, the song's dark theme and repetitive rhythms have inspired multiple interpretations by Norse- and Teuton-centric metal bands (e.g., Rammstein, 2004; Sequester, 2008; Hope Lies Within, 2012). While these amps-at-eleven headbanger versions bludgeon the subtleties of Goethe's poem and Schubert's *Lied*, they testify to the song's enduring hypnotic power and nightmarish appeal.

FULL MOON, DARK HEART

And then a Plank in Reason, broke,
And I dropped down, and down
—Emily Dickinson, "I felt a Funeral, in my Brain," *1861*

In the summer of 1968, a peculiar country-and-western song came and went to little fanfare on a small Nashville record label. Sung by a fading honky-tonker who needed a hit and penned by a successful songwriter who could afford a flop, scant airplay and mediocre distribution consigned the tune to swift oblivion. There it gestated, just out of sight, passed among a fringe of curious listeners drawn to its outré subject and incongruous tone. Over time, hip cover versions and the track's inclusion on album anthologies of oddball songs gave it underground cachet. Neither singer nor composer lived to see this unlikely development.

Bob Dylan, the high priest of cool in 1968, was going country that year—a
stylistic shift as controversial among rock fans as his earlier embrace of rock and
roll had been with folkies. In 2007, he extolled the song, spinning it on his *Theme
Time Radio Hour* and cementing its status. "It never got much airplay," intoned
the aging priest, "but has become quite a bit of a cult favorite." He then added,
changing verb tense: "As is Eddie Noack himself." The song was called "Psycho,"
and Noack sang it while Leon Payne wrote it.

Can Mary fry some fish, Mama?
I'm as hungry as can be
Oh Lordy, how I wish, Mama
You could keep the baby quiet
'Cause my head is killing me

The voice is twangy but smooth, a throwback to honky-tonk crooners like
Lefty Frizzell or Faron Young in balladeer mode. Accompaniment is spare full-
band, minus the syrupy strings and background vocals of the then-dominant
Nashville sound. The arrangement is tasteful, enlivened slightly by tack piano
flourishes and simple shifts of rhythm and meter. A bluesy guitar discretely
supports each verse, and a steady rim-knock from the drummer keeps mid-
tempo time.

The soothing backup belies aberrant words. The lyric is a monologue—not
a soliloquy, as it's all addressed to "Mama." Despite the mild tone, the mood
is tense. It soon grows unsettling, paranoid, though the singer never seems to
break a sweat.

I seen my ex last night, Mama
At a dance at Miller's store
She was with that Jackie White, Mama
I killed 'em both, and they're buried
Under Jenkins' sycamore

The admission is chilling but not unexpected in a song called "Psycho."
Alfred Hitchcock's film *Psycho*, based on Robert Bloch's novel, was eight years
old in 1968, and the abbreviated term for psychopath had entered common
language—shorthand for a killer driven by deviant urges, especially one who's
mild-mannered and seemingly sane on the surface like the Oedipus-addled
necrophile, Norman Bates. There had been first-person murder songs in country
music before, including recent ones such as Porter Wagoner's "The Cold, Hard
Facts of Life" or Johnny Paycheck's "I've Got Someone to Kill" (both released in
1966 and about homicidal responses to adultery). But for all their luridness, these
still traded in familiar themes: love gone wrong, the empty bottle, the prisoner's
lament. Even Johnny Cash's nihilistic "Folsom Prison Blues" (originally released
in 1957 but popularized via the 1968 live version Cash recorded at the prison) is

ultimately contrite. Its killer may have "shot a man in Reno, just to watch him die," but the coldhearted act brings only grief and regret.

Noack's "Psycho" was something new. It starts on grim but conventional ground, with a double homicide triggered by jealous rage, then veers far afield, unhitched from conventional motive or morality.

Don't hand the dog to me, Mama
I might squeeze him too tight
And I'm as nervous as can be, Mama
But let me tell you 'bout last night

I woke up in Johnny's room, Mama
Standing right by his bed
With my hands near his throat, Mama
Wishing both of us was dead

Across six verses, three choruses, and one key change, the song tallies an array of less and less comprehensible killings. The singer recounts them vaguely, as if through a somnambulist fog. Identities are unclear (who is Mary? Johnny?—and whose baby is crying?), highlighting the compulsive nature of the crimes. "You think I'm psycho, don't you, Mama?" goes the chorus, and the singer counters with a Norman Bates smirk: "If you think I'm psycho, Mama / You better let 'em lock me up."

The song's final verses up the transgressive ante: the singer murders a child but, trancelike, has no memory of the incident.

You know the little girl next door, Mama?
I think her name is Betty Clark
Oh, don't tell me that she's dead, Mama
Why, I just seen her in the park

Songcraft excels here, less-is-more style. The scenario recalls the abduction scene in Fritz Lang's proto-*Psycho* film *M* (1931), in which the camera stays unnervingly still as Peter Lorre's whistling child killer buys a balloon for his trusting prey . . . then walks casually out of frame, her little hand in his. Lang later shows us the balloon, lost and tangled in overhead wires, and our minds fill in the dreadful details.

She was sitting on a bench, Mama
Thinking of a game to play
Seems I was holding a wrench, Mama
Then my mind walked away

Payne's nuanced writing, plus Noack's measured vocal, set "Psycho" apart from a slew of morbid novelty tunes—the kind collected on campy anthologies of country weirdness like the Omni label's *Hillbillies in Hell* series. That "Psycho" shows up on some of these (including *Hillbillies in Hell*) is predictable but ironic. Its subject may be grindhouse-sensational, but it's several cuts in quality above bizarro fare like Wayne, Pat, and Keith's devil-be-gone singalong "I'm Tired of You, Satan" (1966) and Billy Barton's echo-drenched dialogue with the diabolical, "The Devil, My Conscience and I" (1958).

These collections are trashy fun but court condescension. Often they're consumed by non-country fans laughing at country music—mocking its bedrock sincerity while conflating the genre with its most extreme progeny. Still, the kinship of "Psycho" with this material raises eyebrows. What were Noack and Payne—the former a past-his-prime but still respected artist, the latter a Nashville Songwriters Hall-of-Famer who wrote

HILLBILLIES IN HELL **COVER ART, 2016**

standards like "I Love You Because" and "Lost Highway"—doing slumming with the suicide, insanity, and Satan crowd? Critics asked the same of Hitchcock in 1960. Today, *Psycho*'s "fine film" status is unquestioned, but, upon release, some sniffed that the director had degraded himself by dabbling in the exploitation field. Hitchcock admitted the dabbling: at sixty-one, four decades into his career, he was trying to stay vital and viable by adjusting to changing tastes. Noack and Payne may have had similar motivations: if darker, more explicit fare was the future, why not execute it artfully?

The artistic bona fides of both are unimpeachable. Payne released a reverent tribute to folk music in 1963 called *Americana: Rare Ballads and Tall Tales.* Noack once called country "the only true American music" and refused to sully himself by branching into rock and roll.[236] Neither man would have risked degrading the form he loved. The B side to "Psycho" was a Noack-penned character study of an ex-con struggling to survive on the outside called "Invisible Stripes." It's the kind of thoughtful, socially relevant song Noack hoped to be remembered for. One suspects he'd have preferred the record's A and B sides reversed.

"Psycho" has a final trick up its ghoulish sleeve. After one last "You think I'm psycho don't you, Mama?" chorus, we learn that Mama—unresponsive throughout the song—is also unmoving. The singer's monologue is a soliloquy after all—sung to a corpse. This O.-Henry-by-way-of-EC-Comics twist provides the song's single instance of unambiguous black humor. As the track fades, Noack deadpans: "Mama, why don't you get up? . . . *Say something to me, Mama ...*"

It reads as both a tension-breaker and a kind of "I've been putting you on"

236 Andrew Brown, liner notes for *Psycho: The K-Ark and Allstar Recordings* (Bear Family, 2013).

wink from Noack, as if he's retaken control of the song and is letting you in on the joke. If so, it's worth considering the nature of the sendup. At whose expense is he laughing—the listener's? country music's? his own? In the context of his life—a trajectory fraught with disappointment and unfulfilled potential—it may have been all three.

Eddie Noack was born in Houston, Texas, in 1930. An only child, his parents soon split, and he was raised mainly by his mother. She later remarried, but those Depression-era, us-against-the-world years forged a potent bond between mother and son. In his teens, Eddie's passions were writing and music. He wrote for his high-school newspaper and, inspired by Ernest Tubb and others, learned guitar and began to play and sing. Merging interests must have seemed simple arithmetic, and, by graduation, he had decided to be a professional songwriter and performer. An anonymous wag placed a cartoon of a guitar-playing hillbilly beside his senior yearbook photo.

He threw himself into the booming local country scene and was soon successfully gigging. From the start, his journalistic and literary bent set him apart from other artists. He used his earnings to finance a college English degree and had a scholar's sense of country music as a historically rich art form. It became his life's ambition to contribute to its canon. In 1948, he recorded original tunes for a fledgling Gold Star Records—early home base to the country, blues, and Cajun legends George Jones, Lightnin' Hopkins, and Harry Choates. After that, his ascent was dizzying.

Noack's songs began to chart locally, both in his own and in cover versions, and the industry noticed. He became a protégé of the influential producer Harold "Pappy" Daily, who signed the twenty-three-year-old to Starday Records, the most prestigious country label in Texas. A two-year stint in the Army put things on hold, but he returned as an in-demand songwriter. In 1956, Hank Snow had a smash with Noack's workingman's ballad, "These Hands" (later a favorite of Cash's), and he broke out of Texas and into the big time. He moved to Nashville in 1959 and signed with the major label Mercury Records as a songwriter the following year. Still young at thirty, he seemed poised for the artistic career he'd dreamt of.

What happened next is hard to say, but Noack's fall was equally vertiginous. For unclear reasons, his songwriting faltered after "These Hands"—ironically, a song about an older man looking back on a life of disappointments. He had trouble producing a commercial follow-up and lost momentum, and backers deserted him in search of reliable hitmakers. He quit performing and focused solely on songwriting. His compositions remained much admired and were covered over the years by blue-chip artists like Jones, Cash, Willie Nelson, Bob Wills, and his early hero Ernest Tubb. But success eluded him.

Mercury let his contract expire, and he spent the rest of his career adrift on a sea of ever-changing small labels. He cut demos, hawked songs, and released occasional, poorly distributed 45s. When Noack's finances grew perilous, he shifted to publishing and later teaching, losing critical time and energy for songwriting to office and classroom work. In 1962 he hit bottom and began recording for "song-poem" labels—vanity studios that financed spotty releases by legitimate but non-headlining artists by setting to music lyrics mailed in by songwriting hopefuls. A fee would be collected and a handful of records issued. Noack sang on these in exchange for studio time to record his own songs.

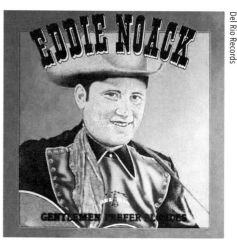

EDDIE NOACK, *GENTLEMEN PREFER BLONDES* COVER ART, 1985

It was a devastating trajectory. In 1968, a cheery notice in the trade journal *Record World* read, "Eddie Noack has agreed to record for K-Ark Records, and his new single, 'Psycho,' a Leon Payne song, is getting great reviews."[237] The tone was triumphant, but K-Ark was a song-poem label where Noack would toil for three years.[238] In a magazine interview decades later, the label's head, John Capps, recalled his tenure tersely: "Eddie would just hang around . . . He was heavy into drinking . . . He was down and out ..."[239] Noack was a private person and wrote no tell-all memoir for a fast (and toward the end, much-needed) buck. But accounts agree that, while normally affable and dependable, he was increasingly crippled by dark moods and drink. In an interview with the researcher Andrew Brown, Noack's half-sister Pat Musslewhite described his volatile spirits as manic-depressive illness, inherited from their mother. She also said that destructive binge drinking nearly killed him twice as a young man— long before things turned sour, when his future still looked bright. Noack's luckless marital history—he had four failed marriages—may further evince his tempestuous, alcoholic nature.

"Dual diagnosis" is the modern-day term for this nightmare cycle of intertwined mental illness and addiction. Treatment resources are plentiful today, but in Noack's time sufferers were typically dismissed as moral failures, especially in conservative enclaves like the Nashville music industry of the '60s. There, they were at best romanticized as rebels or pitied as repentant, Hank Williams–style hell-raisers whose back-and-forth battles with the bottle and bad living were lucrative grist for the country music song mill. Noack's introverted nature and

---

237 *Record World*, 13 July 1968, quoted in Andrew Brown, liner notes for *Psycho: The K-Ark and Allstar Recordings* (Bear Family, 2013).

238 Phil Milstein wryly captured the exploitive essence of these operations by noting their proprietors considered customers "too dumb to grasp the meaning of the simple English word 'lyric'" ("What Is This 'Song-Poem'?", *American Song-Poem Music Archive* website, 2003, www.songpoemmusic.com/what_is.htm).

239 Brown, liner notes for *Psycho: The K-Ark and Allstar Recordings* (Bear Family, 2013).

twinkle-eyed Germanic looks fit neither mold. He never sought help and was probably ashamed of his condition. Notably, despite writing a thematically diverse body of songs—from honky-tonk larks like "Gentlemen Prefer Blondes" (1949) to social realist ballads like "Cotton Mill" (1968)—he never wrote a serious or confessional drinking song.

It was at this low juncture that Noack recorded "Psycho." His motivations are unknown (it's not even clear how the song found its way from Payne to Noack), but he must have felt he had nothing to lose. Perhaps he did it as a prank, a middle finger aimed at a country-music industry he felt had abandoned him. Maybe he hoped that something startlingly different—a modern-day variant on the old murder ballads—would jumpstart his moribund career. Or was he drawn to its dark themes because of the gloomy state of his life?

Serial killers were still rare in 1968. Charles Manson, Ted Bundy, and John Wayne Gacy were just around the corner, but, in the tumultuous year "Psycho" was released, Americans were more preoccupied with civil unrest and social change than with maniacs who hunted humans. The disturbed tone of "Psycho" reflected the tenor of the times, but this probably helped sink the song. Amidst political assassinations, mass protests, and general upheaval, country music's conservative core audience wanted reassurance, not provocation ("Okie from Muskogee" was a big hit the following year).

Payne was a history buff with a storyteller's fascination for news of the weird. His daughter, Myrtie Le Payne, says her father was inspired to write "Psycho" by a conversation with his pedal steel player, Jackie White (name-checked in the song as the killer's first victim), about the horrific killing of eight Chicago nursing students in a single night in 1966 by the sexual psychopath Richard Speck. She said Payne free-associated other details from similar incidents (e.g., the fish "Mary" fries from Albert Fish—New York's "Werewolf of Wysteria," who went on trial for killing and cannibalizing children in 1935, when Payne was eighteen years old). The unhealthy bond in "Psycho" between the singer and his murdered mother seems lifted from Bloch's 1959 novel and Hitchcock's film. The book was a fictionalized account of yet another deviant, Wisconsin's "Butcher of Plainfield," Ed Gein.

Gein is a macabre legend in the annals of twisted minds and bizarre behavior. A simple Wisconsin farmer and odd-jobber, he lived in isolation with a domineering invalid mother who condemned sex as sin and all women as harlots. When she died, the middle-aged Gein went quietly crazy. He robbed graves in a dazed state and fashioned clothing and household implements from their bones and skin like a deranged folk artist. When police finally raided his chamber-of-horrors house, they found body parts everywhere and a missing woman—slain by Gein—hanging from his garage rafters, field-dressed like a deer. Devoted to his mother even after her death, he sewed together flesh scavenged from female corpses that resembled her to make a "woman suit" he would wear to feel symbolically close to her. Gein's influence on popular culture has been vast:

among other cultural artifacts (loosely) inspired by his crimes is Tobe Hooper's infamous film *The Texas Chainsaw Massacre* (1972).

Gein's berserker-style deviance may seem a far cry from Norman Bates, the candy-nibbling hotelier and taxidermy enthusiast in *Psycho*. But the same themes are there: emotional if not literal incest, sexual repression leading to homicidal violence, aberrant interaction with human remains, and depraved acts committed in a semi-conscious state. They're also in Payne and Noack's song.

After "Psycho" stiffed in sales and radio play, Noack soldiered on at K-Ark. He issued another single ("House on a Mountain" b/w "Stolen Rose") to industry disregard, then unexpectedly returned to the murder-and-madness theme of his previous record. The spooky "Dolores" (1970) is essentially a Noack-penned rewrite of "Psycho," framed as a worried husband's warning to his wife to stay indoors because a killer is on the loose. A brisk four verses (with no chorus) tell the tale, and Noack's descriptive writing is strong:

> *Please stay inside the house tonight, Dolores*
> *Lately there's been violence in the streets*
> *The moon is full but hearts are dark, Dolores*
> *Danger in every stranger that you meet*

The song's breezy backing, all Latin-tinged guitar and lightly brushed snare rhythms, is even more perversely pleasant than that of "Psycho." Its melody is lovely—expansive and soaring, where "Psycho"'s was bluesy and clipped.

> *There's a killer in the neighborhood, Dolores*
> *A man who sees a girl and goes berserk*
> *And you're just the kind of woman that he preys on*
> *And my mind stays so upset it's hard to work*

Maybe "Psycho" sold better than is known. It's hard to imagine otherwise why Noack would take another stab at a first-person murder song, unless it was a cutting contest to prove he could match Payne's songwriting chops. If so, he proves himself capably, but "Dolores" too closely resembles its predecessor to make much impression. If anything, it's a little too tasteful—a classicist's take on monsters of the id, minus the borderline batshit qualities that make "Psycho" an unforgettable listen.

Like its predecessor, "Dolores" ends with a *Tales from the Crypt*–style revelation: the singer is, in fact, the killer, and in the final verse, he kills his wife by mistake, then posthumously rebukes her for straying from home into his pathological purview. "Dolores, how could I know that it was you?" he keens in the fadeout, then hums insanely to himself. The song contains a morbid in-joke: Noack's first marriage, undertaken at twenty-two and lasting a year, was to a woman named Dolores.

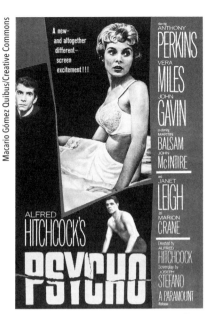

Macario Gómez Quibus/Creative Commons

POSTER ART, ALFRED HITCHCOCK'S PSYCHO, 1960

In Noack's breakthrough song, "These Hands," an aging man tries to make peace with a life of regret: "Now don't try to judge me by what you'd like me to be / For my life, it ain't been much success." The rest of Noack's career tragically mirrored his life. There were cyclical ups. A country superstar like Jones or Cash would occasionally cover a Noack tune, briefly renewing interest in his work, and in the mid-'70s he performed live for the first time in years during a short tour of England. But such highs were followed by letdown and rote dissolution. Renewed interest in his music failed to revive his recording career, and the live dates were, by all accounts, disastrous, with Noack too far gone to deliver the goods. Brief periods of clearheaded sobriety gave way to dark moods and heavy drinking.

In "The End of the Line," a Luke the Drifter–style recitative with spare guitar and steel guitar accompaniment released in 1968 (the same year as "Psycho"), he shares his thoughts on life with a rising star in the music business who might just as well be his younger self. The tone is resigned but not bitter and, after recapping his own bipolar career, he counsels his young charge to think of the job like a marriage:

> *So treat the profession and wife the same way*
> *It's fine while you're making the hits*
> *But if you start to feel either one slipping away*
> *Try once again, and then call it quits*

Noack tried once again at marriage. In 1970, he exchanged vows with his fourth wife, a divorcée from Tennessee named Maudean McDonald. The pair seemed mutually devoted, even happy, but, as with Noack, a hereditary crack lay dormant in his new wife's psyche. She, too, had spent part of her childhood with one parent—her father—while her mother was institutionalized. Like Noack, she also had been thrice married, including to an imposing ex-Marine who brutally murdered a thirty-nine-year-old waitress and mother of three just weeks after Maudean filed for divorce. While he awaited trial, Maudean's fifteen-year-old son from another marriage took his own life. The boy's pitiful note ("... don't cry over me because I'm not that good for anybody") suggests major depression, as does his chosen method—a literally heartbreaking bullet through the chest.[240]

---

240 Jerry Thompson, "Gun Wounds Kill Boy, 15," *Tennessean*, 15 September 1966.

The end of their ill-fated marriage began a few days after Christmas in 1974. The couple had a late-night quarrel about Noack's career direction, which grew heated. According to his half-sister Pat, Noack snapped at his wife, "You're just standing in my way!" Clearly not in her right mind, Maudean retrieved a .38 revolver Noack kept in his car's glove compartment for protection, said, "I'll never stand in your way again," and—like her son—shot herself point-blank through the chest.[241] She died instantly. Noack never fully recovered from Maudean's death or its traumatic circumstances. Wracked with grief, he sometimes lay on her grave, and kept her bloodied nightgown in a dresser drawer until his death.

After that, he mostly called it quits. Music buffs and musicians occasionally sought him out and found him unfailingly gracious and generous, yet his talent and health were spent. He eked out a living transcribing lead sheets for other songwriters and numbed himself in bars. On May 11, 1977, less than three years after Maudean's death, his beloved mother committed suicide in exactly the same way: with a .38 bullet through the heart. She, too, had mental issues, but Noack's family suspected his worsening alcoholism catalyzed her final breakdown. His conviction that the two women he'd loved most ended their lives because of him stole whatever spirit he had left. He died alone on February 5, 1978, with no dreams left to break.

Noack died on the cusp of his rediscovery by a new generation of punks and roots-rockers, gothic and alt-country fans. A fine survey of his wide-ranging legacy is found on two multi-disc Bear Family sets: *Gentlemen Prefer Blondes (1948–1961)* and *Psycho: The K-Ark and Allstar Recordings (1962–1969)*. "Psycho" was out of print for twenty years, but in 1974 a Michigan country singer named Jack Kittel recorded a languid cover version that received scattered airplay. Elvis Costello heard it and recorded his own rendition for his 1981 country homage *Almost Blue*. Various covers followed. These range from engagingly eccentric (the Sadies with Andre Williams, 1999) to respectable but ultimately uninspiring (Steve Wynn, Beasts of Bourbon, Teddy Thompson, T. Tex Edwards). What's striking is how little that's truly new each brings to the song— an unintended nod to Noack's artistry.

---

241 Brown, liner notes for *Psycho: The K-Ark and Allstar Recordings* (Bear Family, 2013).

MURDER IN THE RED BARN

*Logic, n. The art of thinking and reasoning in strict accordance with the
limitations and incapacities of the human misunderstanding.*
—*Ambrose Bierce,* The Devil's Dictionary, *1911*

"Murder in the Red Barn" by Tom Waits presents a challenge. It's a compelling homicidal ballad that paints a haunting picture, but the finished work is indistinct, and remains so under scrutiny. Unlike other songs in this book, Waits's tune has neither basis in fact nor significant links to other music. Rather, it's a stand-alone piece of gothic Americana: an impressionistic mélange of scenes and motifs that evoke a crime—rural, autumnal, seemingly Southern— wherein lines of crisp specificity vie with narrative gaps to tell a fragmented story. Consequently, dissection is tricky: with neither clear scenario nor musical lineage, where to begin?

With the song, of course.

"Murder in the Red Barn" is about halfway through *Bone Machine* (1992), a musical dark ride that sets songs about death and decay to clanging, bare-bones accompaniment that's rough-edged and raw even for Waits. The album is a gloomy highlight of the idiosyncratic singer-songwriter's '80s and '90s mid-period when he transitioned from seedy barroom bard to rootsy latter-day surrealist. The song opens with junkyard percussion—both tuned and tuneless—that's soon joined by minimal upright bass and springy plucked banjo. The tempo is slow, the arrangement sparse, built on a chugging C minor banjo chord that wanders now and then to F and G minor. When Waits's gravelly voice comes in, he sounds distant—as though he were in a well or, perhaps in keeping with the bio-mechanical theme of the album title, hovering overhead in an ornithopter.[242] Lyrics are clear and articulate throughout, starting with the song's (opening) chant-like chorus. Amidst mechanical and barnyard ambiance, it resembles a workman accompanying his labors with a morbid nursery rhyme.

There was a murder in the red barn, a murder in the red barn

It's the only sung line in the song; the rest are recitative, rhythmic with tonal variations, like a rootsy take on the song-speak of eerie atonal operas. Hefty text fills out the song's irregular verses—descriptive phrases, bits of conversation, skeins of omniscient narrative—but, as mentioned, never adds up to a complete story. Instrumentation and vocals integrate, like background and foreground

---

242 The ornithopter's no great reach. Album art features Waits in blurry black-and-white photos (shot by Jakob Dylan, Bob's son), clad in an industrialized devil getup with horns, goggles, and leather jacket. In a (color) video for the album's single, "I Don't Wanna Grow Up" (shot by Jim Jarmusch–Waits doesn't want for talented collaborators), he dons similar attire but rolls up one pant leg to reveal black fishnets and a red pump. He then laughs maniacally and rides a too-small bicycle in circles, his cape flapping in the wind. It's easy to imagine him piloting an unlikely winged contraption in a sister video–perhaps for "Black Wings," the western-style ballad that follows "Murder in the Red Barn" on *Bone Machine*.

merging in a painting. The song is
effortlessly cinematic, transporting
the listener to humid farmland under
serotinal sun.[243] Chickens cluck, a
screen door slams, a bygone swing
creaks on a peeling-paint porch. The
steady clunk-clop percussion evokes
both the geriatric gait of a worn-
out nag and the hammer blows of a
distant blacksmith.

Waits announces crime and
location, then shifts from chorus to
recitation.

**TOM WAITS, *BONE MACHINE*
COVER ART, 1992**

*The trees are bending over, and the
cows are lying down
The autumn's taking over, you can
hear the Buckshot hounds*

Cows lie down when it's about to rain—one pictures a coming cloudburst,
the downpour soothing a late-summer hot spell. Leaves are changing, no doubt
to Halloween orange and chimney red, and hunting dogs bark in the distance.
Without pause, Waits jump-cuts from descriptive exposition to jumbled
narrative.

*The watchman said to Reba the loon
"Was it pale at Manzanita, was it Blind Bob the coon?"
Pin it on a drifter, they sleep beneath the bridge
One plays the violin and sleeps inside a fridge*

Just four lines in, coherence evaporates, replaced by fractured phrases
and dreamlike illogic. Characters with evocative Dylan-esque names come
and go and are never heard from again. Allusions are rich but frustrate our
drearily linear left brain. Is Reba akin to an aquatic bird, is she nuts, or both?
Discrepancies between printed lyrics and what Waits actually sings spawn
riddles: the CD insert reads "Blind Bob the raccoon," but Waits clearly sings
"coon," a loaded substitution given the song's Southern vibe. Manzanita is a
Pacific Northwest beach town but also means "little apple" in Spanish (making
the impenetrable still less penetrable, Waits really sings, "Was *that* pale at
Manzanita," not "it"). Regardless, the second couplet at least returns us to the
crime. Somebody's dead, killed in "the red barn," and the gossip mill's churning
to uncover the facts.[244]

---

243 "I always thought that songs are movies for the ears," Waits told an interviewer in 2016, "and at its best, a film can be like
a song for the eyes" (Andy Gill, "Tom Waits: 'I Always Thought Songs Lived in the Air,'" *Uncut*, 8 April 2016).
244 It's easy to miss, but Waits never names or describes a victim in the song. There "was a murder," we're told repeatedly,

The chorus recurs (*There was a murder in the red barn ...*), as it will five times during the song, highlighting the central theme and giving us a mental breather between blocks of dissociative text. Then, more fragments, more hare-brained names, more riddles—plus a little morbid folk wisdom at verse's end.

Someone's crying in the woods, someone's burying all his clothes
Now Slam the Crank from Wheezer slept outside last night and froze
Roadkill has its seasons just like anything
There's possums in the autumn and there's farm cats in the spring

Junkyard banjo bends a bluesy note, and Waits's singing workman wipes sweat from his brow.

There was a murder in the red barn, a murder in the red barn

Actually, the song's title and chorus provide a tenuous link to other music and historical fact. There was indeed a "murder in the red barn"—a notorious slaying (and subsequent coverup, investigation, and trial) known by that sobriquet that thrilled readers of tabloids and penny dreadfuls in Victorian England. It happened in 1827 in a country village in Suffolk, when a local farmer and con man killed a young woman he'd promised to marry. He then buried her in the earth floor of a community landmark—a semi-remote hillside structure with a red clay-tiled roof known as the Red Barn. The victim was a lowly mole-catcher's daughter named Maria Marten, unmarried but the mother of two illegitimate children when she hooked up with her murderous paramour, a check-forging ladies' man named William "Foxey" Corder. With Corder, she had a third child; the baby soon died, but Marten pushed the father to marry her. Corder said they'd elope in nearby Ipswich and directed Marten to meet him at the Red Barn. She did so on the evening of May 18th, disguised in men's clothing to avoid detection, and was never seen again. Corder relocated and sent letters to Maria's parents claiming the two were happily married; in fact, Corder had married another woman and was planning to flee the country for France.

Meanwhile, Maria's stepmother began having nightmares—recurring dreams that the girl had been murdered and her remains interred in the Red Barn. She urged her husband to investigate and, finally, nearly a year after his daughter's disappearance, he sifted the soil under the red-roofed enclosure—with his mole-catching spike, no less—and discovered her decomposed remains. An inquest was held at the local pub, the Cock Inn in Polstead,[245] where Marten's sister identified the body. Corder was apprehended in London, where he was running a boarding house for women with his new wife (whom he'd met via a lonely-hearts ad in *The Times*).[246] His August

---

and it sets "folks' tongues waggin'." But the body is never identified.
245   Still standing and, according to their website, available for weddings, birthdays, and funerals. (No mention of inquests.)
246   A curious detail in a case not lacking them is that the officer who arrested Corder, James Lea, later apprehended the only serious suspect in the bizarre "Spring-Heeled Jack" attacks of 1837-38. Jack was the epithet given a phantom assailant

1828 trial was a sensation, avidly followed by the public and packed with dramatic testimony (including the stepmother's recounting of her clairvoyant dreams). Cause of death was never established: Corder's green handkerchief was found around the corpse's neck, implying strangulation, but Maria had also been shot, and a dagger may have been driven through her eye. A jury took less than an hour to find Corder guilty. He denied all wrongdoing, then made an eleventh-hour confession. Thousands watched him hang. His body was subjected to sadistic indignities: after dissection and phrenological exam, he was flayed and his tanned skin used to bind a book about his crimes—a grisly memento housed today in a local museum. As for the Red Barn,

EXECUTION AND DISSECTION OF WILLIAM CORDER, 1828

it became a pilgrimage site for the curious, who soon stripped its wood for souvenirs until the structure collapsed.

Infamous acts typically ricochet across a culture, and the Red Barn Murder inspired potboilers in various media: broadsheets, pamphlets, stage plays, even Punch and Judy shows (with Corder as Punch and Marten as Judy). In 1935, the British filmmaker Milton Rosner wove together threads of fact and fiction in the cinematic melodrama *Maria Marten; or, The Murder in the Red Barn*. It starred the notorious ham actor Tod Slaughter as William Corder (recast as a "squire" and middle-aged; in reality, Corder was a common farmer and he and Marten were both in their twenties). The film is visually boxy, revealing its theatrical roots, but an effective if overripe thriller. Inevitably, a topical ballad appeared soon after Corder's execution, "The Murder of Maria Marten" (Roud 215), first published in the mid-nineteenth century and sung from the killer's point of view. Like most topical songs, it's heavier on plot than on poetry, but Corder's heartlessness is chillingly conveyed.

> *"If you will meet me at the Red Barn, as sure as I have life*
> *I will take you to Ipswich town and there make you my wife"*

---

with cape, claws, and helmet who terrorized Londoners and assaulted several women. He evaded capture, but, in 1838, Lea arrested a man who bragged in a pub that he was the culprit; a trial followed, but a teenage victim failed to identify him. Jack sightings continued sporadically for decades (in 1877, a soldier reported an encounter at Aldershot Garrison). The legend's perplexing mix of the tangible and weird delights both folklorists and Forteans. Jack's attacks were material–vicious and real–but witnesses also swore he had glowing eyes, spat white-blue flames, had cold, corpse-like skin, and could hurdle tall fences (hence his springy nickname).

With overtones of "Pretty Polly," the slayer coaxes his trusting lover to a remote place where he's been excavating.

I then went home and fetched my gun, my pickaxe, and my spade
I went into the Red Barn, and there I dug her grave[247]

Typically, this would be the place to compare Waits's "Murder in the Red Barn" with its musical progenitor and the facts that inspired it. But that road is indelibly blocked. Other than the title and the shared crimson edifice, the songs have nothing in common. Nor does the Red Barn Murder relate in any way—factually, thematically, culturally—to the (admittedly) splintered scenario in Waits's song. The Marten case has a clear cast of characters with discernible motives; Waits's "Murder" doesn't even name a victim. Similarly, the real-life crime involves archetypes of love, lust, and betrayal that coalesce in a coherent story; the Waits song, by contrast, meanders, touching on familiar motifs but eschewing clarity. And the Red Barn Murder is quintessentially nineteenth-century British, from its bucolic East Anglian setting to its inquest in a country pub; Waits's oddball names, slang, roadkill, and hobo in a fridge are classic (modern) Americana.

So why did Waits name his *Bone Machine* ballad after a crime and song with no relation to its content? It seems inconceivable that an eclectic like Waits, a collector of offbeat esoterica and a self-described murder-ballad fan, was unaware of either. Probably, he heard and loved the title, tucked it away in his dark-carnival subconscious, and later cut his homicidal song from whole cloth.

Back at Waits's Red Barn, the plot thickens with a biblical injunction and some fatalistic philosophy:

Now, thou shalt not covet thy neighbor's house or covet thy neighbor's wife
But for some, murder is the only door through which they enter life

Waits comes closest to spilling the beans here: he implies a green-eyed motive for the slaying, then describes a lynch mob–like seizure of a suspect and adds a few more names. But the sharper focus is fleeting—if broadsheet ballads like "The Murder of Maria Marten" privilege plot over poetry, Waits's "Murder in the Red Barn" reverses the model.

Well, they surrounded the house, they smoked him out, took him off in chains
The sky turned black and bruised and we had months of heavy rains
Now, the ravens nest in the rotted roof of Chenoweth's old place
And no one's asking Cal about that scar upon his face

---

247 The song is little recorded, but a brooding folk-rock version by the English singer Shirley Collins, backed by the Fairport Convention offshoot the Albion Country Band (with Richard Thompson on guitar), is a highlight of her 1971 debut album *No Roses*.

Like the moody landscapes of Romantic painters, in Waits's world, nature seems to reflect or comment on human activity. Black birds and thunderclouds offset the wretched figure dragged through the smoke, presumably to his doom. Red leaves and rust mirror lust and spilt blood. If "Murder in the Red Barn" has a palette beyond autumnal, it's surely black and red—primordial colors of death and fire, the void and sex.[248] In the next lines, Waits explicitly links red with violence.

'Cause there's nothin' strange about an axe with bloodstains in the barn
There's always some killin' you got to do around the farm

Historians suggest that the ubiquity of red barns in the U.S. stemmed from using iron oxide in homemade wood-preserving varnishes. These were cheaper than store-bought paints and stained wood reddish-orange, over time establishing red as the standard barn color. Today, the bright red barn with white trim is a nostalgic national icon—a Rockwell-esque symbol of self-sufficiency and simpler times. Cheery facsimiles filled with animals were once popular toys. Such heartwarming associations make Waits's choice of homicidal locale unsettling—except that, like so many beloved American symbols, this one's been sanitized. Lost in the Grandma's-apple-pie vibe is the color red's other association with barns—the ubiquitous bloodletting that goes on there, from livestock slaughter to vanquishing vermin and predator animals. In Waits's song, this routine butchery is perverted by leaving *human* bloodstains in the barn, but the farm cycle of birthing and killing is as natural as the sun and seasons. As is the eternal return of death to earth—whether roadkill, random carcasses, or bodies in boxes. Decay replenishes the soil, transforming once-living things into rich ground for renewal. This occult process occurs across the countryside but remains mostly unseen, just out of sight.

The woods will never tell what sleeps beneath the trees
Or what's buried 'neath a rock or hiding in the leaves

Years ago, an article described Waits as a "lexicographers nightmare."[249] This was during his aforementioned shift from bourbon-soaked poet of urban twilight to shamanic ringmaster of the American psyche. Waits launched a startling transformation a decade into his career with the 1983 album *Swordfishtrombones*. He evolved from a conventional if offbeat warbler of sad and seedy songs into something more: a multimedia artist (musician, actor, dramaturge) who fashioned innovative songbooks and performance works from a dizzying array of musical styles (roots music, circus bands, Brecht and Weill), and literary influences (the Beats, Bill Hicks, Carson McCullers) to create a dreamlike shadow-portrait of

---

248 It's also the color scheme of Waits's hermaphroditic devil outfit in the Jarmusch video–scarlet cape, cowl with horns, and high heel, with black fishnets and suit. His undersized bicycle is also red. Come to think of it, Waits's getup also recalls Spring-Heeled Jack, with his (black) cape, helmet, and diabolical countenance.
249 I'd happily credit the scribe who coined the phrase, but I can't find the article online or in my music-mag archive.

America.[250] He did so during the heyday of postmodern critical theory—a time when critics used hyper-intellectual schemas of interpretation to break down books, films, music, and art into supposedly immutable parts.

Hence the "lexicographer's nightmare." A lexicographer is a compiler of dictionaries, a sorter of words and phrases into coherent compendiums. In postmodern discourse, the term also applies to the "texts" beloved by deconstructionists—the cultural artifacts they reduce and dissect. But Waits doesn't deconstruct well. He integrates his sources and styles so fully you can't pry them apart. Thoroughly analyzed, his annotations need annotations. This trait places Waits in a pantheon of similarly irreducible eclectics like Charles Ives, Sun Ra, and Captain Beefheart, and, like those visionaries, Waits is closely associated with soundscapes—seamlessly constructed aural collages that play, to use his synesthetic phrase, like "movies for the ear."

In the final reel of "Murder in the Red Barn," Waits sketches one last scene of rustic intrigue. While it provides no whodunit closure, it effectively tweaks the song's eerie amalgam of shadows and secrets in the harvest-time earth.

Now, a lady can't do nothin' without folks' tongues waggin'
Is this blood on the tree or is it autumn's red blaze?
When the ground's soft for diggin' and the rain will bring all this gloom
There's nothing wrong with a lady drinking alone in her room

Then junkyard percussion, twangy banjo, and a closing reminder:

But, there was a murder in the red barn, a murder in the red barn ...

WHEN YOU GET TO THE BOTTOM, WE'LL KISS YOU TO SLEEP

And so, all the night-tide, I lie down by the side
Of my darling—my darling—my life and my bride,
In her sepulchre there by the sea—
In her tomb by the sounding sea.
—Edgar Allan Poe, "Annabell Lee," 1849

"Lie Down" by the Handsome Family is a song about drowning. Short and simple, it lacks grand ambition yet remains an atmospheric chiller that triggers rich associations between water and death. Its brevity and vagueness resemble a hard-to-shake dream—a montage of haunting images glimpsed in sleep that evoke unplumbed themes after waking. And like a potent dream, each listen reveals new connections.

---

250 Critical to this evolution was his wife and muse, the actress Kathleen Brennan, whom he met and married in 1980. By 1992, she was his full-time co-writer and artistic collaborator.

Tuesday at dawn, Michael's glasses washed ashore
With a styrofoam box and two broken oars
He'd been digging for clams in the muddy swamp weeds
When he heard the saltwater whisper to him

The song is the second-to-last track on *In the Air* (2000), the follow-up to the critically acclaimed *Through the Trees* (1998)—the breakthrough record by the husband-and-wife duo of Brett Sparks (music, vocals, guitar) and Rennie Sparks (lyrics, bass, banjo). Both albums collect songs about life, death, and mystery. But *In the Air* is a tad warmer in tone than its brooding predecessor. The narrative in "Lie Down" is minimal; it has just two verses and a chorus (sung twice). The song is built on three guitar parts: rhythmic chords, an eerie rising-and-falling lead melody, and a distorted mid-song solo. Brett's voice, typically gruff, is here well-water clear, and he harmonizes with himself on the disarmingly lovely chorus.

Lie down, lie down in the dark, rolling sea
When you get to the bottom, we'll kiss you to sleep
Lie down, lie down in the dark, rolling sea
When you get to the bottom, we'll kiss you to sleep

A chestnut of music-buff discourse is the penultimate-track rule codified in the ex-Go-Between Robert Forster's entertaining book *The 10 Rules of Rock and Roll*: No. 2: "The second-last song on every album is the weakest."[251] This was especially true in the LP days when albums needed strong opening and closing tracks on both sides to maintain interest and compel listeners to flip the record. Consequently, the most anemic song was often slipped in before the anthemic finale. Superficially, "Lie Down" fulfills this expectation. Nestled between the Sparks' reworking of a gospel standard, "Grandmother Waits for You," and their own perversely sunny murder ballad "My Beautiful Bride," the song is a brief sketch, and, next to full-blown *In the Air* narratives like the whimsical "Sad Milkman" or the stately "Up Falling Rock Hill," "Lie Down" is a definite placeholder. Yet its modest nature is its greatest asset: like a quirky 45 B-side or between-the-cracks film, it sticks with you like an afterthought amidst larger-scale statements.

"Lie Down" tells its tale in concise lines that are detailed yet obscure. The song opens like a police procedural or true crime book ("Tuesday at dawn …"). Michael, we learn, went clamming in the swampy sea. He didn't return, but his personal effects floated ashore. These include broken oars but no boat, implying mishap or sabotage. The second and final verse throws the listener a few more clues, confirming Michael's fate and his role in his own undoing.

Michael threw his glasses in the cold green water
Hermit crabs ran as he dove down under
One of his shoes bobbed on the waves
Seagulls circled 'til it finally sank

251   Robert Forster, *The 10 Rules of Rock and Roll: Collected Music Writings 2002-11* (London: Jawbone Press, 2011), p. 13.

PeterJ1977/Creative Commons

THE HANDSOME FAMILY, 2008

But the cold heart of the song is its sleepy-time chorus. Something in the water whispers, cajoles, seduces Michael to plunge in and sink: to founder to the seabed and sleep there, sedated by sensual but deadly kisses.

Lie down, lie down in the dark, rolling sea
When you get to the bottom, we'll kiss you to sleep
Lie down, lie down in the dark, rolling sea
When you get to the bottom, we'll kiss you to sleep

Rennie Sparks is a fiction writer and musicologist, and both vocations enrich her songwriting. Her evocative language and mining of cultural motifs are as seductive as the siren call that elicits Michael's doom for literate listeners drawn to the darker side of alt-country. "Lie Down" packs a lot of specificity into sixteen lines (twelve, really—four lines repeat) but leaves much unanswered. Who is Michael? A bespectacled introvert who shouldn't go boating alone, from the sound of it. And why does he throw his glasses in the water? Does it symbolize shedding persona and truly seeing in the face of death? Or is it just easier to swim without them? None of this would matter, except we want to know more because Michael seems to commit suicide. Except what he really does is answer the call of a mysterious force and then sort of mate with death. Except that's clearly a metaphor. Except maybe it isn't.

"Lie Down" is a modern take on an ancient trope: being haunted by a water spirit and dispatched to a sunken grave. Every culture has such tales and many concern mythical species that lure mariners to their deaths, like the aforementioned sirens. These monstrous bird-women, immortalized by Homer, mesmerized sailors with enchanted singing, causing shipwrecks (though other accounts describe them boarding ships and ripping entranced men to pieces). Related are mermaids who, despite image-softening in the age of Disney and *Beach Blanket Bingo,* were feared as aquatic femmes fatales or demonic beings by seamen as varied as Christopher Columbus, Henry Hudson, and Edward "Blackbeard" Teach, all of whom claimed to see them. These humanesque creatures were not exclusively female: sirens appear as both sexes in pre-Classical Greece, and mermen are the lesser-known masculine counterparts to Ariel and her sisters, but, over time, the idea of men bewitched and drowned by alluring female sea-beings came to dominate sailors' accounts.[252]

Berggruen Museum/Creative Commons

ARNOLD BÖCKLIN, *SIRENS,* 1875

Bodies of water are deeply linked with the feminine and maternal—womb-like loci of regeneration and birth, with the sea our ultimate source. And sex is a watery affair—a moist coupling in which procreation depends on an alchemical commingling of bodily fluids. These are archetypal associations embedded in our psyches, but, contrary to Western preference, archetypes are double-edged, with light and dark aspects. Thus, water both nurtures and kills, and the correlative flip side of sex is death.[253]

Water. Drowning. Mother. We start as aquatic creatures, and our births are a kind of reverse drowning. We gestate contentedly, floating in amniotic fluid, then emerge from the darkness, suffocating until our throats are cleared and our backsides slapped and we begin to breathe on our own. Our primordial ancestors were literal sea creatures, and 400 million years ago some soggy forebear crawled from brine to shore, learned to breathe air, and birthed the terrestrial lifeforms

---

252 Provocative exceptions exist. In Ludwig Binswanger's clinical study of Ellen West (see "Worse than the Thing That Possessed Me" in chapter 4), the psychiatrist notes a poem written by the suicidal woman as a teenager. "[In her poem] 'Kiss Me Dead,'" he writes, "the sun sinks like a fiery ball into the ocean and the gloomy, cold Sea-King is called upon to press her into his arms in ardent love-lust and kiss her dead" ("The Case of Ellen West," in Rollo May, Ernest Angel, and Henri F. Ellenberger, eds., *Existence: A New Dimension in Psychiatry and Psychology,* Rowman & Littlefield, 2004, p. 321).

253 A reversal of the man-drowning aquatic she-demon occurs in a dreamlike horror film called *Let's Scare Jessica to Death* (John Hancock, 1971)–about hippie-era urbanites relocating to a rundown country farmhouse. A recently discharged mental patient (Zohra Lampert) has a terrifying encounter with a nomadic young woman (Mariclare Costello), who turns out to be the vampiric ghost of a former resident who drowned in a nearby cove on her wedding day. The pair go swimming in the cove, and the young woman disappears under the water, only to reemerge as the walking corpse she truly is–pale and cadaverous in her bridal gown. She tries to drown Lampert, who manages to break free and escape.

that spawned our species. Life inextricably links to water, and so does death. Our solid bodies are illusory; after dying, putrefaction liquefies our visceral remains into something rich and strange. History and myth are replete with floods that drown whole populations, forcing collective rebirth. We drink water, bathe in it, sail across it, and rhapsodize about its beauty. But we also die from inhaling it—sometimes accidentally, other times by murderous force, and occasionally with intentional self-harm.

Drowning and burning top many lists of most feared ways of dying. Both involve panic, being trapped, and suffocation (the most common cause of death by fire). But only drowning involves the torturous predicament of being forced to inhale water. Interestingly, both are symbols of cleansing and rebirth in the arts and religious ritual. In Bill Viola's notable video installation *The Crossing* (1996), side-by-side life-size screens show the same man facing the viewer. Flames engulf him from below on the left, while water floods him from above on the right. Both figures respond only by lifting their arms as if to welcome the elemental onslaught. Fire and water consume both, leaving nothing behind. Viola has been candid about *The Crossing*'s inspiration: on a boat outing with family at age six, he jumped in a lake, sank to the bottom, and almost drowned. An uncle pulled him to safety, but Viola felt no panic. "I was witnessing this extraordinarily beautiful world with light filtering down," he remembered. "It was like paradise. I didn't even know that I was drowning . . . Later I knew I had crossed the threshold to death."[254]

Another water-drenched work where drowning is a life-affirming metaphor is *Quadrophenia* (1973), the Pete Townshend–penned rock opera by the Who, about a troubled teen's struggles to transcend peer- and parent-based pressures and repair his fractured self. It opens with the calm "I Am the Sea" and ends with the dramatic "Love, Reign o'er Me." In the middle, the protagonist sings a confessional with spiritual overtones, "Drowned," linking suicidal ideation ("I wanna drown / In cold water") with the drive toward individuation:

Let me flow into the ocean
Let me get back to the sea
Let me be stormy and let me be calm
Let the tide in, and set me free[255]

On the darker side, drowning is a persistent, if unpopular, method of non-metaphoric suicide.[256] In Kay Redfield Jamison's study of self-murder, *Night Falls*

---

254   Ben Luke, "How Pioneering Video Artist Bill Viola's Near-Death Experience Influences His Work on Religion," *Evening Standard*, 9 January 2019.

255   Townshend elaborated on the song's spiritual dimension in the liner notes for the 2011 reissue of *Quadrophenia*: "[I]t's a love song, God's love being the ocean and our 'selves' being the drops of water that make it up . . . I want to drown in that ocean." The song is a highlight of Quadrophenia, diminished slightly by Roger Daltrey's unsubtle vocal. A superior version is a live solo cut, passionately sung by Townshend to rapid-fire rhythm guitar, on the Amnesty International fundraiser *The Secret Policeman's Ball* (1979) (www.youtube.com/watch?v=2t9slqL_eSw).

256   According to the Centers for Disease Control (CDC) and Suicide Prevention Resource Center (SPRC), drowning accounts for less than 2% of U.S. suicides. This figure excludes jumping into water, where it is the fall itself that is more likely to cause death (e.g., since 1937, some 1,600 people have leaped from the Golden Gate Bridge, but the vast majority died from the 250-foot drop).

Fast, the psychologist asks whether methods of suicide have symbolic significance, noting that Karl Meininger believed that drowning oneself signified "a desire to return to the womb," while Freud theorized that methods revealed—wait for it—"sexual wish fulfillments." Jamison concludes that "the inventiveness of the interpretations would appear to outweigh the available evidence" and argues that accessibility is the main criterion (i.e., bridge-crossers jump from bridges, gun-owners shoot themselves, etc.).[257]

Certainly, Virginia Woolf—one of the most famous modern cases of suicide by drowning—chose an accessible method. The River Ouse was near her home in East Sussex, a ready option for someone who planned to end it all. Yet there's something indelibly poetic about Woolf, exhausted from declining mental health, writing a suicide note to her supportive husband ("Dearest, I feel certain that I am going mad again . . . [a]nd I shan't recover this time"), then putting on her overcoat, filling its pockets with stones, and walking into the river.[258] Partly, it's her commitment to that torturous predicament: forcing oneself to inhale water. But poignant metaphors emerge from her method: the gradual descent from land to water to underwater mirrors her descent into madness, and both the disarrayed state of her mind and her stream-of-consciousness writing style evoke drowning—sinking irretrievably into a chaos of words, thoughts, and memories.

A darkly comic cousin to "Lie Down"—also an atmospheric sketch and placeholder between more substantive songs—is Tom Waits's "The Ocean Doesn't Want Me," from his morbid masterpiece *Bone Machine* (1992). Atop disjointed percussion and meandering atonal melodies, Waits embodies a quavery-voiced nut job who postpones suicide by drowning because elemental forces are out of sync that day.

> *The ocean doesn't want me today*
> *But I'll be back tomorrow to play*
> *And the strangels will take me*
> *Down deep in their brine*
> *The mischievous braingels*
> *Down into the endless blue wine*

Unlike the Handsome Family's murkily defined underwater nemeses, Waits's oddball narrator knows his well enough to name them—"strangels" and "braingels"—and their neologistic monikers cannily evoke the schizoid duality of the supernatural and psychotic. But the stars aren't right, so death will have to wait:

> *I'd love to go drowning*
> *And to stay and to stay*
> *But the ocean doesn't want me today*

---

257 Kay Redfield Jamison, *Night Falls Fast: Understanding Suicide* (New York: Vintage Books, 1999), p. 139.
258 Ibid., pp. 84–85.

Going "down" or "under" is a recurrent theme in Handsome Family songs. "Down in the Ground," a key track from *Through the Trees* (*In the Air*'s predecessor), substitutes underground descent for underwater submersion. It's a rare lead vocal by Rennie, and, to minimal *art brut* banjo accompaniment, she sings in a grating voice:

> *I am not afraid when you call me down*
> *Down the basement steps, under the house*
> *Down, down in the ground*

It's a declaration of fearlessness in the face of sunken spaces that shelter creepy-crawly things most of us would rather avoid. But it's also a mission statement for the Handsome Family, who explore what's hidden below via the unlikely framework of American country music, with its dualistic treatment of light and dark, good and evil. The Handsome Family defuse this dualism, portraying life in more balanced terms than our sentimental, denial-immersed culture finds comfortable. So a love song is followed by a murder ballad, a portrait of grief with a rumination on decomposition, a life-affirming story with a tale told by an idiot, full of sound and fury. In "Down in the Ground," Sparks, too, is called down. As with doomed Michael and his seductive sirens, hidden forces compel our passive selves from comfort to realms of confrontation and mystery.

> *Black cows are limping, the white dogs bark*
> *Crickets are screaming, smoke in the barn*
> *Just like a field snake eating a mouse*
> *Just like a bluegill, hook through its mouth*
> *Down, down in the ground*

Aquatic themes recur in Handsome Family songs. In "The Forgotten Lake" (*Singing Bones*, 2003), an underwater repository hides human refuse, old and new: "Covered wagons and the wings of missing planes / Float between black fish underneath the velvet waves." But myth and anomaly are never far away: "Strange lights fly across the rocky beach / Girls in white nightgowns wander barefoot in their sleep." The "down, down" motif returns—this time applied to both human beings and their talismanic belongings:

> *Down, down*
> *Float them down*
> *Let the waters float them down*
> *To where they'll remember everything*

Fear of water takes various forms, but, at its most extreme, it divides roughly into two categories. Aquaphobia is a generalized fear, and sufferers typically have water-related traumas in their past: a near-drowning, a boating accident, a witnessed death. These stressors amplify reasonable unease into heightened anxiety. But aquaphobes frequently recover through mastery of their environment—by gradually acclimating themselves to water, learning to swim, or acquiring nautical skills. A related condition is harder to reduce and remedy: thalassophobia, a morbid fear of deep bodies of water.

If aquaphobia is an irrational response to a rational threat, thalassophobia is rooted in something less tangible—a primal sense of dread triggered by two watery traits: depth and darkness. These attributes provoke reasonable fears—of reduced visibility, sinking, or unseen objects and animals—but, for the thalassophobe, such signifiers highlight murkier, metaphoric realms. Depth and darkness are rich in psychological associations, often integrated into everyday speech (e.g., "I'm in too deep," "I'm treading water," "I feel like I'm sinking"). But more unsettling meanings lurk below. "Water," Carl Jung wrote, "is the commonest symbol for the unconscious."[259] And, since the fundamental precept of Jung's psychology is that the unconscious remains mostly hidden but is the source of our most profound insights, to emerge from its darkness requires a potentially frightening deep dive to map and explore its turf.

"The Forgotten Lake" invokes this transformative process in underwater and aboveground spaces:

Golden flash at the corner of your eye
Those shadows that climb
Your darkened walls at night
They open a door lit with forgotten light

Deep water also evokes the void of the existentialists—the bottomless pit of meaninglessness that haunts souls, fosters despair, and threatens life and well-being. At metaphysical levels, it extends this gut-wrenching unease to the cosmos and reality itself.

These elements coalesce in a brief but pivotal sequence in that great American novel of deep water and leviathan beasts, *Moby-Dick* (1851). In chapter 93 of Herman Melville's masterpiece, the cabin boy Pip has a mind-blowing encounter with the ocean's depths. Pip is a young African American, beloved by the crew but so physically small and inexperienced that he's kept aboard the *Pequod* for his safety when the whaleboats head out. When a sailor is injured, Pip takes his place, but when a whale strikes the boat, Pip panics and jumps into the sea. He becomes entangled on a line, and, in the process of saving him, the crew loses the whale. The second mate, Stubb, rebukes Pip and warns him they'll leave him at sea if this happens again. When Pip leaps into the water a second time, the sailors abandon him to pursue other whales. The *Pequod* later retrieves him, but the crew finds he is forever changed.

259 C. G. Jung, *The Archetypes and the Collective Unconscious*, translated by R. F. C. Hull (New York: Princeton University Press, 1980), p. 18.

The sea had jeeringly kept his finite body up, but drowned the infinite of his soul. Not drowned entirely, though. Rather carried down alive to wondrous depths, where strange shapes of the unwrapped primal world glided to and fro before his passive eyes ...

Pip's abandonment, isolation, and glimpse of the vast unknown overwhelm and transform him. He achieves a kind of cosmic consciousness but perceives ultimate truth as alien and empty, "indifferent as his God," which terrifies and diminishes him.

He saw God's foot upon the treadle of the loom, and spoke of it; and therefore his shipmates called him mad. So man's insanity is heaven's sense ...[260]

The episode prefigures existentialist philosophy. It also mirrors themes in more lurid literature, like the cosmic horror of H. P. Lovecraft, whose prewar tales of monstrous alien gods lurking outside our reality underscore human incomprehension and insignificance. "The most merciful thing in the world," Lovecraft wrote in "The Call of Cthulhu" (1928), his eerie tale of an inter-dimensional being, trapped on the seafloor, that contacts humans in their dreams, "is the inability of the human mind to correlate all its contents."[261]

Fear of unseen objects and animals in deep water also resounds with claimed encounters with lake monsters—eel-like or saurian creatures glimpsed while surfaced before they plunge back below. Such sightings confound easy categorization. While most are hoaxes or misidentifications, a stubborn few remain ambiguous, and, like apparitions and funny lights in the sky, people go on seeing them despite widespread disapprobation, including competent witnesses who shun publicity. The most famous such beast lives in Scotland's Loch Ness—a thalassophobe's nightmare with 900-foot depths and water so thick with peat that underwater visibility is practically nil. The loch's elusive inhabitant, "Nessie," is a clear variant on the legendary kelpie or water horse. But modern-day sightings challenge simple distinctions between real and unreal. Such encounters—simultaneously folkloric and anomalous—subvert Western taxonomies. Hence the obsession with proving or disproving their veracity. But lost in the endless debate over "Can such things be?" are startling implications about perception and reality. While sober-faced amateurs and a handful of scientists theorize about post–Ice Age plesiosaur survival, other researchers introduce hair-raising concepts about psychic projections, synchronicities, and multiple realities.[262]

---

260 Herman Melville, *Moby-Dick; or, The Whale* (New York: Book-of-the-Month-Club, 1997), p. 370.

261 H. P. Lovecraft, *Tales* (New York: Library of America, 2005), p. 167.

262 A striking example of this shift from materialist to immaterialist views is the case of Ted Holiday, an English naturalist and angling expert who hunted for Nessie in his spare time. Holiday assumed a scientific source for the monster and wrote a measured account of his theory that Nessie proved the survival of a prehistoric slug-like creature: *The Great Orm of Loch Ness: A Practical Inquiry into the Nature and Habits of Water-Monsters* (1969). But he soon concluded there was more to water monsters than meets the eye, and in *The Dragon and the Disc* (1973) explored connections with UFOs, psychic phenomena, and

This uneasy union between the tangible and visionary is another Handsome Family domain. A strength of the band is their ability to keep metaphoric contexts fluid so that a seemingly straightforward story—whether Michael's drowning in "Lie Down," Rennie's descent in "Down in the Ground," or the submerged mysteries of "The Forgotten Lake"—can function on multiple levels at once. Ultimately, these explorations "down" and "under," though troubling, need not be threatening. "The Forgotten Lake" offers this assurance against the terrors of depth and darkness:

In dark water the gray veil falls away
We'll see with closed eyes
And drift softly in the rain

The song ends with a final exhortation to sink into the water and be illuminated by its mysteries:

Down, down
Float us down
Let the waters float us down
To where we'll remember everything

It's a seductive recast of the band's siren call to "drown"—to confront unknown depths for a glimpse of transcendent, possibly transformative wonder.

demonology. One of the things that puzzled Holiday about Nessie sightings was the fear and dread they inspired; rather than marvel at the sight of an unknown animal, observers were more often disquieted and disturbed. Despite his scientific outlook and experience as an outdoorsman, the loch began to unnerve Holiday as well: "After sunset, Loch Ness is not a water by which to linger. The feeling is hard to define and difficult to explain …" After many strange experiences, he tried to summarize his ideas in a book called *The Goblin Universe* but died of a heart attack before publication (it was printed posthumously in 1986) (quoted in Colin Wilson's Introduction, Ted Holiday, *The Goblin Universe*, London: Xanadu, 1986, p. 2).

STEVEN L. JONES, *OPEN HYMNAL #4*, 2019

CHAPTER SIX: LOST AND FOUND

WRECKS ON THE HIGHWAY

Williams College Museum of Art/Creative Commons

GRANT WOOD, *DEATH ON RIDGE ROAD*, 1935

Come back. Even as a shadow, even as a dream.
—Euripides, Herakles

Shards of shattered windshield, mangled steel, the stink of burning rubber. Torn clothes drenched with liquor, pungent on the breath of a dying man whose blood mingles with that of his passengers on a moonlit road. Lives cut short by reckless decisions and a stranger stumbling upon the scene, helpless to intercede. Moans of pain as eternity beckons, then death rattles as hearts cease to beat. Crackling flames, perhaps a still spinning tire. Otherwise, silence and night.

"Wreck on the Highway" uses spare language to describe a tragic tableau caused by human folly that affords no hope of survival and perhaps no redemption. Even in a musical genre—old-school country—in which melodrama is an accepted means to an artistic end, the song stands out for its bleak fatalism. In its original form—the 1938 recording by its composer, Dorsey Dixon—the song was a temperance homily, sincere if moralistic. But the trimming of some lyrical

fat and a rhythmic rethink in later
versions transformed the song and
its forlorn "I didn't hear nobody pray"
chorus into something less preachy
and more universal in tone.

> *Who did you say it was, brother?*
> *Who was it fell by the way?*
> *When whiskey and blood ran together*
> *Did you hear anyone pray?*

Dorsey Dixon (1897–1968) wrote
message songs. A poor textile mill
worker from South Carolina, he
channeled a flair for songwriting into
a part-time career as a singer and
guitarist in the hillbilly style. Local
radio exposure led to his recording

DORSEY DIXON WITH GUITAR, 1962

over fifty sides for RCA Victor in the 1930s in a fiddle-and-guitar format with
his brother Howard. Dixon drew from life experience in his songs, and, after
"Wreck on the Highway" (inspired by a newspaper story about a fatal crash—
original title: "Didn't Hear Nobody Pray"), his best-known tunes are labor
songs like "Weave Room Blues" and "Babies in the Mill." The latter critiqued
child labor, a familiar social ill for Dixon: Dorsey had started millwork at age
twelve and Howard at ten, while their sister Nancy worked as a spinner from
age eight. His lowly origins drew mockery from factory bosses; his New Deal
sentiments, accusations of communism. Like many dirt-poor Southerners, he
took refuge from personal pains and disappointments in a deep religious faith.
A posthumously published memoir was titled *I Don't Want Nothin' bout My Life
Wrote Out, Because I Had It Rough in Life.*

Struggle and frustration also marked his music career. None of the Dixon
brothers' recordings escaped the hillbilly ghetto, and, when the "King of
Country Music," Roy Acuff, scored a hit with the retitled "Wreck on the
Highway" in 1942, unable (or unwilling) to recall the song's provenance, the
Grand Ole Opry star took writing credit. Dixon reluctantly sued, and an out-
of-court settlement awarded him the copyright, $1,700 in unpaid royalties,
and a percentage of future profits. It proved to be the pinnacle of his success.
A quixotic relocation to New York City to promote his music (during which
he worked in a New Jersey rayon factory) gained him no ground; he stopped
performing and returned to millwork in the South. Within a few years, his
eyesight failed, forcing him to retire. His wife left him, and his brother died
on the job. When Dixon himself died a decade later, despite a modest revival
of interest in his music during the '60s folk boom, he remained a footnote in
country music history.

I didn't hear nobody pray, dear brother
I didn't hear nobody pray
I heard the crash on the highway
But I didn't hear nobody pray

What's mostly kept his legacy alive is "Wreck on the Highway," specifically Acuff's now-classic version and its many descendants. Acuff, a commercially savvy entertainer with a background in medicine shows, knew how to tweak the tune to preserve its tragic narrative and hillbilly style (both marketable novelties in 1940s America) while smoothing its edges to broaden its appeal. Thus he altered the song's feel by replacing the original's choppy oom-pah-pah meter with a more sensual waltz-time sway, and supplanted Dixon's gruff vocal recitation with a fluid country croon. Critically, he augmented the chorus with mournful harmonies that it's now impossible to imagine the song without.

He also excised unnecessary words: a redundant second verse that needlessly delays the action and an awkward coda that provides an unnecessary moral in the form of an explicit quit-drinking-and-turn-to-Jesus message that narrowed the song's appeal.

Please give up the game and stop drinking
For Jesus is pleading with you
It costs him a lot in redeeming
Redeeming the promise for you

Such criticism isn't meant to disparage Dixon's obviously earnest religious beliefs, but the lyrics Acuff kept are a testament to both less-is-more aesthetics and the raw artistry the more seasoned performer must have admired when he first encountered the song.

When I heard the crash on the highway
I knew what it was from the start
I went to the scene of destruction
And the picture was stamped on my heart

There was whiskey and glass all together
Mixed up with blood where they lay
Death played her hand in destruction
But I didn't hear nobody pray

Aside from a changed word here and there, these central verses—which describe the wreck's aftermath with cinematic vividness—are sung as Dixon wrote them. Only a cynic could remain unmoved.

I wish I could change this sad story
That I am now telling you
But there is no way I can change it
For somebody's life is now through

Their soul has been called by the master
They died in a crash on their way
I heard the groans of the dying
But I didn't hear nobody pray

All subsequent versions of "Wreck on the Highway" derive from Acuff's template. Instrumentation and tempo change, but renditions impress mainly on the merits of their singers. Perhaps unsurprisingly, the best come from artists of backgrounds similar to Dixon's: Southerners steeped in old-time religion and the hardships of rural life. Many also have a more than passing familiarity with the destructive side of drinking.

Ira and Charlie Louvin recorded "Wreck on the Highway" late in their career. The volatile duo—Alabaman brothers whose talent for close-harmony singing helped them escape a violent father and backbreaking labor farming cotton— finally went their separate ways in 1963 after two decades of performing together, their partnership a victim of Ira's out-of-control drinking. Recorded in 1962, less than a year before they called it quits, their version of "Wreck on the Highway" is slightly marred by bland instrumental backing. But their voices, guileless and pure, bring chills, transporting the listener to the heart of the song's pitiful scenario. On record, the Louvins always sound like their best or better selves, as if their gravest conflicts—with each other, their inner and outer lives, God, and a devil that was painfully real for both—could be set aside and forgotten only when they sang together.

Ironically, Ira was sober when he and his fourth wife, Anne, died in their own wreck on the highway—a 1965 head-on collision between cars in a Missouri construction zone. Compounding the irony, the other driver *was* drunk, and Ira, when he died, had an outstanding warrant for driving under the influence. A wretched alcoholic—amiable when sober, violent when drunk—Ira Louvin died at forty-one and was outlived by nearly fifty years by his more even-tempered brother.

Like the Louvins, George Jones had a doleful voice of such emotive power he tapped depths of feeling rarely heard in country music before or since. Like Ira, he also was bedeviled all his life by demon alcohol (plus various drugs), a circumstance that led to multiple hospitalizations, public breakdowns, and periods of outright madness, despite commercial success and widespread admiration for his vocal gifts. For years he ranked high on celebrity death pools, but a drunken car wreck in 1999 seems to have scared him straight. He died thirteen years later, age eighty-one, of a respiratory infection.

Jones recorded "Wreck on the Highway" in 1965, in an unlikely duet with the teen idol Gene Pitney, and gave the song the sort of sensitive, soulful reading that characterized all his best material ("I sing because I love it," he told *Billboard* a few years before his death, "not because of the dollar signs").[263] Like the Louvins, when Jones sang, he seemed to find an inner peace that eluded him in daily life and in his struggles with addiction. While his version falls short of his best work, hampered by the song's awkward duet format and Pitney's lesser vocal talent, it's still an affecting performance.

Alcohol suffuses the narrative in "Wreck on the Highway," but redemption is its true theme. The subtext of the song's woeful chorus (*I didn't hear nobody pray*) is salvation through Jesus—the forgiveness of sins and promise of life after death central to Christian theology, especially in its literalist forms, achieved through heartfelt confession and embrace of Christ as savior. If the song's narrator hears no regretful last words, no anguished cries to God at the "scene of destruction," an already senseless tragedy might mean a fate worse than death, with souls lost forever beside cold, stiffening bodies.

It's easy to mock this simplistic scenario, to dismiss it as claptrap or treat it with bemused condescension. The excesses of the Christian Right predispose many to have little sympathy for modern-day fundamentalist beliefs. But today's conservative evangelicals have little in common with their rural, working-class predecessors. For them, daily existence was often a life-or-death struggle between fearsome external forces—economic, political, environmental, medical—over which they had limited control. Such conflicts found natural expression in the dualistic creeds and iconography of a blood-and-thunder religious faith with few shades of gray. A vivid example is the Louvin Brothers' 1959 album *Satan Is Real*, a poignant set of songs about spiritual crisis and alcoholic desperation (e.g., "The Drunkard's Doom," "The Kneeling Drunkard's Prayer") that's sadly better known for its kitschy cover art than for the anguish and yearning within its grooves.

As modified by Acuff, "Wreck on the Highway" is actually fairly nuanced. Minus Dixon's explicit temperance plea to Jesus, "I didn't hear nobody pray" grows flexible, able to accommodate various faiths and views of redemption, or simply signifies death so cruelly sudden that a final prayer—desired by many in their last moments, with or without the promise of eternal life—is impossible. Liberally approached, it might even evoke an agnostic's or atheist's cry (i.e., "I didn't hear nobody *answer*," either). Consequently, a modern-day country-punk band like the Waco Brothers—irreverent, left-wing, anticlerical—can play the song in a fiery version atop a thunderous Bo Diddley–esque beat with full conviction and zero disdain.[264]

A version of "Wreck on the Highway" in title and subject only, Bruce Springsteen's 1980 variation which closes his album *The River* provides a glimmer of hope, compromised but extant, at the end of a double LP of songs that portray an economically battered America on the cusp of the Reagan revolution. In

---

263   Ray Waddell, "George Jones: The Billboard Interview (2006)," *Billboard*, 26 April 2013.
264   On the band's 1997 album *Cowboy in Flames*. It's also a highlight of their scorching live shows.

Springsteen's adaptation, the singer stumbles upon a nighttime crash but finds a survivor: a young man who cries out not for God but for help and is soon sent away in an ambulance. Later, in bed with his "baby," the singer is haunted by his memory of the injured driver. He imagines "a girlfriend or a young wife … and a state trooper knocking in the middle of the night" to inform her of his demise. The singer holds his lover tightly.

Springsteen followed *The River*—which despite its beleaguered tone, was a full-tilt rock album—with *Nebraska* (1982), a genuinely despondent, all-acoustic set of songs about murder, hard times, and driving all night. (The record's moody title track was inspired by the chilling 1958 Starkweather–Fugate killings; see chapter 2.) *Nebraska* also closes with a "hopeful" song, "Reason to Believe," but its opening image of a man poking an unmoving dog with a stick to see if it's dead sets its tone of diminished expectations. If Springsteen's "Wreck on the Highway" seemed to say that, no matter how bad things get, love will see you through (with an exhortation to never take it for granted), "Reason to Believe" implied that hope was little more than a reflex born out of desperation.

Another song, another wreck. This one captured on film in a moment of sublime calm, like the magic hour between sunset and dusk.

In one of the most memorable sequences in *Dont Look Back*, D. A. Pennebaker's 1965 *cinéma vérité* film about Bob Dylan, the young, already iconic musician and his most intimate circle enjoy a rare quiet night in a hotel room, unmolested by fans, journalists, or hangers-on. The folksinger Joan Baez strums her guitar and gracefully sings an unreleased Dylan song while the soon-to-go-electric troubadour writes lyrics at a typewriter. The mood is warm and tranquil, and both Dylan's clownish sidekick Bob Neuwirth and his bearlike manager, Albert Grossman, remain uncharacteristically still, seemingly entranced by the music.

Bad news, bad news
Came to me where I sleep
Turn, turn, turn again
Sayin' one of your friends
Is in trouble deep
Turn, turn to the rain
And the wind

It's a stunning song, and the viewer is struck that Dylan has so much good music under his belt that he can leave this choice composition unreleased (as it would remain for another twenty years).[265]

"Percy's Song" is an outtake from *The Times They Are A-Changin'* (1963). Its tune and recurring "rain and the wind" refrain are indebted to the folkie Paul Clayton and the traditional song "The Twa Sisters" (Child 10), but "Percy" transcends its sources. What's most remarkable about the song—especially

---

265 It finally appeared on the Dylan box set *Biograph* (1985).

given its spellbinding effect, so evident in that long-ago late-night hotel room—is how little happens during its whopping sixteen verses and seven-minutes-plus duration. Its story is simple: a man is sentenced to life imprisonment for vehicular manslaughter ("There was four persons killed / And he was at the wheel"), and his friend (the song's narrator) confronts the sentencing judge, protesting that the punishment is too harsh. They argue, but the sentence stands. Unlike "Wreck on the Highway," in "Percy's Song" no external cause for the crash is suggested. The song's most dramatic moment—which, in print, hardly seems dramatic at all—comes when the judge rebuffs the singer:

At that, the judge jerked forward
And his face it did freeze
Turn, turn, turn again
Saying, "Could you kindly leave
My office now, please?"
Turn, turn to the rain
And the wind

Duration, distance, and repetition are critical here. The singer travels some distance to meet the judge and, when he achieves nothing, he faces the same journey home. The song's slow pace and limited action mirror his trek. As his mission's futility sinks in, the song's mood shifts from weary to despondent, its rain-and-wind refrain from stoic to cruel. "The Lonesome Death of Hattie Carroll," also written in 1963, uses similar song length, structure, and straightforward language to tell a story brimming with detail, as does 1964's "My Back Pages," but in Dylan's lyrically abstract, stream-of-consciousness mode. Perhaps by 1965, "Percy's Song"'s orthodox form and prosaic language seemed stifling to its stylistically restless creator. The song creates a numbing sense of helplessness by slowing down the film, as it were, almost beyond endurance. The listener waits in vain for plot development, a concrete injustice (beyond harsh punishment), or a narrative twist that might assuage the trauma of forced and unexpected separation.

Like Dixon's "Wreck on the Highway," Dylan's "Percy's Song" suffers slightly from rhythmic stiffness (as does the 1970 folk-pop version by Arlo Guthrie)—a shortcoming remedied by the song's own Roy Acuff in the form of England's doom-haunted electric-folk pioneers, Fairport Convention. An early line-up of Fairport introduced the singer–songwriter–musicians Richard Thompson and Sandy Denny to the world and first blended traditional British folk music with rock. They covered "Percy's Song" on their 1969 album *Unhalfbricking*, lending Dylan's tune a lilting, dancelike feel by trading his boxy 4/4 meter for a looser 3/4 sway. Essential to this shift was the drummer Martin Lamble, whose inventive, jazzy style was a linchpin of the band's early sound.

Fairport's other inspiration was to gradually build their arrangement from an *a cappella* start to a full-band finish—adding guitar, bass, drums, dulcimer, and organ, one instrument at a time, so that volume and sonic richness increase with each verse. Layed on top of this backing, Denny gives one of her most moving vocal performances. The result is mesmerizing, haunting, and heartbreaking.

But I knew him as good
As I'm knowing myself
Turn, turn, turn again
And he wouldn't harm a life
That belonged to someone else
Turn, turn to the rain
And the wind

"The narrator [in Dylan's version of "Percy's Song"] comes off as a grief-stricken kid who's put out because a sentence can't be overturned by a sincere character reference," snarked the music writer Tim Riley in an otherwise positive assessment of the song.[266] Perhaps. But part of the power of "Percy's Song" is its ability to conjure that first epochal encounter we all have with irreversible loss and its attendant agonies in a non-patronizing way. Its subject may be a troubling social reality: the sometimes irreconcilable collision between subjective character and objective law. But its true theme—present in Dylan's version but perfected in Fairport's—is the cold, flat, unyielding reality of loss. And part of a life fully lived is re-experiencing that first shock and agony each time we lose someone new.

I walked down the hallway
And I heard his door slam
Turn, turn, turn again
I walked down the courthouse stairs
And did not understand
Turn, turn to the rain
And the wind

And I played my guitar
Through the night to the day
Turn, turn, turn again
And the only tune my guitar could play
Was the old, cruel rain
And the wind

Maybe it takes a bunch of "kids" to make this signify. Fairport's relative youth when they recorded "Percy's Song" (the bassist Ashley Hutchings was the oldest, at twenty-four, and Lamble the youngest at nineteen) may have been vital to their heartfelt interpretation. Regardless, the song proved tragically prescient,

---

266   Tim Riley, *Hard Rain: A Dylan Commentary* (New York: Vintage Books, 1993), p. 79.

FAIRPORT CONVENTION WITH MARTIN LAMBLE, SECOND FROM RIGHT, 1969

a potent omen of an imminent grief storm. 1969 was a pivotal year for the band: they garnered critical raves and expanded an already burgeoning fan base through live performance and an excellent sophomore LP, *What We Did on Our Holidays*. The band seemed poised for a major breakthrough. But, less than a month after the sessions for *Unhalfbricking* ended, the band's tour van, returning from a gig in the predawn hours, struck a barrier on the M1 motorway and careened off the road, somersaulting down a hill into an adjacent field. Injuries ranged from superficial to severe. Both Lamble and Jeannie Franklyn, Thompson's girlfriend, were killed. The van's driver, Fairport's road manager, had fallen asleep at the wheel. Charged with vehicular manslaughter, he served six months in prison.

Fairport Convention eventually recovered and reformed, but the momentum they had built was lost, and they never became a major band. "[I]t was devastating for me," Thompson recalled years later. "I felt in a state of shock for a couple of years. It broke my perspective for a while—I couldn't get an overall picture of something. It was like . . . seeing the world piecemeal instead of as a whole thing."[267] In the aftermath, tragedies and reversals of fortune dogged them. Denny left for a solo career, and Thompson eventually followed. In 1971, a truck ran off the road, knocking out a wall of their "Big Pink"–style communal home and rehearsal space. The band was unharmed, but the driver was killed. In 1978, Denny, a boisterous personality with a taste for alcohol that expanded to drugs, fell down a flight of stairs and died.

267 Patrick Humphries, *Richard Thompson: The Biography* (New York: Virgin Books, 1997), p. 75.

Six years after the crash that took Lamble and Franklyn, Thompson released an elliptical song inspired by the tragedy. Almost hidden in the middle of the uncharacteristically sunny *Hokey Pokey* album (1975)—the second of six he recorded with his first wife, Linda (*née* Peters)—"Never Again" was written shortly after the accident. It's one of three known Thompson compositions that obliquely address it (the others are "Crazy Man Michael," recorded with Fairport in 1970, and the unreleased "Bad News Is All the Wind Can Carry"). "It's strange," Thompson said of "Never Again," "I don't really think I wrote it. It just came from somewhere."[268]

Mystery pervades its lyrics as well. Sung by Linda in a voice that's equal parts dignity and pain, "Never Again" is cryptic yet clear, a requiem for a fallen friend or lost lover and nothing of the sort:

> *The time for dividing, and no one will speak*
> *Of the sadness of hiding and the softness of sleep*
> *O will there be nothing of peace till the end?*
> *Or never, O never, O never again*

The tone is deferential, distinct as the haunting words, yet no easier to pin down. Like so much great music, the song ultimately resists analysis. It just has to be heard.

IN THE COOL ROOM

> *The purpose of rhythm, it has always seemed to me, is to prolong the moment of*
> *contemplation . . . by hushing it with an alluring monotony.*
> —William Butler Yeats, "The Symbolism of Poetry," 1900

In the fall of 1967, an eerie song about death and disease spun cheerlessly on the hi-fis of hippies and rock fans, dulling the Summer of Love's already fading lysergic sheen to a sobering gray. "T.B. Sheets" by Van Morrison was a new song about an ancient ailment—a hypnotic blues sung from the point of view of a young man spooked by his lover wasting away from tuberculosis. Modern in sound, it looked backward for content, mining a centuries-old motif that by the mid '60s was fading from historical reality: the dying loved one, stricken with incurable, infectious disease, and the accompanying bedside vigil. Countless songs, books, and films tell of lovers parted by premature death and the attendant sorrow of partners left behind, but "T.B. Sheets" stands out for its oppressive ambience and the inner turmoil of its anguished yet unheroic protagonist. Dying-lover narratives often portray surviving partners as heartbroken paragons, steadfast and true. But Morrison's singer is all too shamefully human: unable to cope

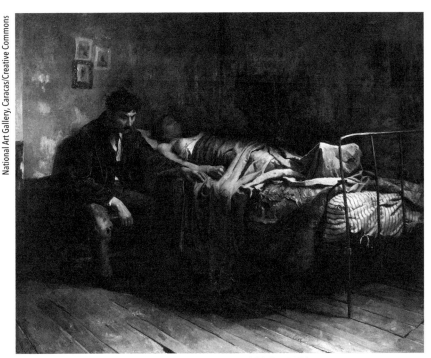

National Art Gallery, Caracas/Creative Commons

CRISTOBAL ROJAS, *LA MISERIA*, 1886

with his lover's illness and approaching death, he comforts himself with false promises and abandons her.

> *Now listen, Julie baby*
> *It ain't natural for you to cry in the midnight*
> *It ain't natural for you to cry way in the midnight through*
> *Into the wee small hours long before the break of dawn*
> *Oh Lord*

Tucked halfway through an LP that opened with the jaunty "Brown-Eyed Girl"—one of the era's sunniest songs and a hit single the previous spring—"T.B. Sheets" no doubt shocked listeners expecting an album's worth of "Sha-la-la, la-la, la-la, la-la, l'la-te-da." Harrowing and hopeless, the song's stark realism rested uneasily next to groovier fare in that season of *Sgt. Pepper*. Only the Doors' doomy debut and the little-noticed *Velvet Underground and Nico* charted similar territory. But rock's other Morrison was a self-conscious Romantic, and the defiantly anti-bluesy Velvet Underground eschewed emotional engagement for cool detachment. Less Romantic than expressionistic, "T.B. Sheets" is a nine-minutes-plus, two-chord groove for drums, bass, guitar, and organ that pulls the listener deeper into the singer's claustrophobic state of mind with each successive bar. Instrumental accompaniment varies little: tempo and dynamics are constant, making Morrison's irregular vocal interjections sound all the more desperate. A tambourine beats time like a morbid metronome, counting breaths or heartbeats. Occasionally, a harmonica shrieks. Morrison's largely free-verse lyrics are half awkward conversation, half taxing internal monologue—semi-improvised, but neither jazzy nor artful, and spat out with long pauses in between. He stutters and gasps for breath. He's in the room with the dying girl, trembling and sweating. And to sit through the song is to join him there.

And the sunlight shining through the crack in the windowpane
Numbs my brain
And the sunlight shining through the crack in the windowpane
Numbs my brain
Oh Lord

Released against his wishes on an LP he never approved, "T.B. Sheets" was one of a handful of tracks recorded in March 1967 ("Brown-Eyed Girl" was another) and set aside for Morrison's debut as a solo artist. The moody singer, late of Belfast's working-class blues rockers Them, only learned of the material's release when a friend mentioned he'd bought the album. *Blowin' Your Mind!* was an embarrassment for its stupid title, condescending cover art, and disrespect for its creator—a cynical move by a tone-deaf industry still consigning rock to the teenybopper ghetto. But its songs capture Morrison at a creative crossroads, on the verge of the breakthrough that produced 1969's masterful *Astral Weeks*, with its unique blend of folk, jazz, rock, and impressionistic, alternately dark and light lyrics. In many ways, "T.B. Sheets" is a dry run for complex song-portraits like "Slim Slow Slider" and "Madame George."

The song's chorus—its only recurring lyric—is a devil's whisper, urging the singer to flee:

The cool room, Lord, is a fool's room
The cool room, Lord, is a fool's room
And I can almost smell your T.B. sheets
And I can almost smell your T.B. sheets

The words are visceral, evoking sense memory so specific ("I can almost *smell*...") the sick room appears with repellent realism. The song's tone is pained and resentful throughout, emotions that often accompany prolonged illness but are typically repressed in polite company. One phrase in the lyric—a fleeting, unspoken thought—jars the listener with its impenetrable mix of grief, anger, and self-loathing: "your little star-struck innuendos, inadequacies, and foreign bodies." It is agonizing to watch a partner die, and part of us resents them for putting us through this misery.

So open up the window and let me breathe
I said open up the window and let me breathe
I'm looking down to the street below
Lord I cried for you, I cried, I cried for you
Oh Lord

The musicians play on, prolonging contemplation with alluring monotony, and the singer grows frantic. His girl begs him to stay and asks him to bring her a drink of water, but he's already backing out the door: "I gotta go, I gotta go, baby." And then, pathetically: "I'll send somebody around *later*." A friend is coming later, he says, with a bottle of wine they'll share, as if her condition warranted a party. He turns on a radio, offering music, at least, in lieu of human companionship: "If you wanna hear a few tunes, there you go, there you go, baby." He then flees, leaving her in the darkness.

The listener leaves, too, forced by the track's fade-out (originally followed by the LP's end-of-side-one run-off groove; one imagines a stunned shaking of heads with no one rising to flip the record). The song's relentless focus on the young man's thoughts, plus Morrison's gut-wrenching performance, compel identification with its protagonist, and by the song's end, with no catharsis possible, the sense of panic and dread is such that we want out too. Consequently, it's hard to listen without feeling complicit in his abdication.

Old documents are a rich source of insight into the lives of ordinary people of past generations. Sifting through census, birth, marriage, church, military, prison, burial, and other records proffers a graphic glimpse into the otherwise undocumented lives of poor and working-class Americans. The Internet makes available for perusal in minutes a wealth of such documents that once required serious legwork to uncover at libraries and historical societies. Poring over old death certificates (mainly from the early twentieth century, when death records were formalized) is especially enlightening. Everybody dies, so it's interesting to see what everybody dies *of*, especially during an era that seems both grandparent-near and sepia-tone-far.

Then as now, most people died of depressingly familiar ailments. The Big Three remain: heart disease, cancer, and stroke. Old people often died of "senility" ("old age" in prewar parlance). Accidents were common, sometimes with an antique flavor ("run over by street car") or ballad-like air of tragedy (e.g., a married couple with their children "drowned in the river" when their car slid off a river ferry).[269] At times the tone darkens. Methods of suicide include "carbolic acid poisoning," "gunshot to the heart," and, in the case of an unemployed, recently divorced World War I veteran who ironically last worked as a "stove fitter," "heating gas asphyxiation." In 1927, a teenage girl repulsed her father's predatory "advances" with a "gunshot wound to the abdomen." In 1938, a middle-aged farmer's death

---

269 All examples come from death certificates collected by the author.

certificate lists two startling
causes: "lightning strike" as
primary and "insanity" as
secondary.

More prosaic are the many
victims of once lethal, now
largely eradicated infectious
diseases—maladies   that
terrified   our   ancestors
but are now neutered by
childhood needle jabs, such
as diphtheria, smallpox,
measles,   whooping
cough, polio, typhoid, and

**BEDS ON A TERRACE AT WAVERLY HILLS
SANITARIUM, LOUISVILLE, KENTUCKY, C. 1940S**

tuberculosis. In nineteenth-century America, it was not unusual for every
second or third child born to die of such an illness. As a result, with birth control
and inoculation both distant dreams, many women spent much of their lives
pregnant *and* grieving a recently lost child.

Tuberculosis is ubiquitous in those old death certificates. Caused by airborne
bacteria, the contagion most often settled in the lungs, causing gradual weight
loss and suffocation. The poor and city dwellers were hardest hit. Victims who
could afford it drew their last breaths in private sanatoriums: long-term medical
facilities offering bed rest and palliative care instead of a cure. (The first effective
treatment, Streptomycin, wasn't available until 1949.) In advanced cases, dire
surgical procedures—the removal of ribs and temporary collapsing of lungs—
also occurred.[270]

Equally malignant in Van Morrison's home, Northern Ireland, tuberculosis
ravaged the province, partitioned by the United Kingdom in 1921, well into
the twentieth century, and remained a leading cause of death among children
until after the Second World War. While Europe overall made strides in
combating the disease, reducing mortality rates from 25% of all deaths at the
turn of the century to under 10% by the 1950s (when Morrison was a child),
Northern Ireland lagged behind. Substandard living conditions and lack of
access to medical care, exacerbated by prejudice, left the province vulnerable.
Consequently, for natives of Morrison's generation, T.B. remained a fearful
childhood memory.

Speculation that "T.B. Sheets" was inspired by such a memory, neither
confirmed nor corrected by its taciturn composer, dog the song. Morrison can

270 In Kentucky, sufferers often convalesced at Waverly Hills, a handsome brick facility of leviathan proportions that housed
T.B. patients by the thousands between 1910 and 1961. Treatment at Waverly focused on the curative powers of fresh air and
sunshine, so patients' beds were rolled onto open-air balconies, even in winter. The long-abandoned structure still stands
and is best known today for its low-incline, 500-foot underground tunnel once used to discreetly transport bodies of the dead
from the building to waiting hearses. The complex regularly appears on lists of Most Haunted Places and was the site of a
notoriously un-restful extreme metal festival in 2008, never repeated due to neighbor complaints. (One wonders how local
haints, lacking access to phone or alderman, responded to the likes of Gwar and Hatebreed.)

be a prickly interview and specifically dislikes expounding on his work ("I just sort of write down what I get," he told an interviewer in 1985, "without censoring or questioning what it is and what it means, you know?").[271] Thus conjecture abounds, including a recurrent rumor that Morrison contracted but survived the illness as a child. If so, this might explain the song's subjective intensity. But the shift of infection from himself to a girlfriend is curious. Perhaps it was easier to recall the experience by externalizing the disease. Or perhaps there's some psychological significance to splitting himself into a female felled by infection and a male unable to cope or assist.

Autobiographical or not, "T.B. Sheets" is rooted in the reality of Morrison's life and times.

"T.B. Sheets" is rarely covered or performed. It's hard to imagine what other artists could bring to the song and equally difficult to picture concert audiences (including Morrison's) raising lighters and boisterously chanting, "'T.B. Sheets!' 'T.B Sheets!'" Unsurprisingly, given the song's roots in the blues, its only notable cover is by a blues legend who remakes it as his own.

John Lee Hooker recorded "T.B. Sheets" on his 1971 studio album *Never Get out of These Blues Alive,* in a small-band rendition featuring spine-tingling violin by the jazz musician Michael White. Characteristically, the Boogie King takes Morrison's already minimalist original and decelerates it further, trading its mid-tempo 4/4 groove for a sepulchral 6/8 sway. Lyrically, Hooker sings a line from the original here and there but mostly wings it. He alters the narrative, deleting the lover and assuming the victim's voice. As the track fades, his growling voice intones: "I don't weigh but ninety pounds . . . I won't be here . . . raise up the window . . . let me see daylight . . . one more time ..." Hooker's version has stark power, but its reductive, single-character scenario denies it the creeping despair and psychological complexity of Morrison's original. The first-person substitution does, however, link Hooker's version to earlier blues.

The Depression and war years were rife with fatalistic, un-squeamish blues songs about myriad illnesses: influenza, meningitis, alcoholism, drug addiction, even "Jake leg," the crippling paralysis caused by drinking improperly distilled hooch during Prohibition. The poor Blacks that wrote these songs were intimately familiar with each ailment; like the Irish, poverty and prejudice kept disease rates disproportionately high in their communities. In 1927, Okeh Records released "T.B. Blues" by Victoria Spivey. The first of several songs the pioneering blueswoman wrote and recorded about tuberculosis, it's memorable for its moaning vocal and wearily repeated words:

Too late, too late, too late, too late, too late
It's too late, too late, too late, too late, too late
I'm on my way to Denver, and mama mustn't hesitate

---

271 Al Jones, "Nights in Copenhagen with Van Morrison," radio interview, 24 March 1985.

Colorado was a common destination for T.B. patients. Home to numerous sanatoriums, its convivial weather and high elevations were thought to relieve symptoms.

T.B.'s all right to have if your friends don't treat you so low-down
T.B.'s all right to have if your friends don't treat you so low-down
Don't you ask 'em for no favors, they'll even stop coming around

Spivey's song was covered, reworked, and imitated by a range of artists, including Josh White, Lead Belly, and Champion Jack Dupree. Like Hooker's version of "T.B. Sheets," all are subjective accounts sung from a victim's perspective. A recurring theme present in Spivey's original is abandonment by friends:

I used to have friends, but none of them that I can see

—Buddy Moss, "T.B. Is Killing Me" (1933)

Well, now here I am here sick, baby, you know
And I'm laying here in my bed
And now even won't none of my friends come
And even rub my aching head

—Sonny Boy Williamson [I], "T.B. Blues" (1939)

Friends. Abandonment. The words seem wildly incongruent in the context of terminal illness. Yet it's not uncommon for friends, even family members or spouses, to do just that: abandon a dying loved one at their time of greatest need. It sounds unbelievably callous, self-centered, and cruel. But when the chips are down, some people flee—for a time or forever, just like the singer in "T.B. Sheets" ("I gotta go, I gotta go, baby"). A poignant fact about Morrison's song is how our irritation, even disgust, at the singer's selfishness never turns to contempt—a testament to its creator's humane artistry and the realization spurred by the song that we have the capacity and instinct for the same wretched behavior.[272] Dark as "T.B. Sheets" is, it's imbued with a kind of grace—a deep compassion for human frailty, partly bred from the knowledge that the singer will likely be haunted by his actions for the rest of his life.

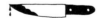

---

272 Ironically, the cantankerous Morrison's own capacity for wretchedness was on display during a more recent grappling with contagion—the COVID-19 pandemic. Frustrated by a lockdown that kept him from performing live, the aging contrarian joined forces with a similarly peeved Eric Clapton to release a pair of "message" songs—"Stand and Deliver" (2020) and "This Has Gotta Stop" (2021)—that condemned mandates to contain the virus as "slavery" and extolled their rejection as "freedom."

ON THE RAILS, ALIVE AND DEAD

The girl I love / Is on that train and gone
—"Worried Man Blues" (Roud 4753)

Johnny Cash, *American Recordings* series, Volume V: *A Hundred Highways.* The first posthumous collection, released in 2006, three years after his death. The Man in Black sits as he's shown on the cover, before a microphone and music stand in semidarkness, scanning a lyric sheet through bifocals. When the playback hits his headphones—simple guitar, later augmented with understated overdubs—he strains against the accumulated aches and pains

of hard living, multiple surgeries, and the recent death of his wife to find his voice and give the song life. The resulting vocal is measured, slightly over-enunciated, but still stirring. Like Billie Holiday's end-of-career *Lady in Satin* period, Cash's final recordings find his once-booming voice diminished, at times a near croak, but, as with Lady Day, this frailty affords him a new emotional frankness as aesthetic nicety slips away.

JOHNNY CASH, *AMERICAN V: A HUNDRED HIGHWAYS* COVER ART, 2006

Facing death, country music's lion in winter sings about it. He channels long-gone Hank Williams in a song the Lost Highwayman wrote (co-credited to his wife Audrey) but never recorded, an earnest tune about loss and separation that mines Victorian parlor songs and hillbilly ballads for inspiration and finds its main metaphor in America's once-vast train mythology. Cash sets the scene in near-slow motion, pausing so deliberately in the middle of lines that he turns them into couplets.

I heard the laughter ... at the depot
But my tears ... fell like the rain
When I saw them place ... that long white casket
On the baggage coach ... of the evening train

Setting and tone are sketched in a few strokes. For a modern listener, the non-Amtrak train and baggage-car coffin set the song squarely in an archaic past, a lost time when trains and railroads were ubiquitous settings for experiences lived and imagined. But the dissonant juxtaposition of laughter and tears rings across generations, familiar to anyone who's suffered a profound loss and been

Christine Cano and Martin Atkins

jarred by others going about their business, unaware that the world has changed. The next verse—the second of just four, though the last repeats (there is no chorus)—swiftly fills out characters and defines the tragedy.

> The baby's eyes ... are red from weeping
> Its little heart ... is filled with pain
> "Oh, Daddy," it cried ... "They're taking Mama
> Away from us ... on the evening train"

The best *American Recordings* are deftly minimal—music and voice stripped to essences that maximize emotional power and favor singer over song. The care given to every facet of their stark design—sonic, thematic, presentational—by the producer and Cash collaborator Rick Rubin extends to song selection and an old-school, album-as-songbook concern with running order. Tracks on each volume are treated like chapters in an unfolding narrative. "On the Evening Train" falls halfway through Cash's last album—the end of side one on vinyl, and that moment when you flip the LP over or set it aside for later listening. Either way, the break prompts a reflective pause; in the current context, it's both mournful and nostalgic. "On the Evening Train" is the only song on *American V* set unambiguously in the past, in a bygone era when people, both living and dead, mainly traveled by train.

> As I turned to walk ... away from the depot
> It seemed I heard ... her call my name
> "Take care of my baby ... and tell him, darlin'
> That I'm going home ... on the evening train"

June Carter Cash, Cash's wife and bedrock partner of thirty-five years, died suddenly during the sessions for *American V,* and her incorporeal form seems to hover over its songs and their bereaved singer. Listening to "On the Evening Train," it's easy to place her in the song's long white casket and her widower at the depot—dazed and silent, his only solace the knowledge that he'll soon be joining her and his religious faith that the reunion will be literal. After June died, Cash told Rubin, "I want to work every day, and I need you to have something for me to do every day. Because if I don't have something to focus on, I'm gonna die."[273] So the pair put scores of songs on tape, starting the day after her passing, during the mere three months that Cash outlived her.

American V opens with a prayer: Larry Gatlin's weary "Help Me," a country gospel tune popularized in the early '70s by Elvis Presley and Kris Kristofferson. It closes with "I'm Free from the Chain Gang Now," a prison-release song first recorded in 1933 by a dying, T.B.-wracked Jimmie Rodgers. (Rodgers, the Singing Brakeman, also recorded scores of songs during his final months; his last session, cut with

273 David Camp, "American Communion," *Vanity Fair,* October 2004.

the singer resting on a cot between takes, occurred just two days before his death.) Both were recorded by Cash earlier in his career and are revisited in slowed-down, simplified versions—thematic bookends to the album's end-of-life chronicle that resemble the invocation and benediction of a Protestant church service.

In between are songs of struggle and acceptance, of love for June, even sardonic reflections on success and fame. In "Like the 309," another train song and Cash's last recorded composition, he grouses wryly about his asthma-addled lungs and calls for an electric fan to cool his "gnarly ol' head." "Then load my box on the 309," he sings, ready to go. "Gonna get outta here on the 309." As in "On the Evening Train," death is this engine's ultimate engineer. But Williams' song and Cash's performance are too grief-stricken for levity, because, as many people discover, in the end, dying is far easier than being left behind.

> *I pray that God ... will give me courage*
> *To carry on ... 'til we meet again*
> *It's hard to know ... she's gone forever*
> *They're carrying her home ... on the evening train*

Historical shifts end eras of shared experience but leave rich residues of anecdote and artifact in their wake. "Today," wrote the folklorist Norm Cohen in *Long Steel Rail: The Railroad in American Folksong*, "it taxes the imagination of young people to appreciate the impact that the rails once had on their grandparents."[274] Trains once crisscrossed this country in staggering numbers, consigning passengers and freight the way veins and arteries pump blood through the body. Between 1830 and 1945, they transformed life—reducing travel time, connecting far-flung communities, depleting wilderness (and Native Americans), and streamlining capitalism. They inspired a sweeping mythology that permeates folklore and the arts to this day.

All this is common knowledge, but the fact that passengers sometimes *were* the freight—lifeless cargo stored a short stroll from coach car seating—is less remembered. It's the sort of private-sphere detail more likely to turn up in art or memoir than in historical record, and a common enough feature in train songs to merit a chapter in Cohen's massive 1981 tome. But the "young people" he refers to are now middle-aged and possibly grandparents themselves. As the last generation disappears that remembers the railroads' heyday, such details risk fading as well.

"On the Evening Train" was written in 1949, after a final crescendo of railroad travel saw millions of American servicemen routed cross-country during World War II. Hundreds of thousands were also shipped to hometowns or federal cemeteries for burial. The gradual supersession that followed—of trains by planes and automobiles—extended to transport of the dead. Bodies moved by hearse, jet, or *freight* train became the norm. Postwar America also saw death increasingly sanitized and hidden away. Like bodies kept in parlors

---

274 Norm Cohen, *Long Steel Rail: The Railroad in American Folksong* (Champaign: University of Illinois Press, 1981), p. 14.

or family burials on private land, the conveyance of the dead by train now feels fabled and unfamiliar.

The song was first recorded, also in 1949, by the country singer Mollie O'Day. Little remembered today, O'Day was the unvarnished real deal—a coal miner's daughter from Appalachia who sang in a gutsy alto, not unlike the country matriarch Sara Carter. She recorded thirty-six sides for Columbia from 1946 to 1951, before tuberculosis and a nervous breakdown curtailed her career (she survived the former, and withdrew into church work and occasional gospel singing after the latter). Five of these were Hank Williams tunes, and the last, "On the Evening Train," may have been written with her in mind. Details on the song's composition are scant, but its split authorship with Audrey, the only such credit in Williams' songbook, raises eyebrows. Their turbulent relationship aside, Audrey's musical ability was slight (she never wrote or co-wrote another song), but her professional ambition was boundless.

In contrast to Cash's funerary reading of the song, O'Day's—in a string-band arrangement with prominent harmonica—pulses with life. Her homespun performance may hint at the vulnerabilities that felled her; it's hard to imagine so openhearted an artist surviving the music industry intact. A 1962 rendition by the bluegrass singer Wilma Lee Cooper echoes O'Day's exuberance and ups its stridency.

"Death train" songs are as old as the railroads, and nineteenth- and twentieth-century variants recount wrecks, chases and battles, funeral processions, and "Sweet Chariot"–style journeys to heaven. Beside these, Williams' song stands out for its brevity and compacted narrative. Williams drew on ballads but excelled at snapshots, an early genius of the two-and-a-half-minute single format that swept midcentury radio and jukeboxes. The few verses and fewer adjectives of "On the Evening Train" set it apart from its Victorian and hillbilly ancestors.

Two such precursors, long-form *fin-de-siècle* ballads, are attributed to Gussie Davis, an early Tin Pan Alley scribe and one of the first commercially successful African American songwriters. "In the Baggage Coach Ahead" (1896) and "He Is Coming to Us Dead" (1899) are typical tear-jerkers of their time—parlor songs of a tragic bent that found their way over time from the drawing room to the street. Formulaic and sentimental, the best of these, like silent film melodramas, can still connect with modern audiences able to adapt to their stylization.

Both date from the early sheet-music era, when copyrights were less regulated, and seem partly derived from non-original sources, including printed verse. Both deal with bodies shipped by train, center on narrative twists, and were widely covered, often in versions with melodic or lyrical variations. It's beyond unlikely that Williams—an unschooled songwriter who sharpened his skills by listening—never heard them.

"In the Baggage Coach Ahead" is the better-known tune and tells of a crying child, held in its father's arms on an overnight Pullman trek, who arouses the ire of fellow passengers. "Make that child stop its noise / For

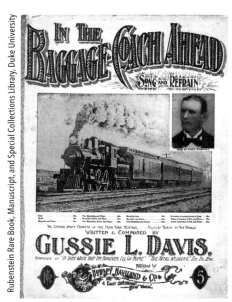

**GUSSIE DAVIS, *IN THE BAGGAGE CAR
AHEAD* SHEET MUSIC, C. 1896**

it's keeping us awake," the men hiss from their berths in Vernon Dalhart's 1925 recording. A woman intercedes:

> *"Where is its mother? Go take it to her"*
> *This, a lady then softly said*
> *"I wish that I could," was the man's*
> *sad reply*
> *"But she's dead in the coach ahead"*

The revelation is not unexpected, but the writing is restrained. The sobbing, motherless child evokes the "baby's eyes ... red from weeping" from "On the Evening Train." When the women on board rise to collectively comfort the child, the act is both touching and a reminder that trains were by nature communal—small villages of cramped but interactive travelers, so different from the depopulated sedans and wagons that supplanted them.

> *Every woman arose to assist with the child*
> *There were mothers and wives on that train*
> *And soon was the little one sleeping in peace*
> *With no thought of sorrow or pain*

The vaudeville balladeer Imogene Comer debuted "In the Baggage Coach Ahead" on stage in turn-of-the-century Boston, quaintly accompanied by stereoscopic slide projections. But the song remained unrecorded until 1924-25, when a slew of hillbilly versions—by Ernest Thompson, George Renault, Fiddlin' John Carson, and Dalhart—introduced it to a new generation. Vernon Dalhart (birth name Marion Slaughter) was a significant figure in the evolution of country music: a classically trained tenor, Texas-born but New York–based, who preferred opera to old-time music. He recorded *thousands* of light-classical, dance-band, and hillbilly sides under a hundred aliases from 1916 to 1939.

His version of "In the Baggage Coach Ahead"—country in spirit yet beholden to the parlor-song style—straddles bourgeois and busker modes, making hick music safe for respectable folks while deflating Gilded Age pomp. He trims Davis's wordy original but still sings eight verses and two choruses. This chorus is especially unnecessary, a tearful contrivance ("For baby's face brings pictures / Of a cherished hope that's dead") that dulls the genuine emotion generated by the verses.

The song's scenario is entirely plausible, which no doubt contributed to its wide-range appeal. Davis's sheet music was marketed as "based on fact" (with no substantiating details)—a common promotional gimmick. Yet stories circulated for years that the song had a real-life protagonist: a Missouri medical doctor named James B. Watson, who in 1869 accompanied his wife Abigail's body to their home state of Pennsylvania for burial. Various writers, including the folklorist Vance Randolph, repeated these claims and named a daughter, Nellie Klapmeyer (*née* Watson), as the song's distraught child.[275]

The musicologist Sigmund Spaeth went further, positing that Davis (who once worked as a Pullman porter) personally witnessed the event that inspired the song. This claim would preclude the Watson theory since Davis, born in 1863, would have been six years old when Abigail died. More likely is a similar assertion—that Davis encountered the tale via another eyewitness, a conductor and former porter named Frank Archer. Archer dabbled in poetry and published an obscure poem depicting a similar scenario called "Mother" in the waning years of the century (the Davis and Archer compositions share no text). Muddying already cloudy waters, a handful of other nineteenth-century poems, published after the Civil War and possibly set to music, give comparable accounts.

The second Davis song, "He Is Coming to Us Dead," concerns neither a fraught child nor a bereaved husband but a grieving father. An aged man stands on a train platform. He tells an inquiring clerk that he's waiting for his son, who's "coming home today." The clerk informs him he's at the wrong terminal—a freight depot—and tries to redirect him to a passenger station "just o'er the way."

"You do not understand me, sir"
The old man shook his head
"He's not coming as a passenger
But by express instead"

Once more, a passenger is freight. As with "In the Baggage Coach Ahead," the twist is predictable but subtly rendered. When the train pulls in with its precious cargo, a crowd gathers, "showing signs of grief and tears," and surrounds the man in solidarity—recalling the women who comfort the child in the previous song. A "long white casket" is lowered to the ground, evoking the identical vessel in "On the Evening Train."

The final verse adds another twist: we learn that the old man's son is a soldier, presumably killed in action and that his grieving (off-screen) mother predicted the boy's death when he enlisted.

"He broke his poor old mother's heart
Her fears have all come true

275 Much of this is verifiable by public records. The doctor's name was John E.–not James B.–Watson; otherwise, names, dates, and places line up. Watson (1839-1881), a Montgomery County physician, married Abigail Benscoter (1839-1869), who gave birth to Nellie Forrest Watson in 1867. Abigail died two years later, and her widower remarried in 1871 and fathered additional children. In 1885, Nellie married a Kansas City banker, James Klapmeyer, and they raised a family of their own. She died in Nebraska in 1926. There's no mention of the train journey or grieving child, but the bare bones are there.

She said it's the way he'd come back
When he joined the boys in blue"

Like its predecessor, "He Is Coming to Us Dead" found its way from Victorian venues to 78 rpm discs during the hillbilly boom. First recorded in 1927 by the old-time duo Grayson and Whitter, the pair mostly retain Davis's lyric (while altering his melody) but recast the song in down-home style, complete with folksy spoken interjections ("Take warning, good people!") between stanzas. Later versions—by Doc Watson (1964), the New Lost City Ramblers (1966), and Ralph Stanley (1996)—derive from their template.

Despite the song's 1899 copyright, the appellation "boys in blue" probably refers to Union troops and a Civil War setting, since imperialist ventures in Cuba and the Philippines at the turn of the century were seeing khaki uniforms replacing military blues, and romantic ardor surrounding the War Between the States remained high. Grayson and Whitter's final spoken interjection, heard after the song's last couplet ("She said it's the way he'd come back / When he joined the boys in blue") is acerbic—perhaps unsurprising in a recording made in 1927, just nine years after the War to End All Wars took 117,000 American lives:

A lot of them come back that way, too

"He Is Coming to Us Dead" was revisited during the '60s folk revival, often with an antiwar flavor. A singular version by Steve Ledford, cut in 1971 when the former Carolina Ramblers String Band fiddler was sixty-five and had seen his share of wars, explicitly updates the song as "He's Comin' from Vietnam." A somber rendition by Ron Thomason of Dry Branch Fire Squad, regularly featured in the bluegrass band's twenty-first-century live shows, retains Grayson and Whitter's quip and refashions the song for our era of endless war.

Dying people often talk of travel. They think and dream about it, sometimes startling bedside attendants by emerging from the fog of deep sleep to make crystal-clear pronouncements like "I'm going on a trip," or "I'm checking in my luggage," or "I'm getting on the plane." This preoccupation with gathering one's things and moving on is clearly symbolic—a moribund message about life's final journey shared as conscious and unconscious minds merge before death. This integration of dreams and "reality," of material and immaterial realms, evokes the blurring of both in creative expression. "We begin to see," wrote the physician and poet William Carlos Williams of his dying patients, "that the underlying meaning of all they want to tell us and have always failed to communicate is the poem, the poem which their lives are being lived to realize."[276] In the past, the dying no doubt spoke of trains.

Davis's parlor-turned-hillbilly ballads and their kin use a once familiar circumstance—the transport of bodies by rail—and a metaphoric sense of

---

276   William Carlos Williams and Robert Coles, "The Practice," *The Doctor Stories* (New York: New Directions, 1984), p. 125.

train travel as the passage to an afterlife to process grief over wrenching loss. While archaic in theme and tone, they express universal desires for meaning and closure. Cash's "On the Evening Train" recalls both its singer's restless life and the travel metaphors invoked by the dying. By modern standards, it, too, is old-fashioned, but a listener who meets the song halfway will likely end up, in some sense, on the platform as well, reliving their own losses as the baby weeps and the casket loads.

Such songs didn't end with Davis or Cash; they continue to be revived and rewritten, their features sifted for new ways to tell eternal stories. But their heyday ended with that of the trains. A closing example follows a now-familiar practical path. Written by the professional songwriters Joseph Ettlinger and Billy and Dedette Lee Hill in 1931 and first recorded by hillbilly singers Asa Martin and James Roberts in 1933, it was later a chart hit for the country superstar Hank Snow in 1958. It also captures their timeless melancholy.

> *There's a little box of pine on the 7:29*
> *Bringing back a lost sheep to the fold*
> *In the valley there are tears as the train of sorrow nears*
> *The sun is gone, the world seems dark and cold*
>   —Martin and Roberts, "There's a Little Box of Pine on the 7:29" (1933)

CODA: HURT

All things are full of labor; man cannot utter it: the eye is not satisfied
with seeing, nor the ear filled with hearing. —Ecclesiastes 1:8

The first thing you notice is the face: worn, haggard, bloated, and uneven. Its oversized features, once ruggedly handsome, now puffy and pale. Awkward to contemplate, painful to see. When he sings, he opens his mouth crookedly, as if he's had a stroke. His half-blind eyes look haunted; the familiar shock of thick, dark hair is reduced to wispy strands of gray and white. He remains a mesmerizing presence but now radiates fragility and doubt. He will be dead soon and looks it. Strikingly, his frailty is undisguised by makeup or lighting or special effects. The result is jarring; it's rare to see mortality addressed with such directness in as mercenary a marketing tool as a music video.

It's the last video the man will make, and it's as unforgettable as the song it's set to. It manages two uncommon feats: the imagery genuinely enhances the music, rather than trivializing or distracting from it; and the song—a genre-crossing cover—both bests and supplants the original (in the words of the man who wrote it, "[T]hat isn't my song anymore").[277] Popular consensus names it one of the best-ever cover songs and one of the best-ever videos.[278]

The music is lean, the imagery lush. It starts with a simple arpeggiated guitar pattern. We see bronze statuettes (a sylvan deity, a Remington cowboy) and an ornate vessel filled with fruit. Then a banquet table dressed like a Dutch Baroque still life, those sumptuous visual celebrations of postwar prosperity.[279] These images evoke romance, riches, and Dionysian indulgence. But *vanitas* themes proliferate: depictions of abandonment and decay, lost loved ones and dead times. In the video's central image, the singer strums a guitar with difficulty and sings in carefully measured phrases. It ends with glimpses of the crucified Christ and pealing chords on a piano. Weathered hands close the keyboard lid, pristine and white, as the tones echo in our ears. It feels like a funeral in a country church—the lid a visual rhyme for the coffin.

In between, a flow of images documents a life. Grainy and overexposed film clips, family photos, and homely mementos mix with the banquet scene—a reverie of memories built on dichotomies of success and failure, matter and spirit, set to a heart-like pulse. Through it all, the singer's familiar baritone, still clear but quavering, anchors music and visuals. The words are biting, but references to self-harm and addiction transcend specificity toward something universal.

I hurt myself today, to see if I still feel
I focus on the pain, the only thing that's real
The needle tears a hole, the old familiar sting
Try to kill it all away, but I remember everything

---

277 Geoff Rickly, interview with Trent Reznor, *Alternative Press*, no. 194, September 2003.
278 In 2011, Time magazine listed "Hurt" in its "30 All-Time Best Music Videos." The same year, *New Musical Express* declared it the greatest music video of all time.
279 The Eighty Years' War ended in 1648 with an independent Dutch Republic and an explosion of exuberant Dutch painting.

The chorus is heartbreaking, an end-of-life lament:

What have I become?
My sweetest friend
Everyone I know goes away
In the end

And you could have it all
My empire of dirt
I will let you down
I will make you hurt

"Hurt," as sung by Johnny Cash, was released in late 2002 on his final album, *American IV: The Man Comes Around*—the last of four Rick Rubin–produced collections that revitalized his career and expanded his audience during the final decade of his life. (Two posthumous volumes followed.) The video, Cash's first since 1994, was created by the director Mark Romanek from footage shot at the singer's Hendersonville, Tennessee, home in early 2003, interspersed with archival footage from throughout his life. In May of that year, Cash's beloved wife June died unexpectedly after heart surgery (she makes a brief, indelible appearance in the video, standing on a stair watching her husband sing, her face fluttering with emotion). Cash, afflicted with severe health problems, died in September.[280]

American IV got good reviews, but "Hurt" initially made little impact. Radio and television play were limited, leaving word of mouth to generate interest. Awareness of the song peaked with Cash's death, cementing its status as a public requiem. Over time, "Hurt" developed a life of its own (as of September 2022, there were 168 million views on YouTube)—as an intro to Cash, to country music, or simply a rare popular work about death that neither wallows in sentiment nor pretends emotion and spirit don't matter.[281]

In a sense, "Hurt" began as another song entirely. A strength of the Rubin–Cash collaborations was their mix of covers and originals, the former ranging from classic country (Hank Williams, Kris Kristofferson, David Allan Coe) to pop standards old and new (Dean Martin, the Beatles, Leonard Cohen). Most compelling were songs by non-mainstream rock artists, particularly dark and introspective material by idiosyncratic musicians like Soundgarden, Will Oldham, and Glenn Danzig. Rubin thought these outliers might resonate with Cash—an artist rooted in rock as well as country, and no stranger to darkness or introspection. The best of these were genuine reinterpretations: stripped-down, Man in Black versions of alt-rock, Americana, metal, even synth-pop, built

---

280 Those health problems included diabetes, autonomic neuropathy, lungs weakened by pneumonia, heart, liver, kidney, and foot ailments, plus a painful jaw condition.

281 A recent spate of reaction videos–wherein novices new to Cash or country respond in real time to "Hurt," invariably with strong emotion–attests to this.

around Cash's iconic voice and filtered through his life and experience. These unlikely covers served a dual function: they recast a late-career artist, abandoned by the country mainstream, as an interpreter of current, edgy music, drawing a new, younger audience in the process, but they also allowed Cash to express late-life thoughts and feelings through non-country material, unhindered by the strictures of Nashville.

"Hurt" was one such cover. The song debuted on *The Downward Spiral* (1994), the second album by the industrial angst-rockers Nine Inch Nails—a chilly soundscape of negation forged from processed noise and mechanized beats whose guiding aesthetic was succinctly captured in the title of their first album, *Pretty Hate Machine* (1989). Written by the auteur and front man Trent Reznor, "Hurt" is *The Downward Spiral*'s closing track and stands out for its musicality and restraint in comparatively dire surroundings: still bleak but almost hopeful, a kind of coda to chaos. Rubin, whose forte pre-Cash was metal and rap, was a fan of Reznor and sneaked "Hurt" onto one of the CDs of potential covers he burned for Cash when they were trawling for songs for *American IV*. At first, Cash didn't bite. But Rubin persisted, resubmitting the song and urging Cash to focus on the words.

I wear this crown of thorns,[282] *upon my liar's chair*
Full of broken thoughts I cannot repair
Beneath the stains of time, the feelings disappear
You are someone else, I am still right here

Rubin was right. Whatever misgivings Cash had about the Nine Inch Nails version, the lyrics—inspired by a romantic breakup and Reznor's heroin addiction—have power and humanity beyond their trappings in obsessive post-adolescent gloom. They fit perfectly with the ailing singer's mood and circumstances.

Reznor was initially unsure of the match as well. "It didn't sound bad," he said about first hearing Cash's cover, "it sounded alien."[283] Unable to distance himself from the original, it felt like some "other person inhabiting my most personal song."[284] Romanek's video changed that. Its synthesis of sound and vision snapped like a sheet of paper in Reznor's mind, freeing him to experience the song unfettered by his own associations. Then, it "really, really made sense, and I thought what a powerful piece of art."[285] Romanek had lobbied hard to make the clip. A veteran producer of big-name videos (including for Nine Inch Nails), low on art and high on promotion, he was frank about the limitations of his vocation: "Videos are supposed to be eye candy—hip and cool and all about youth and energy." "Hurt" gave him a rare opportunity to pay tribute to a hero and craft something personally meaningful in a commerce-focused field. "I didn't want to make a phony video," he

---

282   "Crown of shit" in the original—a tossed-off line that Cash exchanged for the Christian symbol of Jesus's humiliation before death, trading desultory self-loathing for possible redemption. He made no other changes.

283   Paul Goodman, "Johnny Cash, 'Hurt': The Story Behind the Video," *Spinditty*, 17 January 2022.

284   *Sun*, 1 August 2008, via Chris Vinnicombe, *Musicradar*.

285   Robert Hilburn, *Johnny Cash: The Life* (New York: Back Bay Books, 2013), pp. 606-607.

Mark Benney/Creative Commons

TRENT REZNOR, CIRCA 1994/5

said at the time, "I wanted to tell the truth but not be insensitive, because Johnny is not in the peak of health right now."[286]

Contrasting the Cash and Reznor versions of "Hurt" reveals both common ground and dramatic divergence. That the same words and tune can yield such polarities, yet be of a piece, is striking. Both are minimalistic in their way, built from simple guitar and vocal foundations. And both express the thoughts of troubled men at turning points in their lives, wracked by psychic and physical pain from which they seek release. But there the kinship largely ends.

Reznor's "Hurt" is a studio creation, its backing an icy collage of textures, drones, and loops beneath sinister-sounding guitar chords (B minor/D/E). Each sound is drawn out and dramatized, and sudden dynamic shifts startle the ear. Reznor's vocal swoops from a barely audible, devil-in-the-ear whisper to an anguished Goth-metal yell. He acts the song as much as sings it. *Life is wretched, a joke and a travesty* is the prevailing mood. The overall effect is stark and horror-movie-ish, self-conscious in the extreme. But not ineffective. Song and album end with a thunderous guitar clang followed by a two-minute fadeout of staticky *musique concrete*, like an industrial '90s nod to the Beatles' final "A Day in the Life" piano chord. In a 1995 live video of the song, Reznor hunches over a microphone, all stringy hair and sunken eyes, before a scrim of black-and-white movie projections: war atrocities, atomic explosions, decomposing animals. Subtle it's not. But neither is youth in its contemplate-suicide mode. If Reznor's sensibility fetishizes depression, at least in "Hurt" he wants out.

Cash, by contrast, keeps it simple. Guitar, piano, a live ambience and steady vocal. Fixed dynamics except for a crescendo in the insistent piano of the chorus. A change of key (chords: A minor/C/D) vastly alters the song's feel, from

286   Gil Kaufman, "Johnny Cash's 'Hurt' Delves into Life of Former Hell-Raiser: VMA Lens Recap," MTV.com, 26 February 2003.

eerie-but-corny to mournful-but-warm. *Life is hard and then you die, in the end I'm no different from you* is the prevailing mood. No fadeout, just a final piano chord that lingers in memory after it ends. An air of dignified despair dominates, matched in the video by complementary visuals: a robust Cash piloting a steam train, incongruent beside the diminished figure we see singing; forlorn views of the abandoned House of Cash museum, its shelves empty, a gold record shattered; Cash at his banquet table, spilling wine from a goblet on rotting delicacies like an enfeebled feudal lord. The most famous passage from Ecclesiastes—the Bible's dourest book—seems to haunt the proceedings: "Then I looked on all the works that my hands had wrought, and on the labor that I had labored to do: and, behold, all was vanity and vexation of spirit, and there was no profit under the sun." Near death beside the woman he loves (and soon will lose), seated on a throne in his tomb-like home, he lays bare the clot of unresolved feelings, regret, and yearning for personal peace that accompany dying.

If Reznor's "Hurt" is a glimmer of hope in darkness, Cash's feels like darkness smothering hope. What's left is faith—not in his legacy but in something vaster. Differences of style aside, what really separates one "Hurt" from the other is belief and age. Both were essayed by brooding, conflicted men with self-destructive tendencies, but Cash has a transcendent refuge—the Christianity he embraced after June helped him kick the drug habit that nearly killed him—while Reznor is adrift. Put crudely, Reznor is the existential nihilist, and Cash is the believer felled by sin. But the difference is largely superficial. Cash's "sin" has less to do with hell-raising or pill-popping or Mammon than with simple remorse and fear. And Reznor's nihilism is clearly the refuge of a wounded Romantic, down to its simultaneous rejection of religion and longing for God.[287] Most relevant is season of life. Reznor's "Hurt" is a young man's song, sincere but solipsistic; Cash's is an old man's, rueful and wracked with doubt.

At times this sense of generational interpretation took on literal father–son overtones. Before his death, Cash paternalistically praised Reznor's "Hurt" as "the best anti-drug song I ever heard,"[288] rooting its essence in the great existential crisis of his life: his near death and recovery, imperfect but committed, from addiction, and consequent rebirth as an artist, husband, and family man. A decade after his death, Reznor said of Cash's version: "[I]t came at a very insecure time in my life and it felt like a nudge and boost and a hug from God. It said, 'Everything's okay and the world is bigger than what's just in my head.'"[289]

A working title for this book was *In My Time of Dying*, after the traditional gospel blues about preparing for death after a hard life.[290]

---

287   Which grew as he got older. "I do [believe in God]," he told an interviewer in 2014. "I take comfort in thinking there's some purpose and higher power of some sort. I'm not affiliated with any particular religion, but that gives me some sense of comfort" (Dave Kerr, "Came Back Vaunted: An Interview with Nine Inch Nails' Trent Reznor," *The Skinny*, 6 May 2014).

288   Eric R. Danton, "Years Take Toll on Cash's Voice," *Baltimore Sun*, 11 November 2002.

289   "Interview: Trent Reznor," *Uncut*, 4 May 2005.

290   Also called "Jesus Make Up My Dying Bed" and best known in versions by Bob Dylan (1962) and Led Zeppelin (1975). Both derive from Josh White's 1933 Piedmont blues, but the gravel-voiced Blind Willie Johnson's riveting "holy blues" version (1928), with mostly different lyrics, is the essential cut.

In the time of dying, I don't want
nobody to moan
All I want my friends to do, come and
fold my dying arms

Josh White's influential recording
is almost jaunty, a gem of delicately
picked guitar and smooth, reassuring
vocals that belie the mortal concerns of
the lyrics. (Dylan's version, on the other
hand, is raspy and barbed, Zeppelin's
thunderous and witchy.) Billed in the
'30s as the Singing Christian, White
was not a haunted figure, nor was he
dying when he recorded the song.
His version is a tonic for grief with
comforting salvation imagery—music
you can imagine wanting to hear on
your deathbed.

Rubenstein Rare Book, Manuscript, and Special Collections Library, Duke University

JOSH WHITE, 1964

Well, well, well, so I can die easy
Well, well, well, so I can die easy
Well, well, well, so I can die easy
Jesus gonna make up my dying bed

As a title, *In My Time of Dying* was discarded for a simple reason. In a book
about songs of death caused by sudden, often violent reversals of fortune and
what they say about processing trauma and grief (from the Introduction), it
aligned neatly with the trauma and grief part, less so with the sudden reversals of
fortune. Because few of the characters in these songs had the luxury of preparing
for their deaths.

Such preparation, for both dying and loved ones, makes a difference. It's folly
to say if the devastation caused by drawn out versus sudden death is worse;
both involve trials that anguish the departed and those left behind. But there's a
welcome sense of peace and resolution that comes with setting affairs in order
and having time to think, process, remember, reconnect, make amends, and
say goodbye. An adjunct crime to murder, insult-to-injury fashion, is robbing
human beings of this last, basic right.

Cash's "Hurt" is a kind of farewell song. While not conceived as such, the
singer knew the end was nearing, and that awareness imbues both recording and
video with a sense of reckoning, bravely shared not just with friends and family
but with a vast network of fans.[291] A significant achievement of the clip is how it

291 The video was so unflinching and Cash's portrayal so vulnerable that nearly everyone involved–Cash, June, his
management, even Rubin–was unsure if it should come out. But his daughter Rosanne was unequivocal: "It was a work of art,"

casts a leveling gaze on grief without lapsing into self-pity and dramatizes Cash's spiritual struggles without devolving into grandiosity. As a farewell, it offers two generations of fans benediction. For old-timers, whether raised on stalwart country or rebellious rock, it's a parting gesture of bedrock earnestness. For newcomers—Gen X-ers more ideologically afloat and apt to take refuge from insecurity in reflexive snark—it's an unaffected confrontation with unvarnished truth. Perhaps this was Cash's final career accomplishment: he made sincerity safe for ironists.

Certainly "Hurt"'s closing lines, written by Reznor but brought to life by Cash, are a testament to dropping persona, irresolutely and for all time:

If I could start again
A million miles away
I would keep myself
I would find a way

---

she told Cash's biographer, Robert Hilburn, "excruciatingly truthful. I thought, 'How could that be wrong in any way?'" Cash ultimately approved its release (Hilburn, *Johnny Cash: The Life*, p. 603).

OUTRO

What doesn't transmit light creates its own darkness.
—Marcus Aurelius, Meditations

If I could start again ...

In the end, death robs us of more than life. It also depletes our finite reserve of second chances. In America, with its fervent belief in fresh starts and re-creation—in proving F. Scott Fitzgerald's "no second acts" maxim wrong—this is a bitter pill. So long as life appears endless, or at least long, our propensity for denial and procrastination can flourish. Out of sight and out of mind, death remains distant and indistinct. But brushes with death—our own or another's, real or imaginary—can burst our escapist cocoon and force a confrontation. Whether we metamorphose into someone more fully alive or swaddle ourselves in comforting illusion is up to us.

In 1946, a merchant seaman named Hubert Selby, Jr., took ill with tuberculosis. Frail and poor, he spent years recovering in New York hospitals. As part of his treatment, surgeons removed ten ribs and half of one lung. Several times during his convalescence, he almost died.[292] Once discharged, his doctors predicted a drastically reduced lifespan. He tried to return to everyday life, marrying, fathering a child, and working various clerical jobs. But recurrent respiratory illness landed him back in the hospital for much of a decade, while chronic pain and despair led to heroin and alcohol dependence. His wife eventually left him, and poor health made employment difficult.

During this bleak period, he had an epiphany, a road-to-Damascus insight so pure it transformed him forever. For the rest of his life, he told and retold the tale:

> [I] *knew that someday I was going to die. And just before I died, two things would happen. Number one, I would regret my entire life. And number two, I would want to live my life over again . . . And that terrified me . . . So I had to do something. I had to do something with my life.*[293]

Selby was unschooled but had an interest in writing ("I knew the alphabet," he later recalled, "so I figured I could write").[294] He bought a typewriter. Not knowing where to start, he first wrote a letter, then a short story. For six years he labored, working desultory day jobs and writing at night until he amassed enough material for a book. He shaped this into a novel called *Last Exit to Brooklyn*, published in 1964 to critical acclaim and public controversy.

---

292 Selby's intimacy with death began in the womb. Choked by his own umbilicus, he started life with cyanosis and minor brain damage. "Thirty-six hours before I was born, I started to die," he later recounted. Consequently, "[d]ying became a way of life" ("Memories, Dreams, and Addictions: Ellen Burstyn Interviews Hubert Selby, Jr.," DVD/Blu-ray special feature from the 2000 film version of Selby's novel *Requiem for a Dream*).

293 "Memories, Dreams and Addictions: Ellen Burstyn Interviews Hubert Selby, Jr."

294 Ibid.

Last Exit to Brooklyn is an unflinching portrait of urban outcasts—a brutal look at the lives of gangsters and hoodlums, hookers and sailors, drag queens and drug addicts, by a self-taught author driven to portray harsh reality by the harsh reality of his life. Selby gives voice to their rage and pain, compassionately and without judgment, uncovering a stratum of misfits and pariahs swept under the societal rug. The book's coarse language and taboo subject matter provoked censorship battles, and the avant-garde leaped to its defense. Allen Ginsberg predicted the novel would "explode like a rusty, hellish bombshell over America, and still be eagerly read in a hundred years."[295] Six decades later, Selby's rough-hewn prose and shrill portraiture still startle. Yet, despite the book's underground cachet, it lacks all bohemian self-consciousness. Its most striking quality remains how resolutely Selby honors human suffering by giving it an impartial voice.[296]

I introduce Selby late in this book because his life and epiphany resonate with its themes. In the Introduction, I described the dynamic of tragic songs as one of despair, documented, then disseminated—as a commemorative and cathartic cycle that affords a soul-reckoning with the ineffable. Like Selby, many of the songwriters and performers in these pages were driven by mortal circumstances to make penetrating statements about devastating loss. Others were drawn to such songs by brushes with the same. But most were compelled, like Selby, to make something of, if not their life, at least the wounds inflicted by their encounters with death.

Like the author of *Last Exit to Brooklyn*, many were also instinctive artists: novices, outsiders, or unknowns who used raw, often minimal skills to musically depict their rage, pain, numbness, and confusion. Some, of course, were seasoned pros. But the preponderance of roots music—folk ballads, hillbilly and blues songs, plus later DIY variants like punk and post-punk—speaks to the ubiquity of untrained responses to traumatic loss and their emotive power.

One last song, by a roots-inspired punk band who stuck out from the pack for their earnest desire to not just rant at injustice but also make sense of the world.

In 1980, the Clash released *Sandinista!*—a massive three-LP set of stylistically diverse, tonally all-over-the-place anthems, jokes, and experimental filler that both confounded and exhilarated listeners. Tucked in the middle of side two was a powerful if offbeat rocker: an old-school punk rave-up, but punctuated with weird carnival keyboards and echoey street sounds. Its subject was murder, the shock of its occurrence and its jarring finality vividly captured in the line "Goodbye, for keeps, forever."

---

295 Eric Homberger, "Obituary: Hubert Selby Jr," *Guardian*, 28 April, 2004.

296 Selby's impartiality scandalized some readers, who complained he was too tolerant of his characters—that his refusal to privilege abused over abuser, or even differentiate between the two, and condemn them for their life choices was amoral. But Selby believed all suffering deserved a hearing and that trauma begat trauma in a vicious cycle that precluded finger-pointing. He also considered pain and suffering interrelated but discrete, the latter resulting from not fully feeling the former. "[T]he function of suffering," he said in 2001, three years before his death (at seventy-five; Selby long outlived his doctors' early death prognosis), "is to let me know that my perception is skewed . . . [that] the resistance to the natural phenomena of life causes tremendous suffering" ("Memories, Dreams and Addictions: Ellen Burstyn Interviews Hubert Selby, Jr.").

THE CLASH, 1980

Somebody got murdered
His name cannot be found
A small stain on the pavement
They'll scrub it off the ground

"Somebody Got Murdered" was inspired by an encounter with a corpse—a random collision with arbitrary homicide. In early 1980, the Clash were recruited to write a "heavy rock number" for a Hollywood crime thriller.[297] The singer and guitarist Joe Strummer took the commission over the phone. Years later, he recalled the composition's circumstances tersely: "[S]o I said OK. I hung up and went home and there was this guy in a pool of blood out by the car parking kiosk. That night I wrote the lyric."[298] A parking attendant had been slain during a robbery, apparently for mere pounds, and left bleeding on the pavement. Strummer gave the lyrics to his bandmate Mick Jones, who set them to music.

The resulting song circles its source like the calliope sounds that engulf it. Strummer's lyric (sung by Jones) transcends the personal and becomes an everyman monologue about sudden, violent death. The singer observes and re-observes the inert body, asking questions, trying to make sense of the tragedy. There were witnesses, he notes, but now no one is talking ("But where they were last night / No one can remember"). The paltry sum for which the victim died makes him shudder—it could easily have been him there on the ground instead ("And you're minding your own business / Carrying spare change"). He can't fathom the killer's cruelty, looks inward, and wonders what might drive him to take a life ("I been very hungry / But not enough to kill").

---

297 The film was *Cruising* (1980), William Friedkin's controversial neo-noir about a serial killer targeting gay men in New York City and an undercover cop (played by Al Pacino) who infiltrates the S&M and leather scene to find him. The Clash's song went unused in the film and was instead released on *Sandinista!*
298 Liner notes, *Clash on Broadway* box set, 1991, p. 56.

But nothing explains or erases the dismal sight. One soul fewer now occupies the world, but life goes ineluctably on. Still, as the singer transitions from reflective silence to everyday street noise, he finds himself changed:

As the daily crowd disperses
No one says that much
Somebody got murdered
And it's left me with a touch

It's a haunting song that confounds expectations—a would-be anthem undone by its desolate theme and disorienting ambience. Though rousing and infectious, the song's chorus provides no inspiration, release, or reassuring punky call to arms. It simply reiterates the shock of no more second chances and end-of-life regret, honoring human suffering by giving it an impartial voice. The chorus also distills the essence of this book into a single cause-and-effect couplet—two lines that return us to square one in our reckoning with death:

Somebody got murdered
Somebody's dead forever

Goodbye, for keeps, forever. Amen.

ACKNOWLEDGEMENTS

"The symphony," said Gustav Mahler, "must be like the world. It must embrace everything." I share the composer's ideal of all-encompassing works—multi-layered constructions with recurring themes, shifting perspectives, and associative reach beyond subject matter. But books are finite artifacts with page limits and deadlines. Consequently, preparing one for publication requires balancing high aims with practical realities.

Many people assisted in this process, but two made vital contributions. Catherine Murrell has reviewed my writing for two decades and proofed and commented on every scrap of text created for this book. Her support was unwavering, her critical eye indispensable. My editor, Christina Ward, similarly scrutinized every word and helped hone a sprawling manuscript into a focused statement without sacrificing my voice or vision. I'm deeply grateful to both for their insightful critiques.

I'm also grateful to Feral House—a fabled publisher whose offbeat tomes I special-ordered for years from indie bookstores, never dreaming that someday they'd publish my own opus. Thanks to managing editor Jessica Parfrey for welcoming me to the family, copyeditor Laura Smith for fine-tuning my text, and designer Ron Kretsch for imbuing the book's look with a musical sensibility.

Many individuals and institutions lent practical support. Photographers John Ingledew, Frank Loose, Jason Thrasher, and Sue Zechini generously contributed critical photos. And the Ekstrom Library of the University of Louisville, Ramsey Kanaan and PM Press, the Ralph Rinzler Archives of the Smithsonian Institute, Rani Singh and the Harry Smith Archives, and Aaron Smithers and the Wilson Library of the University of North Carolina at Chapel Hill provided evocative historical images. Special thanks to Yard Dog Gallery and Tom Van Eynde for superb art documentation.

Portions of this book appeared previously in different form in online and print publications. A chance encounter with Ken Bigger at a "murder ballad event" at Chicago's Packer Schopf Gallery in 2015 led to my first published work on the subject in the Murder Ballad Monday feature of *Sing Out!* magazine that Ken cofounded. Sincere thanks to Ken and the executive director of *Sing Out!,* Mark Moss. Thanks also to Bertis Downs IV, attorney and manager of R.E.M., who read and promoted my work, and David Daley, former editor-in-chief of Salon, who crossposted my essays and dramatically enlarged my audience. I first wrote about "Strange Fruit" and lynching photography in a 2005 review of an exhibit at the Black History Museum and Cultural Center of Virginia in the Richmond arts paper *Style Weekly.* Thanks to those establishments. And thanks to Virginia Commonwealth University and the

School of the Art Institute of Chicago for letting me try out ideas in art and music history lectures that found their way here. And to my students for their enthusiasm and engagement.

Unsurprisingly, musicians crucially impacted this book. Profound thanks to Patterson Hood and Jon Langford, two of the hardest working folks in music and mensches to boot, for interviews, feedback, and photos. Kudos also to Tom Greenhalgh, Kristin Hersh, Todd Menton, and David Stenshoel, who gave enlightening interviews. David—a multi-instrumentalist with Boiled in Lead and other genre-busting ensembles—tragically succumbed to cancer in 2021. He spent his last weeks jamming with friends on an inspiring set of YouTube videos dubbed the "Oud and Hospice Music Sessions." Godspeed, David. Other musicians who answered questions and offered feedback were Janet Bean, Lu Edmonds, Kevin Lycett, Brett Sparks, Rennie Sparks, and Sally Timms. Guitar virtuoso John Szymanski patiently proofed chord progressions in the text and corrected errors. Heartfelt thanks to all. And tremendous goodwill to Tim and Katie Tuten—co-owners of the Hideout, Chicago's premier space for roots rock and Americana—who staged a musical launch for the book. Without music, there'd be no book, and without musicians, there'd be no music. But without venues, musicians would have only the streets.

Fellow writers provided both modest and substantial assistance. Shoutouts to Martin Billheimer, Aaron Cohen, Abbott Kahler, Rick Kogan, Duncan McLean, Bill Meyer, James "Chip" Nold, and Stuart Shea for encouragement and counsel. At some point in this book's gestation, each of them inspired me to stay the course and keep moving—in Rick's words—"onward!"

Acknowledgments typically treat professional and personal thanks as discrete categories. For me, there's too much overlap to divide without difficulty, but I'll close with a more subjective set of felicitations.

First off, eternal gratitude to my late parents for introducing me to music. I spent countless hours in my mother's lap listening to my father's choral group before I could speak. Consequently, melody, harmony, and rhythm affect me more than language—a foundation which might explain my lifelong drive to use language to describe music. My papaw—my mother's father—introduced me to rougher-hewn sounds on his guitar during visits to the country. And my brother Doug, my first creative collaborator (we wrote books and enacted elaborate fantasies together), taught me more than anyone how to write. My late wife Susan championed me as a writer when I thought I was just an artist. And Carole and Millard, my second parents, boosted my morale during a difficult patch writing this book. Thanks to all, and also to my cousin Lori and myriad Kentucky ancestors whose modest, often arduous lives inspire me.

My first great teachers, Bill Walsh and Steve Worful, provided my earliest opportunities for serious writing. P-Form magazine published my first art criticism in college, and during grad school, professors Morris Yarowsky and Barbara Tisserat, sadly gone, mentored me as both a writer and painter. Every up-and-coming misfit needs a stomping ground, and I cut my creative teeth during the '80s in Louisville's underground music scene, mostly at Tewligan's Tavern, where my band Folks on Fire regularly played and in Chicago's performance art community, where I mixed music and monologue at Club Lower Links and Randolph Street Gallery. Sincere thanks to all who partook in my formal and informal education. Thanks also to Jim Dempsey and Aron Packer, unstuffy art world types who share my love of old-time music, everyone who played in the Feckless Hayseeds (a band waiting to be reborn!), and Matthew Johnson, who commissioned the *Open Hymnal* paintings printed in this book for an unrealized music project. I'm glad they found a home here.

As everyone knows or eventually learns, life rarely accommodates personal agendas. The year and a half during which I wrote this book was fraught with challenges, and I'm deeply grateful to those who helped me through it. My dear friend Heidi Lang kept me sane with gargantuan weekend phone calls, as did weekly sessions with my therapist, George Hogenson. (George, an author, also provided pointers on book completion.) In a season of much work and little play, evenings out at Chicago nightspots like Montrose Saloon, Lizard's Liquid Lounge, the Hideout, and Old Town School of Folk Music offered precious recreation with live music and friends.

Finally, perpetual belly rubs for my late dog Mojo—a pear-shaped Beagle mix whose provocative blues-lore name contrasted comically with his mild, middle-aged nature. Diagnosed with terminal cancer just days into my rough draft, he snoozed loyally beside me for five months and 95,000 words, seemingly trying to hang on until I finished my task. Alas, he died a week before completion. He was a dear companion who deserves his own folksong. Months later, as I revised the manuscript, I adopted a scrappy rat-hunting mutt named Queequeg.

To everyone named herein, and to those I've inevitably forgotten, I quote Big Star without irony: "Thank you, friends / Wouldn't be here if it wasn't for you."

—SLJ, Chicago, May 2023

SONG LICENSING ACKNOWLEDGMENTS

INDEX: THE VICTIMS, CRIMES, & TRAGEDIES THAT INSPIRED THE SONGS

THE TRAGEDIES THAT INSPIRED THE SONGS